MAD DOG

MAD DOG

THE MAURICE VACHON STORY

Bertrand Hébert *and* Pat Laprade
translated by George Tombs

Original title: *Maurice «Mad Dog» Vachon*
Copyright © Les Éditions Libre Expression, 2015
Published under arrangement with Groupe Librex Inc.,
doing business under the name Les Éditions Libre Expression,
Montréal, QC, Canada

Published by ECW Press
665 Gerrard Street East
Toronto, ON M4M 1Y2
416-694-3348 / info@ecwpress.com

To the best of his abilities, the author has related experiences, places, people, and organizations from his memories of them. In order to protect the privacy of others, he has, in some instances, changed the names of certain people and details of events and places.

Library and Archives Canada Cataloguing in Publication

Hébert, Bertrand, 1971–
[Maurice Mad Dog Vachon. English]
Mad Dog : the Maurice Vachon story/ Bertrand Hébert and Pat Laprade; translated by George Tombs.

Translation of: Maurice Mad Dog Vachon.
Issued in print and electronic formats.
ISBN 978-1-77041-332-0 (softcover); ISBN 978-1-77305-064-5 (PDF); ISBN 978-1-77305-065-2 (EPUB)

1. Vachon, Mad Dog 1929–2013. 2. Wrestlers—Québec (Province)—Biography. I. Laprade, Pat, author II. Tombs, George, translator III. Title. IV. Title: Maurice Mad Dog Vachon. English.

GV1196.V33H4213 2017   796.812092   C2017-902407-8
C2017-902986-X

Editor for the press: Michael Holmes
Cover design: Tania Craan
Cover image: © Pro Wrestling Illustrated
Type: Rachel Ironstone

Printed and bound in Canada by Friesens   5   4   3   2   1

The publication of *Mad Dog* has been generously supported by the Canada Council for the Arts, which last year invested $153 million to bring the arts to Canadians throughout the country, and by the Government of Canada through the Canada Book Fund. *Nous remercions le Conseil des arts du Canada de son soutien. L'an dernier, le Conseil a investi 153 millions de dollars pour mettre de l'art dans la vie des Canadiennes et des Canadiens de tout le pays. Ce livre est financé en partie par le gouvernement du Canada.* We also acknowledge the contribution of the Government of Ontario through the Ontario Book Publishing Tax Credit and the Ontario Media Development Corporation.

To the memory of Guy Laprade, Huguette Caza-Daoust,
Béatrice "Bétisse" Croteau-Bertrand, Roddy Piper, Fernand Ste-Marie,
Bob Leonard, Jim Fanning, Ivan Koloff, Frenchy Martin,
J Michael Kenyon, and Régis Vachon

TABLE OF CONTENTS

PREFACE AND ACKNOWLEDGMENTS

When we last met Maurice Vachon in July 2013 we knew we might never see him again. He seemed a shadow of his former self: wracked by illness, physically weak, he had lost the keen wit that had once been his trademark.

It was heart-wrenching to see him like this, but for brief moments a radiant smile would suddenly light up his face, and he would speak to us as if he were still at the height of his powers. With a great sense of gratitude, we remember playing cribbage with him and hearing him speak French to us, the language of his youth.

When we took his photograph, his last words were *"De rien, mes amis,"* or "You're welcome, my friends." We still shudder when we remember that voice of his — still slightly hoarse and always full of life.

With the publication of this book, we offer our thanks to Maurice Vachon one last time. This book celebrates his life, his career, and the legend he became. We heard news of his death the morning we were scheduled at the Montreal Book Fair, launching the French version of *Mad Dogs, Midgets and Screw Jobs: The Untold Story of How Montreal Shaped the World of Wrestling*. We were busy all that day, giving media interviews and promoting the book by the same token. While meeting a stream of readers at the Book Fair, we couldn't help thinking that before dying, Maurice had given one final helping hand to two fellow Quebecers — ourselves. Like he had done so many times throughout his life. But then Maurice Vachon was an exceptional human being: throughout his life he had demonstrated unparalleled generosity towards others.

That very evening, as we turned over the events of an emotion-packed day in our minds, we realized we were in a position to take on a new book project, telling his personal story as completely as possible, focusing not just on the good sides of his character but also on the darker side.

We hope that in reading his story, you will find the courage and determination to find your way through the trials and tribulations of life. May you live to fulfill your dreams the way "Mad Dog" did.

We wish to thank our families, especially Monique, Zakary, Elayna, Jean-Krystophe, Françoise, Gérald, and Josihanne for helping and supporting us throughout this project.

We also wish to thank the team at Libre Expression, which published the original French-language edition of this book. They believed in this project. We would particularly like to mention our publisher Miléna Stojanac for the precious support she offered while we wrote the previous book, and also this one. We would also like to thank Michael Holmes and ECW Press for believing in this version and for giving us our first break.

A special thanks to World Wrestling Entertainment (WWE) and Steven Pantaleo for permission to use exclusive photos of Maurice.

Thanks also to Linda Boucher and Élise Boucher for access to their fantastic collection of photos, as well as for the research they conducted on our behalf.

Thanks to the Vachon family (Kathie, Paul, Guy, the late Régis, and Mike), as well as Nicole Chaput, for always being so available and ready to grant us many hours of their time.

Thanks, finally, to all those who helped us to complete this project, whether by granting us interviews or helping us in other ways too numerous to list here. Know that we are grateful. Thanks to Yves Thériault, Greg Oliver, Vern May, Christian Lavoie, Michel Longtin, Paul Leduc, George Schire, Jim Fanning, Bob Oldis, Roddy Piper, Rick Martel, Pat Patterson, Raymond Rougeau, Jacques Rougeau Sr., Armand Rougeau, Ivan Koloff, J.J. Dillon, Bill Apter, Fernand Ste-Marie, J Michael Kenyon, Tim Hornbaker, Al Friend, Nick Bockwinkel, Dick Beyer, Karl Lauer, Mike Lano, Dave Cameron, Scott Teal, Adam Simpson, Dave Meltzer, Luc Denoncourt, Michel Jasmin, Mike Rodgers, Dean Silverstone, Denis Gauthier Sr., Gilles Poisson, Neil Guay, Angelo Mosca, Merv Unger, René Goulet, Ross Hart, Stu Saks, Bob Leonard, Jim Cornette, Kevin Cerutti, Danny Hodge, Jeff Sharkey, Gerald Brisco, Anne Béland, Claude Tousignant, Jim Raschke, Guillaume Lefrançois, Terry Funk, Dory Funk Jr., Jean-Pierre Coallier, Fumi Saito, Don Leo Jonathan, Éric Salottolo, Michel Piché, Bob Kapur, Serge Savard, Régis Lévesque, Angélique Richer, and François Poirier.

Pat Laprade and Bertrand Hébert
September 2017

FOREWORD

My brother Maurice "Mad Dog" Vachon had two distinct personalities. For the public, he was a "rabid dog": a detestable and fiendish wrestler who could stoop to do the most despicable things. He did such a good job and he was so talented that he became a legend in his lifetime. But over time, the public bought into this image of the villain so much that fans considered "Mad Dog" their very own villain — an endearing member of the family. That's the public image he has left behind.

But in his private life, Maurice was the opposite of the image he cultivated in public. He was a loving, generous man whose heart went out to his family first: his mother, his father, his brothers and sisters. He shared his love with us equally, but he also loved his children and their mothers. He loved life just as much as he loved his wife Kathie. I was fortunate to receive his unconditional love, and I have always said how grateful I am, how privileged to have had him as a brother.

But Maurice didn't just share his love and joy with his family. He was always willing to reach out and help people he knew, even when they hadn't asked for anything, just because it made him happy. First, I think of all his fellow wrestlers: he gave them advice, suggested they adopt a new name, supported them in making a new decision or in developing new tactics. He helped them advance their careers, without expecting anything in return. It would take too long to make a definitive list of all the people he supported over the years, and besides, a list like that would doubtless leave out many names. But I can certainly mention one person who benefited greatly from his help and advice. And that person is . . . me.

Maurice, my brother, thank you from the bottom of my heart.

Maurice passed away and I miss him a lot, but I am not going to cry because something of him will always remain with me — with me, and with all those people whose lives he touched.

He went through the greatest trials of life with the dignity and humanity of the great champion he had always been. Through thick and thin, he never felt life had betrayed him. He loved it too much. He died quietly and peacefully in his sleep, the way all of us want to end our days — after reaching the end of a path that had been a fantastic adventure.

Don't spill tears over him. Instead, celebrate the life of this extraordinary and generous man. Tell people about the legend he became, the way this book is about to. Make sure my brother, our brother, Maurice "Mad Dog" Vachon, will be a source of inspiration for generations, helping people fulfill their dreams and face the trials of life, the same way he always did, without letting other people take advantage of him.

I hope you have as much fun reading this book about the life of my brother as I had in knowing him first-hand.

Paul Vachon
October 2014

PROLOGUE

On August 3, 1967, a crowd was packed into the Trois-Rivières Coliseum, halfway between Montreal and Quebec City. The atmosphere inside the Coliseum was heating up. You might think people in the stands had their minds on hockey, but they were actually waiting for the opening bell of a professional wrestling match.

Wrestling had been popular in Quebec since the early twentieth century, but it really took off thanks to promoter Eddie Quinn, the blossoming of local star Yvon Robert, and the advent of television. But in 1967, wrestling had just crawled out of a slump in the province and was only beginning to regain a foothold in popular culture.

Fans in the Coliseum wanted just one thing: to see their favorite heroes, brothers Johnny and Jacques Rougeau, make mincemeat of the much-hated heels, the villainous Baron Fritz von Raschke and Maurice "Mad Dog" Vachon.

The Baron and Mad Dog made a pretty strange team. Fritz von Raschke was actually from Nebraska, but he said he was from East Germany, on the other side of the Berlin Wall, which had only just been put up six years before, a symbol of the Cold War. There was a whiff of both the Nazi and Communist about him. His partner Mad Dog was a French-speaking Quebecer from a working-class Montreal neighborhood, part of a very large family typical of Quebec at that time.

Even stranger was the fact that these two wrestlers had developed their business relationship a few months earlier, in Minnesota.

In the wrestling world, like in other work environments, you don't often find a veteran helping a rookie or youngster get his start. Usually the well-established wrestler is busy fighting to keep his position on top of the heap, so he tends to protect his job, even if it means stifling the potential of the rookie just starting out.

But Maurice wasn't a typical wrestler, any more than he was a typical human being. His own start in wrestling in Quebec had been far from easy, and the difficulties he experienced along the way convinced him his mission in life was to help as many fellow wrestlers as possible during his career. Maurice was often considered altruistic, whether in the wrestling world or in his personal relationships.

Not surprisingly, a friendship grew between the two men. They realized they had a lot in common — not just amateur wrestling but also their love for children. They shared values such as doing their very best. And they shared a common passion — fishing. So when they started traveling together, Maurice took the younger man under his wing: he recognized von Raschke's true potential and showed him all the tricks of the trade.

In the ring, things couldn't have gone better. The Vachon/von Raschke duo worked like magic. The crowd would just go crazy, and riots often broke out at the end of each match.

Maurice told the promoter in Trois-Rivières that he was bringing along quite the young wrestler for the summer. "I was big and ugly," remembers von Raschke, "whereas Maurice was small and ugly, so we made the perfect team. And 'Dog' knew how to drive the fans wild!"

A few months before the match, von Raschke had been too shy to give interviews. But eventually he got the better of the situation. Suddenly he felt a lot more comfortable in front of a microphone and camera. He lost all his inhibitions, put on an accent, and said a few words in German. After all, a Baron could do and say whatever he wanted.

For their part, Johnny and Jacques Rougeau were impressed by the way the Vachon/von Raschke duo brought in so much money. Johnny, who would continue as the key promoter and take full advantage of a wrestling rivalry that would simply set the territory on fire, had signed a contract with the French-Canadian television network Channel 10 the previous year, so the arrival of the Vachon/von Raschke duo was timely.

Then Maurice thought of doing something he had already tried out in Texas. Actually, it was an idea that went back to the early twentieth century, when wrestlers wrestled in county fairs. Before each match got under way, von Raschke would throw out a bold challenge to anyone in the crowd: if any contender could face the German in the ring and still be standing after twenty minutes, then that contender would receive $2,000. The setup worked like a charm. Fans didn't have to rely on experienced wrestlers to avenge them. They had a chance to settle the score for themselves. There were surprisingly good contenders now and then, but von Raschke was such a big fighter he knew he could take on any challenger. The promotion didn't require staged confrontations, choreographed in advance. The challenges were for real, and nobody ever managed to reach the time limit.

That night in Trois-Rivières, Vachon and von Raschke faced Johnny and Jacques Rougeau in the ring. This third match in the series was the main event that night — and it was a Texas death match, a no-disqualification, no-holds-barred affair. The dramatic name given to the match made it seem larger than life.

Early in the evening, Jean-Claude Corbin, a strongman from Cap-de-la-Madeleine, near Trois-Rivieres, challenged von Raschke. Corbin failed, but with the crowd shouting their support, he managed to stay in the ring with the German for more than ten minutes, which was a feat in itself.

The evening was a success: the Coliseum recorded its largest crowd of the summer, Corbin thrilled fans, and the Rougeaus won the match. The Coliseum saw attendance double during the summer of 1967, thanks to Maurice's idea of the challenge and his teamwork with von Raschke. Between the first match opposing the two teams, on July 13, and the last, on August 13, attendance rose from 1,982 to 4,300 fans.

Things were paying off for Maurice. Vachon and von Raschke were facing off against the crowd's favorites, plus the duo had a wrestling style that was thrilling to watch. They knew a lot about amateur wrestling and added their own unbridled and ruthless rough-and-tumble style — a definite crowd-pleaser. Fans would sometimes throw their chairs into the ring after the match was over, if they were unhappy about the outcome. Sometimes the crowd got so out of control that Maurice and von Raschke practically had to force their way out of the ring and back to the locker room. This kind of response was nothing new for Vachon — he had learned how to whip the crowd into a frenzy years earlier when making his name in the United States.

A few years later, Maurice reminisced about the matches that summer in the Trois-Rivières Coliseum. "It took us fifteen minutes to get to the ring because people had destroyed the cage before the bell. People just went nuts, flipping cars over and smashing the Coliseum windows. I never really understood what happened. After all," he said, with a sly smile, "it wasn't like we had done anything wrong."

The reality was, Maurice had everything going for him. His wrestling style was based on punches, kicks, and the use of many objects. Because of his style, he would be able to continue wrestling this way for twenty more years. Deep down, wrestling was a way for Maurice to externalize the violence he had lived with from a very early age: this was the main reason he had trained for amateur wrestling.

The year 1967 seemed full of promises. But then in August, Maurice was injured in a car accident that should have ended his career or even killed him. Over the years, Maurice was to experience the hammer-blow of fate time and time again: just when things seemed to be going well, something traumatic would happen. It would take von Raschke and Maurice another decade to wrestle together on a regular basis. And while Maurice was convalescing, the first of his three wives filed for divorce. Things had definitely taken a turn for the worse.

Von Raschke needed to find a partner to replace Maurice, so he teamed up with Hans Schmidt, and even became singles champion in Montreal in November 1967. Then, in 1968, the Sheik offered him work in Detroit, so the Baron left Montreal. At that time he shortened his ring name to Baron von Raschke, dropping the Fritz. He would go on to enjoy an exceptional career, becoming one of the best heels of his era. Recalling the importance of Montreal to their lives, his wife, Bonnie Raschke, can still speak some French, and their daughter has dual U.S.-Canadian citizenship.

"Without Montreal," the Baron said a few years ago, "little Jimmy Raschke would never have had such a successful career. I improved my delivery in interviews, I got over my discomfort, I worked with so many good wrestlers. . . . Montreal had lots of talented wrestlers. Maurice became both a mentor and a friend. He taught me everything I needed to know to get crowds to hate me. Without Montreal and without Mad Dog Vachon, I would never have had such a fascinating career."

Maurice was a discreet mentor. But gradually his reputation became legendary as the behind-the-scenes stories became available. Pat Patterson, René Goulet, Roddy Piper, Paul Vachon, and many more could have said what von Raschke did: there is no way to measure what these wrestlers owed to Maurice.

Montreal was blooming in 1967 with the completion of its first Metro network and by hosting the Universal Exposition. But for Maurice Vachon, 1967 was a rollercoaster, both on a professional and personal level. Mad Dog's career and Maurice's life had always been subject to dramatic twists and turns, and in '67 the man became the wrestler, and the wrestler became the man.

Twenty years earlier, he had taken part in the Olympic Games, and in the '50s he'd made his debut as a professional wrestler. Now mid-career, he had to spend the rest of the year on the sidelines, unable to participate in the sport he loved.

At the time, Maurice had no way of knowing that 1967 would mark just a short pause in his life story: the second half of his life was about to begin. In the twenty years that followed, he would experience lasting love, find financial stability, and enjoy unbounded popularity, but he would also face another divorce, overcome a difficult relationship with his children, and survive a hit-and-run accident that left him maimed right up to his death in 2013.

After doors closed to him in his native province of Quebec at the end of 1967, he would eventually achieve star status there, becoming the public figure he had dreamed of after returning from Auckland, New Zealand. In fact, he would become more than that. He would become a legend!

A THUG IN THE MAKING

The epic story of Maurice Vachon starts in 1929 in Ville-Émard, a working-class neighborhood in Montreal. Ville-Émard is located next to the city boroughs of Verdun and LaSalle, between the Lachine Canal and the Aqueduc Canal. It was annexed to the City of Montreal in 1910 and is now part of the South-West borough. Other well-known personalities come from there, such as ice hockey legend Mario Lemieux, and many factories were built there in the early twentieth century, giving the neighborhood a working-class character.

Maurice's father, Ferdinand Vachon, was born on March 7, 1905, in St. Raphael, a small Ontario village that no longer exists, a few dozen miles north of Cornwall and west of Valleyfield, Quebec. When Ferdinand and his twin brother, William, were ten years old, the family moved to Ville-Émard. Maurice's mother, Marguerite Picard, was born on September 13, 1905, in the small Ontario village of Huntsville. The village has about two thousand inhabitants and is located some three hundred miles west of Ottawa and sixty miles south of North Bay. Her family moved to Montreal when she was just two months old, and she was already living in Ville-Émard by the time her future husband moved there. These two young Franco-Ontarians had connecting backyards, so they saw each other on a regular basis while growing up. They got married on October 29, 1927. Between 1928 and 1951, Ferdinand and Marguerite, devout Catholics, had a total of twelve children and adopted a thirteenth.

Maurice Régis Vachon was born on September 1, 1929, a little over a month before the stock market crash heralding the beginning of the Great Depression, and ten years to the day before the start of World War II. He was baptized at Notre-Dame-du-Perpétuel-Secours Church, a parish with many English Catholic families, and was named Maurice for his godfather, Maurice Picard (his mother's brother), and Régis for his paternal grandfather, who had died nearly two decades beforehand.

The firstborn in the family was Marcel. Coming next was Maurice, born in the first family home on Briand Street. By the time their third baby, Guy, was born in 1930, the family had moved to 6873 Jogues Street, where Maurice would grow up. This second-story apartment wasn't exactly a penthouse: it was the upper half of a duplex, with a room for the boys and a double room for the girls and the parents. Considering the Vachons raised twelve children here (their last child, Diane, was not born on Jogues Street), the apartment must have felt cramped. But many other families in working-class areas of the big city had similar living quarters. The rent varied from $14 to $25 a month, not much in today's world, but salaries were not what they are today.

Ferdinand Vachon, who was nicknamed Fred, worked as a dock worker at the Port of Montreal, then as a police sergeant, earning $75 every two weeks. During the Depression, this was good pay, although with many mouths to feed it wasn't a fortune. The Vachon children made their own toys, and, as in all large families, the youngest of them wore hand-me-downs from their older siblings. Marguerite shopped for food at the grocery store, Blain, on credit, not so much because she had to but because it was convenient. The children went to a store in downtown Montreal where for just forty cents they could buy bread, cakes, and donuts fresh from the day before. Fred had a job that brought certain advantages. For example, when he recovered a truck full of stolen clothes, the store owner offered him a set of free clothes for all his children. Nowadays, such practices would be considered unethical, but during the Depression, any donation was welcome. All in all, every penny counted in the Vachon household, but the children never wanted for anything.

So for young Maurice, money was not a concern. In fact, he was busy getting into mischief, fighting with English kids, and hating school. The Vachon children all went to Saint-Jean-de-Matha elementary school nearby. This was not the right kind of place for Maurice, who later described himself as a shy child who had a hard time speaking and expressing his feelings.

Making matters worse, he was left-handed. This is considered normal today, but at the time, being left-handed was often seen as a handicap or an illness. Schoolteachers — often Catholic priests and nuns — forced several generations of youngsters to write with their right hands. And using the word "force" is not an overstatement: left-handed children had their knuckles rapped with a wooden ruler until they learned to stop writing with their cursed left hand. So, like many other left-handers, Maurice wrote with his right hand and did everything else with his left hand.

School discipline was harsh, and that didn't exactly make him feel like attending on a regular basis. "I was scared when I went back to school," Maurice recalled in the 1980s. "I wanted to die. I would go see the principal and get the strap. I felt like I was in prison. I was someone with lots of energy to burn off."

And Maurice burned off a lot of energy.

Going to class was agonizing, but leaving at the end of the day was a different story. His day really got going once the final bell rang at 4:00 p.m. — that's when the fights started. Sometimes they were triggered when classmates called him "Vachon le cochon" ("Vachon the pig"). Other times classmates threw out a challenge: "Why do you want to fight me? Why not take on Maurice instead? You'll see it isn't easy." He usually wore a white shirt, frequently spattered with some other kid's blood, and some of his own too.

Maurice told the story many times of how he would come home from school with blood on his shirt. "My father would ask if I had been fighting. I would answer yes. Then he would ask if I had won. I would answer yes. Then he would say, 'OK, that's fine then.'"

Fred Vachon was a loving father, but he was also a man of his generation. Without realizing it at the time, he embodied something dark that Maurice would later integrate into his own personality: Fred had a bad relationship with violence. With hindsight, the schoolyard fistfights of children can be downplayed, but being so close to violence became probably the most long-lasting aspect of Maurice's life, apart from wrestling.

Once Fred Vachon the policeman had finished interrogating Maurice about his school day, the boy would head outside looking for mischief, and that's when the real trouble would start.

The "Vachon Gang" became well-known in the neighborhood, and for good reason: they broke windows, they got into misadventures, they fought with English kids. There was no stopping them.

The gang consisted of Maurice, his brothers Marcel and Guy, and some of their buddies, the Fichaud and Bélec brothers. Marcel was born in July 1928 and Guy in December 1930: they were only two and a half years apart. Maurice was clearly the boss — he was the one developing new schemes. He was respected by the others as much as by his own brothers. "You couldn't fight against Maurice for very long," recalls Guy.

At the end of Jogues Street were "Crazy Field" — so named because it was close to the Douglas Psychiatric Hospital in Verdun — and a forest that would later become Angrignon Park. At the time, Ville-Émard was working-class but it still had a very rural character, as shown by the wooden boardwalks along the streets, from before the era of concrete sidewalks. For the youngsters, the forest was their secret realm. It was also the place where Maurice and his gang fought with English kids. As we will learn shortly, a better way of putting that would be: it was the place where Maurice and his gang *beat up* English kids. These fistfights no doubt reflected childhood rivalries, but they were also typical of the era. In the 1930s, there was a big divide between English-speaking and French-speaking Montrealers. People speaking English were perceived as belonging to the upper class of society, whereas people speaking French were an uneducated and exploited labor force. This divide affected not just adults but also children.

Parents are responsible for the values transmitted to their children. Marguerite Vachon never hid her deep hatred for the English, despite the fact she and her husband were both originally from Ontario. In a neighborhood with two communities living side by side, there was bound to be friction. "The English called us 'French pea soups,'" Maurice later recalled. "We called them 'blokes' and 'limeys.'" These were not exactly cruel slurs, but for children in a politically charged environment, it didn't take much to come to blows.

No English-speaking residents of Ville-Émard have ever given their side of the story, but it seems clear the Vachon Gang treated beating up English kids as a blood sport — and the gang came out on top most of the time. The Vachon Gang claimed Crazy Field as their own territory, so no self-respecting English kid would venture there. The only exception was when an English kid could speak French. And if English kids were accompanied by their fathers, then the Vachon Gang would go into hiding and be proud of not getting caught. A few years later, Maurice's brother Marcel was the first of the family to show an interest in girls, and he went out with an English girl from Verdun. Considering the territory, this meant, ironically, that the girl's brother had probably already been a victim of the Vachon Gang!

But beating up English kids wasn't the gang's full-time occupation. Actually, they seem to have spent more time breaking windows. One school in Ville LaSalle had to replace its windows over and over again: Maurice had broken all of them three times in a row. The fourth time, the school janitor caught him in the act and wanted to call the police. Maurice then started to cry, vowing never to do it again so he wouldn't have to face the wrath of his father. So ended his career as a window breaker.

Marguerite Vachon, a diminutive woman weighing just 105 pounds, had her hands full with such a turbulent brood. She was from a large family, and thanks to a strong character she didn't overreact. She disciplined her children, though, bringing out the strap or a stick only to scare them. At the same time, she recounted only parts of their misadventures to her husband, which spared them far more severe punishment at his hands. The family hired a maid named Ross who helped around the house from time to time. At $3 per week, this was a luxury the family could afford.

Ferdinand played his fatherly role well, but the fact that he was a policeman meant his son could often wriggle his way out of facing consequences. Youngsters in Ville-Émard looked up to Maurice for all the wrong reasons, but more generally the Vachon brothers enjoyed special consideration because their father was a policeman. At the time, this position brought more respect than it does today.

Even so, fathers came over to the Vachon household to complain about Maurice beating up their sons or to report on the latest mischief he had gotten into. Ferdinand sometimes took his son on patrol, probably to show him how easy it was to get out of line. This would be unthinkable nowadays.

The one time when the Vachon children didn't make such a ruckus was when they were playing with their dog, a border collie named Mickey. The dog's presence spread good cheer all around, and he often accompanied the brothers on their escapades. Mickey was a full member of the Vachon Gang. He was as impertinent as any boy, and he chased after other dogs on the slightest pretext. They paid him back in kind, however: Mickey died of wounds after being attacked by two rival dogs.

Whenever his children needed to burn off energy, Fred would take them, and especially his boys, fishing and camping on Lake of Two Mountains. At the same time, he was always ready to take out the strap when they got into serious mischief. Nowadays, child services would be brought in right away, but in those days corporal punishment was the norm in many families. Maurice later remembered, "At times, I would rather have gone to jail than face the brunt of my father's punishment."

The Vachon boys made a point of not telling their father everything. That proved to be a wise decision. "We got up to a lot of mischief," Maurice later recalled. "We got some good thrashings, and I suppose we deserved them."

But their father's attitude was paradoxical. He was proud of his sons' bad-boy reputation and he would immediately call them to order if they seemed cowardly. One day, while sitting on the balcony of the apartment, he saw his three oldest boys running home with their school bags. This time they were fleeing, with English kids close on their heels. Instead of demanding they return home immediately, he shouted out to them there would be no dinner unless they turned around and beat up the English kids.

Despite the fistfights and other misadventures, the Vachon family were devout and regular churchgoers, like most Quebecers of the time. Maurice went to Mass regularly, even becoming an altar boy. Early in the morning he would go to church, then come home again to change, then head for school. On Sundays, Marguerite would bring her children to St. Joseph's Oratory, a Catholic basilica and Canada's largest church.

Maurice didn't like academic subjects, but he made an exception in the case of geography because he had big dreams of traveling the world. Ferdinand spent a lot of time telling his sons about the criminals he had arrested. Some were Italians, others were Poles or Americans, but all had a story and a particular path in life. Ferdinand probably had the most influence on his children through his storytelling, because most of them would go on to travel and work all over the world.

Maurice had two hobbies that enabled him to develop his passion for geography: collecting stamps and raising carrier pigeons. Everyone knows about stamp collecting, but raising carrier pigeons takes some explanation. Carrier pigeons were trained to routinely return to their dovecote, and they were used especially in wartime to send messages from one base to another. Maurice raised pigeons until he was twenty years old.

One day he decided to head out, carrying a dozen pigeons in a potato sack. Once he got near Châteauguay, across the St. Lawrence River from Montreal, he sent the following message home via pigeon: "Don't worry, Mommy, I am going to the United States, I will be back in five years." Marguerite got into a bit of a panic, but Fred remained calm. "There's no cause for concern," he said. "You'll see! Maurice is bound to get hungry and then he will come home!" Around 11:00 p.m., Fred's prediction came true.

Maurice fed his fantasies and dreams with stamps. They enabled him to travel the world while staying at home. Some of these stamps were from France, Belgium, or Germany, and they were a welcome escape from school, where he was unhappy.

Beyond hobbies and periodic misadventures, Maurice also discovered professional wrestling. At a quite young age, he accompanied his father to see "la p'tite lutte" — light heavyweight wrestling matches. In the 1930s, wrestling was undergoing a big revival in Montreal. Thanks to the French wrestler Henri Deglane, former Olympic champion in Greco-Roman wrestling, the sport was gaining in popularity. Light heavyweight matches were held all over the city in places like the Exchange Stadium, the Ontario Stadium, the Mile End Stadium, and many others.

One time, a wrestling show was held at the Saint-Jean-de-Matha Stadium, near Maurice's school in Ville-Émard. His father introduced him to Paul Lortie, one of the stars at the time. Maurice was all of four or five years old, but he was already fascinated by the world of wrestling that would become his. From 1939, heavyweight wrestlers fought at the Montreal Forum under the rule of promoter Eddie Quinn. But light heavyweights wrestled in the city's smaller stadiums, occasionally replacing heavyweights at the Forum (home to the Montreal Canadiens) or wrestling in the openers.

Maurice was obviously interested in the big leagues. He and his buddies would walk a few miles just to have a look at the stadium posters announcing the upcoming matches. They occasionally attended the matches and discovered the big stars of Montreal wrestling. Their favorites were the Dusek brothers, Lou Thesz, Maurice Tillet, and Bobby Managoff, among others.

"We bought tickets for seventy-five cents and then sat in the ringside seats going for $2," Maurice later recalled. "We were always the first to arrive."

There was nothing surprising about his love for wrestling. Once Maurice entered the fray, he would always showboat while fighting. He liked to humiliate his opponents before beating them. He would pull their shirt up over their head, then twirl them around in a circle. He loved provoking them just enough for them to lose their concentration. That's when he would close in for the knockout. "Maurice developed his talents as an entertainer at a young age," Guy Vachon recalls. And Guy had eye-witnessed quite a few of his older brother's escapades. But Maurice was the only member of their group of buddies who truly loved wrestling — and since he was the leader, the others followed along, whether they wanted to or not.

Maurice also worked for a time for Elmer Ferguson, a well-known journalist who at the time covered hockey and professional wrestling. A reporter at the *Montreal Herald*, Ferguson employed Maurice as a clerk, paying him $10 a week for his services. But Maurice discreetly stole some of the best photographs, which he pinned on a wall at home that was already decorated with photos of wrestlers from the papers. Needless to say, Maurice didn't keep the job very long.

Of all the wrestlers Maurice idolized, one stands out in particular: Yvon Robert. In the late 1930s and early 1940s, Robert was exceptionally popular, although he would become even more famous later on. Clearly, he was the new darling of wrestling in Quebec. A native of Verdun, not far from Ville-Émard, Robert came from the same kind of social background as the young Vachon. Maurice considered Robert the perfect example of a man from a modest background who succeeds at what he does and travels the world. As Maurice would later say on several occasions, "Yvon Robert was like a god to us."

Interest in wrestling flagged somewhat in the late 1930s, but all of that changed with the arrival of Eddie Quinn the promoter and the blossoming of local star Yvon Robert. Hockey was not as popular in Montreal as it later became in the 1950s, and baseball was even less popular. The Vachon boys knew how to skate, but they weren't hockey fans. Wrestling, meanwhile, was gaining ground by leaps and bounds: in those days, wrestling matches were held in Montreal more times than there are days in a week.

Maurice found wrestling fascinating, but it would take a decade before he made a career of it. Robert's popularity actually worked against Maurice in his first years as a wrestler, but then years later it would offer him a golden opportunity.

Meanwhile, his personal life seemed like one long series of misadventures and fistfights. Maurice often got away with it and spent only a few hours in jail. But having a well-respected father in the police force proved to be a double-edged sword. On the one hand, it prevented Maurice from getting into serious trouble, but on the other hand, his father was far from pleased with the situation, although paradoxically and without realizing it he encouraged his son to indulge in bad-boy behavior.

Two events then took place that would change the course of Maurice's life forever.

Maurice had many flaws and he had gotten into a lot of trouble. But his heart was always in the right place. That's the way he was. He had to channel that voracious energy of his one way or the other, but he wasn't always sure how. When anyone took on someone from the Vachon Gang, it was like attacking Maurice himself. And this was even more the case when his own brothers were involved. He knew his role was to protect and to defend them. He hated acts of injustice: when one gang outnumbered another and abused its strength, or when the stronger attacked the weaker without the slightest pretext. He ended up defending others more often than he defended himself. These were the first signs of a character trait he would go on to demonstrate throughout his life: generosity.

Over the years, the Vachon family grew. After the first three sons (Marcel, Maurice, and Guy) came Jeannine, Régis, Marguerite, Paul, Arthur, Pierre (the son of Marguerite's sister, he had been part of the family since birth), Claire, André, Lise, and Diane.

One time, the children were playing on the sidewalk when a local kid, who happened to be English, gleefully started shooting pellets at them with an air rifle. Another time, when Régis (or Paul, depending on the version of the story) went apple picking, the same kid stole his bag of apples. This was too much for Maurice. He followed the boy home, subjecting him to a storm of punches to teach him never to steal from a Vachon again. A few days later, as Maurice was on his way to school through the back alleys, the English kid's father came after him on a bicycle and happened to kick him in passing. Maurice gave him everything he had: he showered the man with blows. The father nevertheless managed to escape and reached a clearing not far away. But Maurice hadn't finished yet. He followed him, then jumped on him until the man begged for mercy: "Let me go, let me go!"

Giving kids his age a licking was one thing, but for thirteen-year-old Maurice to beat up an adult was another.

"That's when I realized this made no sense," he later recalled.

When Maurice and his buddies weren't breaking windows or getting into brawls, they were attacking trains, especially by removing the seals on freight wagons. This was illegal, because without those aluminum seals, nobody could be sure of the freight loaded in the wagon. Maurice got arrested and was temporarily detained at the station. His father had to bend over backwards to get him out of trouble.

For Ferdinand, this was one misadventure too many. He had put up with straightforward mischief, broken windows, train damage, fistfights, and Maurice's reluctance to apply himself to his studies. Ferdinand pictured what kind of future his son was headed for, and it wasn't a pretty one. Maurice was developing the same profile as some of the bandits Ferdinand had to deal with on a daily basis.

"Maurice would have taken a wrong turn in life," says Paul Vachon. "He was headed more or less for the life of a thug."

"He liked fighting way too much," adds Guy.

Maurice himself admitted he didn't have too rosy a future: "I think I must have taken the wrong path in life. I got into more and more mischief, then I started doing stuff that was straight-out illegal."

That's when Ferdinand decided to sign his boys up for boxing at the YMCA. "If they have that much energy to spend, they might as well spend it in the right place without hurting anyone," he told himself.

No one could have predicted what was about to happen, but this decision marked a turning point in Maurice's life. The only time he would approach the criminal world again was while working as a doorman in private nightclubs.

For the police sergeant, the boxing lessons at the YMCA certainly came as a relief. But for Maurice, this was the beginning of a new life. He would discover the passion of training. Maurice would continue to train throughout his life. Training would open many doors and help him learn many things, but it would also have tragic consequences.

2

THE ENGLISH ARE COMING!

Before Maurice started training, he made the all-important decision to quit school. Now aged thirteen, he had reached eighth grade. He realized his education was going nowhere. This had to stop. Eloi Gendron, one of his former teachers, recalls disciplining the teenager: "One time I grabbed him by the throat and pressed his forehead against the blackboard and told him not to move."

Maurice idolized not just Yvon Robert but also his own father. Ferdinand had overcome having very little formal education, and practiced a profession that won him respect from the community. Maurice wanted the same.

At thirteen, Maurice began working in construction. During World War II, he even went out to Saskatchewan to harvest wheat. But he nearly died out West. The horse Maurice worked with every day bucked him so hard it sent him flying through the barn wall. Any other teenager lacking Maurice's physical strength would probably not have survived. This was the first serious, nearly fatal accident for Maurice, but it did nothing to change his bad-boy attitude.

Upon returning to Montreal he was back to his usual shenanigans. Ferdinand took control of the situation, determined to provide structure for Maurice, as well as for Guy and Marcel.

Ferdinand liked going to the matches, especially to boxing matches, so he decided to take his three oldest sons to the Verdun YMCA. But no boxing classes were offered there, so instead he took them to the YMCA in downtown Montreal, on Drummond Street. That's where Ferdinand met Frank Saxon, the leading wrestling coach at the Montreal YMCA at the time.

Saxon's real name was Francis Morphet. He hailed from Wigan, England, and was well-known as a former professional wrestler who had coached the Canadian amateur wrestling team at the Amsterdam Olympics in 1928 and the Los Angeles Olympics in 1932. At the Amsterdam Games in 1928, Canada had won three medals in freestyle wrestling. One member of the Canadian team, Earl McCready, would go on to an extraordinary career in pro wrestling. The team didn't do as well at the Los Angeles Games in 1932, but one member of the team that year, another Montrealer, Harry Madison, later had a distinguished career as a professional wrestler.

Ferdinand would have liked his sons to learn how to box, but to his dismay, Saxon recommended they go in for amateur wrestling instead. Saxon was surely ahead of his time, because he believed wrestlers were less likely than boxers to sustain head injuries. With all the controversy about concussions in contact sports nowadays, this was an avant-garde position to take in the 1940s. But as history would show, wrestlers also got head injuries.

Saxon believed the Vachon boys would one day represent their country at the Olympics — but it would take them hard work and a little luck. Maurice relished the prospect. Participating in the Games would mean traveling abroad, a dream he had nourished since childhood. He saw amateur wrestling as his "ticket" to see the world.

The gym was a place where the Vachon boys could finally channel their energy. But Maurice was the one showing the most promise as a wrestler. There was nothing easy about training. He quickly learned this was a whole new world. He could no longer count on dominating kids his own age. It was back to square one. Besides, Maurice's ego took a hit the very first time he turned up at the YMCA. He saw an old man squatting on all fours on two mattresses fifteen feet square, covered with a very rough canvas. This was a typical position in amateur wrestling. The man invited Maurice to wrestle.

"I thought I would quickly get the better of an old man like that," Maurice later recalled. "Ultimately, I did win, but it took me four years to find a way!"

The man in question was Jim Cowley. A fifty-five-year-old measuring about six feet but weighing just 158 pounds, Cowley didn't look like much but he was good at wrestling. A native of Bryn, England, he had been recruited by Saxon in 1913. "Captain" Cowley was both a police officer and a wrestler — his police rank was added to his name. He had an interesting career and spent a lot of time helping young Maurice train.

Saxon and Cowley suggested Maurice strengthen certain parts of his body. They told him to work on his neck so he could resist better when his opponents tried pinning his shoulders to the mat during competitions. They also got him running. Cowley believed that while Maurice might be weaker and less experienced than his opponents, the fact that he didn't get winded would help him win wrestling matches. Actually, Maurice's redeeming quality in the ring was not brute strength — he was no stronger than his brothers, nor even than his sisters . . . Everyone agrees that Paul, Régis, and André were stronger than Maurice, but so were Claire and Diane. The Vachon girls were no pushovers.

Maurice decided to turn the odds in his favor. Like many

youngsters, he loved comics. On the last page of a comic book, he noticed an advertisement featuring the training program of Charles Atlas — "The World's Number 1 Body-Builder." Atlas was a Calabrian by birth established in the New York area who had developed a personal training program based on the principle of dynamic tension. Developing and strengthening a muscle required stretching that muscle to the maximum, then applying a weight to it. Maurice could afford the written program, which didn't require him to buy any expensive contraptions. He ordered a copy and got his father to translate it into French.

He got a few of his brothers to serve as weights. To strengthen his neck, Maurice trained by assuming the bridge position, arching over backwards with both feet on the ground and his head thrown back. Then he would get one of his brothers — Paul, Guy, or Marcel — to sit on his stomach, serving as a weight and applying the pressure required by the Atlas method. That's how he managed to develop an eighteen- to nineteen-inch neck. The Atlas training program also taught him push-up techniques and leg strengthening.

Maurice started running as well, a physical activity he would pursue all his life. He never did anything by halves. Again, he got his brothers involved. Paul was just five or six years old at the time, so when his kid brother was too pooped to continue, Maurice would hoist him onto his shoulders and continue running. This was another application of the Atlas method. "I have been running all my life," Maurice later recalled after retiring. "How far I run depends on the day. Sometimes I run two or three miles. I once ran fifteen miles in a day."

When Maurice started training at the YMCA at age fourteen, he was 5 feet 7 1/2 inches tall and weighed 200 pounds. He already had the build of a man, not of a boy his age. Cowley was his main coach for four years, and Maurice later admitted it was a grueling experience.

Maybe the pendulum had swung back. Considering Quebec's old French-English rivalries, now an Englishman was the one making him sweat. But that was the least of his worries. Maurice wanted to learn, so he threw himself into wrestling morning, noon, and night. He quickly became known as someone who never complained about training, who was never reluctant to fight against stronger and more experienced men. His training program paid off. Maurice's weight dropped to 174 pounds, the weight he would keep throughout his amateur wrestling career.

His father came to watch his boys train a few times, and even joined some of the wrestling training sessions, but his mother didn't really approve of Maurice's new hobby. "I never encouraged him to go in for wrestling," Marguerite once said in an interview. Fred didn't see it the same way. Wrestling meant the boys were no longer fighting in a field or in the street but on a mat, and with wrestling they stood a chance of traveling the world.

Maurice took to the sport like a fish to water. "I loved wrestling the minute I got onto the mat. I was hooked right away. I just loved amateur wrestling. Classes were Monday and Thursday evenings, from 8:00 p.m. to 10:00 p.m., and Saturdays from 2:00 p.m. to 4:00 p.m. I was always the first to arrive and the last to leave."

After several years of hard work, Maurice finally got his first chance to travel. World War II was over, and the Olympic Games resumed after a twelve-year hiatus. In March 1946, London, England, was chosen as host city for the 1948 Games. Maurice's two coaches were from England.

On May 24, 1947, Maurice defeated local wrestler Don Trifinov at the Canadian championships held in Winnipeg, becoming Canadian champion at just seventeen years of age. The same year, at a tournament in Alberta, he faced Eugene Nicholas Kiniski, who would go by the ring name of Gene Kiniski and would become one of the greatest professional wrestlers of all time. Maurice got recognition at the municipal level as well, when he was one of the nominees for the Montreal Athlete of the Year Award, along with Montreal Canadiens goalies Bill Durnan and Gerry McNeil. So what Frank Saxon had seen as possible two years earlier was now becoming a reality. However, Canada didn't have a lot of money to put into amateur wrestling.

On May 11, 1948, fourteen wrestlers representing Quebec in national competitions did a series of exhibition matches to raise funds a few weeks before the national championships, which also served to qualify athletes who would be sent to the London Olympics. The funds would help them participate in the Canadian championships and, for some, the Olympics. To qualify for London, however, a wrestler had first to be the best in his weight class in his province and across Canada. And this might still not be enough, since there was no guarantee all weight classes would be represented. Once champions in all classes had won, a committee of four members of the Canadian Olympic Committee would decide which wrestlers would go on to represent Canada in London.

By the 1940s, Maurice had already won a few municipal, provincial, and national titles, but the title he won on May 29, 1948, in Toronto was the most important of all. Maurice astonished and impressed the crowd, the way he had been doing ever since he started wrestling. He not only won the national championship in his class, defeating fellow Montrealer Gilles Milord, but also made it to the Canadian Olympic team along with two other Quebecers. It just happened that Jim Cowley was one of the four committee members calling the shots. At the age of eighteen, and with just four years of experience to his credit, Maurice was considered a wrestling prodigy and a top-notch recruit for Canada. He had dropped out of school years before; wrestling was now driving his life.

In 1948, he would finally fulfill his dream of traveling abroad. That year saw the young wrestler head overseas for the first time, venturing on the first of a long series of trips spanning several decades.

And who had offered this new life to Maurice? Ironically, it was Frank Saxon and Jim Cowley — representatives of Montreal's English community, which Maurice had seen so differently a few years before. So, after Maurice's boyhood clashes with English kids, now it was English coaches who were stimulating his passionate interest and giving him a whole new motivation in life: wrestling!

AROUND THE WORLD

Today the Olympic Games are synonymous with high-profile media coverage and sponsorship for many athletes, but in 1948 things were very different.

Pierre de Coubertin revived the modern Olympics in 1896, but the Games were not held in 1916, 1940, or 1944 because of the world wars that raged at the time. Even though people still refer to the London Olympics of 1948 as the Games of the XIV Olympiad, they were actually the eleventh Summer Games and the first held since the end of World War II. From 1896 to 1936, the way the media reported on the Games was nothing like today's essentially nonstop coverage. In the late 1940s, the idea of comprehensively televising the Olympics was still far off in the future. Newspaper and radio reporters covered the London Games, but most Canadians were not following them on a daily basis. The previous Summer Games were in 1936, so overall the Olympics were a case of "out of sight, out of mind."

The London organizers were pulling out all the stops, however. They wanted to restore the image of amateur sport, and the London

Games were the greatest sporting event at the time. Between July 29 and August 14, 1948, no less than 4,675 athletes from fifty-nine countries took part in the Games. By comparison, the London Games in 2012 drew 10,519 athletes from 205 countries.

Freestyle and Greco-Roman wrestling occupied a central position in the program. After all, wrestling is the oldest sport in the world. In all, sixteen competitions were held between July 29 and 31, showcasing 219 wrestlers from twenty-nine countries.

Aged eighteen, Maurice was by far the youngest member of the Canadian wrestling team in London. All the other members were thirty and over, with the exception of Maurice's twenty-six-year-old friend Fernand Payette. Maurice and Fernand had trained together and they were now about to experience the Olympics together. Payette fought as a light heavyweight, with Maurice, at 174 pounds, in the middleweight class. The two men were known by other team members as tough and aggressive young men who had the wrestling knowledge of true veterans. Mario Crête, a thirty-four-year-old featherweight wrestler and fellow Quebecer, also made friends with Maurice.

The world was finally within Maurice's reach and he hoped to make a good first impression. On July 13, wiping away a few tears, he left his family on the dockside in Montreal, bound for Halifax, Nova Scotia. There he joined the other Canadian athletes on the trans-Atlantic passenger liner RMS *Aquitania* for the crossing to London, arriving there on July 22. Passengers could cross the Atlantic on propeller-driven aircraft, but this was before the convenience of the Jet Age, and many people still preferred traveling by sea.

The idea of building an Olympic Village and housing all the athletes in the same place was also the stuff of the future. In '48, the Canadian wrestling team was housed at RAF Uxbridge, a Royal Air Force station near London. The war was still a vivid memory for people in England, but spectators at the Olympics were impressed by the opening ceremony, when thousands of athletes paraded through Wembley Stadium. But Maurice focused on one thing alone: July 29, the date of his match against Keshav P. Roy, an experienced wrestler from India.

This was the first international competition for both wrestlers. Six feet tall and twenty-two years old, Roy already enjoyed a solid reputation. It would have taken more to impress Maurice, although he admitted being a little nervous. But he was nervous in a good way. He jumped on his opponent's legs, lifting him bodily from the mat, did a wrist-lock, then pinned him by the shoulders to gain the win. It was all over in just fifty-four seconds, although when the story was told and retold in later years, the time it took for Maurice to defeat Roy was cut even shorter. In coming to London, Maurice had wanted to be noticed, and with this initial match he definitely succeeded. This resounding victory was reported by different newspapers back home. The Montreal daily *La Presse* reported that "Vachon disposed of K. P. Roy in less than the time it takes to say 'Jackie Robinson.'" (Robinson had played in 1946 for the Montreal Royals before breaking the color barrier in major league baseball in 1947 with the Brooklyn Dodgers.)

The *Montreal Gazette* provided solid coverage of Maurice's victory in London. An article on Canadian wrestlers at the Olympics devoted considerable attention to the wrist-lock Maurice applied on Roy before pinning him. The reporter said that Maurice's win served as a catalyst, enabling Morgan Plumb (from Toronto) and Maurice's friend Fernand Payette to win their respective matches. The article also noted Maurice was dedicating this victory to his newborn sister, Lise, and to his loving mother Marguerite. Lise would be the second-to-last child born into the Vachon family.

But above all, the article mentioned this victory as one of the most sensational of the evening: wrestling veterans had only praise for Maurice, who was described as "the shy and uncommunicative son of a Montreal police sergeant." The newspaper coverage made Ferdinand proud, but following Maurice's exploits at the Olympics proved to be complicated for the family. "My father and I had to go downtown to find a radio so we could hear the results of the Games," recalls Paul, who was only ten years old at the time.

But Maurice had a long way to go before picking up a medal. He would still have to win at least two, and perhaps even three, more matches to reach the podium. His next opponent was the Turkish wrestler Adil Candemir, who was also competing for the first time. Candemir was thirty and more experienced than Maurice. During an exhausting encounter on July 30, 1948, neither wrestler managed to pin his opponent. The judges had to make the decision. Wrestling is much like boxing or mixed martial arts today: when a match goes the distance, three judges have to step in. Maurice stood a good chance of winning, according to many spectators, because he had frankly dominated his opponent. But the judges couldn't agree and their verdict was a split decision (2–1) that handed victory to . . . Adil Candemir. The Vachon clan was shocked.

"I was sure I had won my fight," Maurice later said. "Before the judges made their call, someone tapped me on the shoulder. It was the coach of the Turkish team. He said: 'You won this fight.' When the judges made their decision, they gave it to my opponent. That really upset me, because I knew I had won this match."

The Canadian team lodged a protest, but it didn't make any difference. The three judges refused to budge and the decision was upheld. After the 1948 Games, it came as little comfort to learn that the Olympic Committee realized it had to develop a better judging process in sports like boxing, gymnastics, and wrestling.

Paul Vachon remembers the judges' decision: "The Canadian

wrestling team was so short of funds they were managed by a boxing coach in London who didn't know much about wrestling. With a wrestling coach, things might have worked out differently." In fact, Dennis White (who would go on to a great career in the world of boxing) was busy in London, managing both Canada's boxing and wrestling teams, with the backup of Gordon Sauvé and John Morgan Tutte. Frank Saxon was far more knowledgeable about wrestling; if he had been present, it could have made a difference.

Despite the loss, Maurice still had a chance of winning a medal, because this was not a tournament played on a knockout basis. A wrestler would be eliminated by accumulating five bad points. For example, a win by fall didn't add a point to the score, but a defeat by split decision was worth two points. In his next fight, the only way Maurice could be automatically eliminated from the competition was by being defeated by unanimous decision. On the other hand, he could still hope for a medal if he earned a win by fall or by decision.

His next opponent was Paavo Sepponen, a twenty-four-year-old Finn. Sepponen had won his first two bouts, one by fall and the other by unanimous decision. Maurice's lack of experience showed in this bout. On July 31 — the third day of competition — he was physically and mentally worn out after the shock defeat the day before. Maurice was dominated by his opponent, and the judges handed the Finn a unanimous and uncontested victory.

But for Maurice, one positive he left the London Games with is worth recalling. He was just eighteen years old and taking part in his first international competition, and he ended the Games without having his shoulders pinned to the mat. It was a real feat. Overall, Maurice finished eighth and his performance in London heralded a bright future for wrestling in Canada. Of the various opponents Maurice faced, only one got a medal — the Turk Candemir won the silver. This was all the more frustrating considering how their match had been decided. That same day, Fernand Payette needed just one win to earn a medal, but he didn't come through either. Nonetheless, he ended up in fourth place in his class, a very respectable outcome. In the end, after winning wrestling medals in three successive Olympic Games, this was the first time the Canadian team came home empty-handed. On the flip side, Turkey won eleven medals, six of them golds.

So Maurice left London without a medal, but he had gained immeasurable experience and now enjoyed an international reputation. He proved that he belonged on the world stage. Not once did he lash out bitterly or aggressively at the judges. He wasn't that kind of person. He wasn't looking for excuses.

The Canadian athletes weren't the best fed participants in the London Games. Maurice regularly ate two steaks per day at home, so being at the Olympics couldn't have been easy for him. He never used this argument to explain away his defeats: he didn't want to lay the blame on anyone.

With the other members of the Canadian delegation, including a young boxer named Armand Savoie, who once fought Willie Pep, and the marathon runner Gérard Côté, Maurice headed back to sea, leaving London on August 17 for Halifax.

During his trip to Europe, he had gotten to know other athletes. He had always dreamed of traveling, and now he had met people from all over the world, visiting places he'd only dreamed about. He visited Windsor Castle and met former wrestler George Hackenschmidt — nicknamed "the Russian Lion" — one of the greatest professional wrestlers of all time. Moreover, Maurice now felt reconciled with English people, or at least the ones living in England, whom he found nice and friendly.

The London Games were remarkable considering the number of

participating athletes who at one time or another would become professional wrestlers. Some athletes like Charles Istaz (Karl Gotch) and future NWA world champion Dick Hutton competed in wrestling, while others like Harold Sakata competed in weightlifting. Sakata would go on to play the role of Odd Job in *Goldfinger*, the third film in the famous James Bond series, and would become a very well-known wrestler under the ring name of Tosh Togo, one of the famous Togo brothers. In later years, two more athletes from London would become close friends with Maurice. The first was a French athlete of Polish origin, Édouard Wieczorkiewicz, a substitute on the French gymnastics team. Not really surprising, considering he would later become known as "Édouard Carpentier, the Flying Frenchman." Maurice also became friends with Verne Gagne, one of the substitutes on the U.S. wrestling team. Gagne was from Minnesota and would play a key role in Maurice's professional career some fifteen years later.

The London Games had been a dream summer, but Maurice now faced the harsh return to reality. He knew what he was worth, and he was more motivated than ever. The next Games would be held four years later in Helsinki, Finland. He had every intention of returning to Europe and winning a medal.

He barely had time to resume training in Montreal when there was already talk of him returning to another overseas competition. On September 26, 1948, the return of the British Empire Games was announced for Auckland, New Zealand, in 1950.

The British Empire Games brought together all former British colonies, which had recently formed the Commonwealth. (In fact the multi-sport event would be renamed "the British and Commonwealth Games" from 1954 to 1966, then "the British Commonwealth Games" from 1970 to 1974, and finally just "the Commonwealth Games" starting in 1978.) Like the Olympics, these games were not held during

World War II, even though Montreal had been chosen to host the event in 1942. The last British Empire Games dated back to 1938.

Were funds available to send a Canadian wrestling team to New Zealand? Chances were good: not only had Canada participated in the first three British Empire Games, but Canadians had won no less than nineteen medals in wrestling, including seven gold medals in seven weight classes during the first Games, held in 1930 in Hamilton, Ontario.

Maurice again had to take the national title in order to get a chance to participate in Auckland. The Canadian championships would take place on October 22, 1949, after which members of the wrestling team would be chosen for the Auckland Games. This time, Maurice was wrestling on his "home turf" at the Montreal YMCA on Drummond Street. In the final match of his weight class, Maurice defeated Robert Langlois, thereby earning a ticket to New Zealand, the longest trip he had ever made. His dreams were now taking off like a rocket. Only a few years beforehand he had been pitching rocks through school windows, and now he was heading out on a journey to the other side of the world.

He made the trip with his Olympic buddies Morgan Plumb and Fernand Payette, and it involved almost three weeks' worth of travel. Funding was tight, so the first group of thirty-six Canadian athletes (of a total of seventy-two) left Vancouver by sea on December 22, arriving in New Zealand on January 10, 1950. Maurice and other Canadian wrestlers were part of the second group of thirty-six. They left Montreal by train on January 9, making the cross-Canada rail journey to Vancouver in five days. After a three-day stay in Vancouver, they flew to San Francisco, where they were laid up five days because of bad weather, then on to Honolulu, where they had to wait another three days because of more bad weather. Then they flew to Fiji before finally reaching Auckland, New Zealand, a total of fifteen days from Vancouver. Today, making this trip from Montreal would take about twenty-four hours.

The Games took place from February 4 to 11, 1950, drawing participants from twelve countries for a total of nine sports. By comparison, athletes from seventy-one countries competing in seventeen sports events participated in the Glasgow Commonwealth Games in 2014.

No one was overly concerned about the competition. Of the top ten middleweight wrestlers at the London Games two years earlier, only three had come from a Commonwealth country, including Australian Bruce Arthur and Englishman Eddie Bowey, ranked ninth and tenth respectively. According to the Olympic ranking, the favorite this time was the South African Callie Reitz who had finished off the podium. But Maurice had matured — he was now twenty — and he had gained experience since his last international competition.

This time, the Canadian Olympic Committee didn't take any chances: Frank Saxon was appointed to accompany the delegation. This was surely good news for Maurice and his wrestling team, but it might not have been such good news for the boxing and weightlifting teams, since Saxon was coaching those teams as well.

The Auckland Games started on a dramatic note. Fernand Payette was injured during an exhibition match against teammate Henry Hudson, who went on to win the gold in the welterweight class. Payette pulled a neck muscle and had to withdraw and return home without the gold medal he had been hoping for. This would prove the end of his amateur career.

In his first match, Maurice faced off against the New Zealander Peter Fletcher. Maurice earned the win by fall, but it wasn't a massacre. Still, he was mentally stronger than his opponent and beat him relatively easily. In his second bout, Maurice won out over the South African favorite, Reitz. This meant he was headed for the finals and stood a chance of winning the gold.

Maybe it wasn't an Olympic medal, but it was still a gold medal in an international competition. His opponent was the Australian, Arthur. Maurice displayed the aggressiveness and passion that were becoming his trademarks, winning the fight, one bad point to three. He finally won the gold medal he had been hoping for. Arthur won the silver medal, and Reitz picked up the bronze. Cleary, Maurice's experience at the Olympics turned out to be a huge asset in a competition generally considered to be secondary. Maurice was also acknowledged to be the wrestler with the best technique, in all classes. Paul Vachon recalls, "In 1962, when I was in Australia, Bruce Arthur, one of the guys who had wrestled with Maurice in Auckland, told me he was still hurting all over from that match!"

After the medal presentation, tradition required the national anthem of the winning country be played and the national flag raised. But in 1950, Canada didn't yet have its own flag — it was still using the Red Ensign it had been flying since colonial days. The maple leaf flag — the flag we know today — would not be adopted until 1965. As for a national anthem, there was no single "Canadian" song: sometimes it was "God Save the King," other times "O Canada." In a setting like the British Empire Games, "God Save the King" took precedence. That special moment would influence Maurice's political views in later years.

Maurice was very proud of his performance, as evidenced by a statement he made to the daily newspaper *Montréal-Matin*: "Long ago I dreamed of winning, and today I finally pulled it off. I am currently experiencing the greatest emotions of my whole wrestling career."

Getting to New Zealand had been quite the journey, but getting home to Montreal proved to be a true odyssey. Because of budget restrictions, the Canadian organizers decided most married athletes would leave Auckland by air, whereas everyone else — including Maurice — would have to travel by sea. This meant steaming from

Auckland to Sydney, Australia, to catch a passenger liner for Europe. The liner then skirted the coast of Australia, crossing the Indian Ocean to Ceylon (now Sri Lanka), and heading up the Red Sea and through the Suez Canal in Egypt. Once in the Mediterranean, the liner headed for Naples, Italy, then the Strait of Gibraltar between Spain and Morocco. Finally, the ship proceeded around the coastline of Spain and France, landing at Tilbury, England, London's main port. Over the years, the story of these athletes returning from New Zealand to Canada has been told and retold any number of times, and in the telling people have no doubt inflated the number of months it took the athletes to get home again. The voyage nevertheless was long: Maurice and the other athletes left Auckland in mid-February and only reached England on April 17. There still remained the North Atlantic to cross. They sailed from England on April 21, reaching Montreal in early May. Maurice wanted to travel, and travel he did — he had now circumnavigated the globe.

Celebrations upon Maurice's return were short-lived. The homecoming was disappointing. Maurice was expecting a triumphant return to Montreal, but his brother Marcel was the only one who turned up in the Port of Montreal to meet him for the ride home.

Worse, two and a half months at sea had not been good for Maurice. According to Paul Vachon, "My brother gained a lot of weight on the return voyage from Auckland and he never trained again the same way." By his own admission, Maurice weighed 219 pounds when he disembarked. He gave up training altogether, and only had time for wrestling and eating. It was also on the voyage back that Maurice developed a taste for alcohol and began binge drinking. One day he got so drunk he smashed the shipboard toilets to pieces. The Canadian team wanted to strip him of his medal, but Frank Saxon intervened in his favor and the incident eventually was settled internally. His problems with alcohol were just beginning.

This was bad timing for a wrestler who had been fighting at 174 pounds just a few months earlier.

Wrestling was now occupying a more prominent place on the international stage. The first world championships took place in 1951, but no countries from the Americas took part. That same year, the first Pan American Games took place, but again, Canada lacked funds and was not involved. And then there were the Helsinki Olympics, slated for 1952.

Maurice quickly realized that medals filled his heart but not his bank account, and now that he was no longer in such good physical condition, he had lost that motivation as well. He was also disappointed with media coverage and public reactions on his return. Aside from a visit to Montreal mayor Camillien Houde, Maurice's gold medal went practically unnoticed.

"Returning from the British Empire Games with a gold medal, I thought people were going to carry me unto their shoulders. But that's not what happened. I was almost forgotten," Maurice later recalled with a heavy heart.

He didn't take part in the provincial championships in Montreal on May 10, 1950. Ironically, Robert Langlois, the man he had beaten to earn a place in Auckland, won not only the provincial title but also the Canadian title. However, Canada didn't send a middleweight wrestler to the 1952 Olympics and actually would not send any representative from this class until 1968.

At twenty, Maurice wasn't even at his peak. Conventional wisdom held that a wrestler reached his peak in his mid-twenties, and the thought was that Maurice could still compete a few more years. He certainly would have been a medal hopeful at the Helsinki Olympics in 1952 and again at the Melbourne Olympics four years later, by which time he would have been only twenty-six. Reitz, the South African he had beaten in Auckland, who had come fourth in

London, ranked sixth in Helsinki. Maurice was much better than that.

"In 1952, I knew Maurice by reputation and I knew he was a very good wrestler," remembers former amateur and professional wrestler Danny Hodge, from Oklahoma. "In 1952, he would have won a medal in Helsinki, I'm sure. As for 1956, it would have been an interesting match." Hodge was twenty-four when he won the silver medal in the freestyle middleweight class in Melbourne. He and Maurice would then have been at the top of their game.

Maurice suffered because he made a name for himself just when amateur sport was beginning to become better organized, both in terms of visibility and funding. At another time, a man with his talents could no doubt have represented his country at every conceivable venue: the world championships, the Pan American Games, the Commonwealth Games, the Olympic Games, and more. What rank did Maurice occupy in the hierarchy of amateur wrestling? Sadly, we will never know.

Years later, at the end of his career, he would enjoy the distinction of being one of the best amateur wrestlers to turn professional — a member of that select club that includes Brock Lesnar, Danny Hodge, the Iron Sheik, Verne Gagne, and Kurt Angle.

The return from New Zealand marked the end of Maurice's amateur career. The British Empire Games enabled him to travel as never before, to come home with a medal he would long cherish. But the harsh reality of life caught up with him. After struggling to find his way as a teenager, he now had to face the cruelties of the adult world — where dreams and passions have to take a back seat to the salary you need to earn.

Maurice was no longer a child — he had become a man.

4 THANK YOU, ARMAND

Ferdinand Vachon was known for his impressive natural strength. In his earlier years, he had sometimes lifted one of his children at arm's length. By the age of seventy, he could still do seventy one-arm push-ups at a stretch. Even at work he'd often be asked to take part in contests of strength between Montreal's different police stations. Ferdinand was six feet tall and weighed 230 pounds, and he could certainly hold his own on "the Main" (Saint-Laurent Boulevard), where there was a lot of action for a police officer. He was quick to defend himself when attacked — which happened quite often on his beat — and he liked fighting. But by 1948, he'd had enough. After twenty years in law enforcement, Ferdinand decided to return to his roots, buying a farm in the rural village of Mansonville in the Eastern Townships, and moving there with the family members who were still at home, leaving Guy and Marcel to continue their own life in Montreal.

Maurice also stayed in Montreal at the time, training for the London Games. He worked near the Port of Montreal, then at the meat-packing company Morenz Beef, and then in Pointe-Saint-Charles for the Canadian National Railway (CNR), one of Canada's two largest railway companies. His wrestling coach Frank Saxon was a CNR foreman. The CNR even paid Maurice's salary for a month and a half while he took part in the British Empire Games in 1950. An advantage of working for the CNR was that it belonged to the federal government.

While training for the British Empire Games, Maurice landed a job that kept him employed longer than any he'd had previously. But this new occupation was more dangerous than any railway tracks.

Even with his movie star look and the fact he was only eighteen, he became a nightclub bouncer. In Montreal, bouncers were given the fancy title of "maître d'hôtel." But their role was to serve as doormen, welcome customers into the club, and seat them before the show started. Actually, that was the only "fancy" thing about the job.

Montreal was widely known for its nightlife, with many artists, singers, bands, and actors giving performances in nightclubs and cab-arets. Maurice was just eighteen years old, so he wasn't old enough to buy or drink alcohol in a bar. In Quebec, the legal drinking age for alcohol remained at twenty-one years until 1971. But Maurice *was* old enough to be a bouncer in the same establishment.

The greater part of Maurice's work — the part for which he became well-known — was removing unruly customers from the premises when they created a disturbance. Typically, he had to deal with one of two different situations: first, there were the guys who got drunk and rowdy; second, there were those who had gone out with only fighting in mind.

"Many people would take a swing at me. That's the way it was in Montreal in those days. If you looked physically strong in Montreal, some wise guy always turned up and was ready to take a swing at you," Maurice later explained during the French-language documentary *Mad Dog: The Man Behind the Beast*.

His buddy Fernand Payette helped him land the job, which paid between $75 and $100 a night, or what was about the equivalent of $1,000 today. Payette was already working in the business before London, and after Auckland, he was asked to recruit new men and place them in different clubs. In the 1950s, the Beaver Café at the corner of Sainte-Catherine and Bleury was considered one of the toughest nightclubs in Montreal. Guy Larose quit as the doorman there because he couldn't take it any longer. A few years later, he would become widely known in the wrestling world using the ring name Hans Schmidt.

Maurice arrived on the scene when Montreal's cabarets were booming. During the decade following the war, cabarets sprung up all over the city, showcasing international stars and homegrown Quebec stars; Charles Aznavour, Édith Piaf, Frank Sinatra, Jerry Lewis, Dean Martin, Sammy Davis Jr., Oscar Peterson, Oliver Jones, and Félix Leclerc all performed regularly in these clubs.

So Payette sent Maurice to the Beaver Café — and the young man made his reputation just as he had done in amateur wrestling. Nobody fazed him, and no one could overpower him. Then other clubs began calling on Maurice's fighting talents, including the Bistro du Plateau, the Bal Tabarin, the Havana, the Mocambo, and the Montmartre.

An entire book could be written about the fistfights Maurice got into in his hometown nightclubs. His wrestling reputation probably drew men who considered themselves tough guys or big shots, who turned up only because they were looking for trouble and relished the prospect of taking on the legendary bouncer in person. But Maurice always managed to overpower the unending series of wannabe fighters — former boxers, former military police officers, some of the many thugs living in Montreal and the surrounding area. Maurice always claimed he had never started a fight. But it didn't take much provocation to get him into one. And he could get very aggressive if things didn't work out the way he wanted. This was a case of "like father, like son" because Maurice had always had boundless admiration for his father and had always sought to resemble him in terms of physical strength and character.

There could be some debate about whether he ever initiated a fight, but there is no doubt about the fact that he ended every one of them. One of the most striking examples was during a fight outside the Beaver Café. A black man gave him such a powerful head butt that Maurice's lower front teeth were knocked out. Maurice retaliated by repeatedly slamming the man's head against an iron post. Without the intervention of the police, Maurice would have continued battering the man and could have killed him.

"He often fought and he always won, but it's not good business for a club to have too many fights," recalls his brother Guy, who also worked as a doorman in those days.

One challenge Maurice faced was his size. At 5 feet 8 inches tall, he didn't exactly strike fear in the hearts of rowdy customers, and sometimes they felt they could afford not to take his warnings seriously. Maurice's brother Guy was big and beefy enough to get the message across just by standing there. But Maurice had to find another way to get respect. And that's when the trouble would start. He resembled his father in that he completely lacked patience where unruly customers were concerned. Guy took the time to talk sense into customers and help them understand what was likely to happen. But Maurice had no time for chit-chat: he often grabbed customers and bodily removed them from the cabaret and onto the pavement outside.

That's what Maurice became famous for.

One time he was asked to give a hand at the Havana, a cabaret on Frontenac Street, where a customer was creating trouble. Whenever the show started, he would tap the table with his bottle and continue tapping throughout the show. Nobody could control him, so Maurice was called in.

The first evening, he observed the problem customer, who was sitting on the main floor of the cabaret, right next to the door leading to the stairs. The man began tapping with his bottle as soon as the show began. Maurice decided to have a little talk with him.

"If you don't stop making so much noise, I'm gonna get you out of the club."

"Just go ahead and try," said the customer.

While it might be true that Maurice didn't start fights, that kind of remark was usually enough. He came round behind the customer, applying one of his buddy Payette's favorite techniques. It was much easier to bounce a customer who was facing backwards: he couldn't hold onto the door with more than his fingertips, and he couldn't see where he was heading. But this was also true of the doorman: he couldn't see where he was going, which was a problem, especially when there was a staircase.

"So I dragged him backwards, and when we got to the staircase, down he went — boom, boom, boom, boom! I practically reached the bottom of the stairs before he did, and once we got outside, I just let him have it — three or four punches in the face. There, the fight continued another five to six minutes. I gave him a real beating. He was covered in blood; I guess he had a broken nose," Maurice recalled, providing the grisly details.

But he sagely stopped pounding the guy for fear of actually killing the poor soul.

Later in the evening, a rumor reached the cabaret: the ambulance had apparently come to collect the customer, who had died from his injuries. Maurice was stunned by the news. His family had moved to Mansonville, and he now lived in Montreal with his Uncle Armand and his Aunt Alice — she had served in the army and now worked for the police. She wasn't supposed to know Maurice worked at the Havana, but when he got up on Sunday morning, she told him she'd heard about the rumor that was making the rounds. Maurice was astounded. Fortunately, it proved to be just a rumor and the customer was still alive. Maurice later admitted the guy was "beaten up real bad."

A few days later, Maurice was still at the Havana when a police inspector turned up. The inspector was a friend of his father's, and he told Maurice the bad-tempered customer wanted to file a complaint against him for both theft and assault and battery. He also advised him to get a good lawyer. Maurice spoke to the owner of the Havana, Joe Beaudry, who owned several other taverns and nightclubs in Montreal and had a lot of experience. Beaudry told Maurice never to plead guilty and to defend himself in court if necessary. Beaudry knew that kind of customer by heart. Sure enough, no complaint was filed and the affair fizzled out.

"The guy who got beat up deserved it, and things ended right there," Maurice said succinctly. Despite his brave words, he realized that when people couldn't beat him with their fists they would look for other ways to mess with him.

It took Maurice two months to establish order at the Bal Tabarin, on Saint-Laurent Boulevard. That's what he was being paid to do; that was his job. The whole point of bodily removing bad-tempered thugs was to calm things down in the cabaret and make sure anyone disturbing the peace understood he had better keep quiet or he would face the doorman.

Then, one night at closing time, three young men began quarrelling with Maurice. According to one of them, the girl at the cloakroom hadn't given him a ticket so he couldn't get his coat back. Without thinking, he grabbed the girl and began twisting her arm.

"It didn't take me long. I stood up, punched the guy three or four times in the face, then pitched the three guys down the stairs."

The only problem was, one of the young men was the son of the chief organizer of Maurice Duplessis, the premier of Quebec. Maurice was accused of breaking the young man's jaw. He was arrested for aggravated assault, which raised the prospect of a six-month jail term. Up until that point, Maurice had managed to stay on the right side of the law, but he now found himself in the same situation as when he had been a delinquent teenager. He went to see his father in the Eastern Townships. Ferdinand always defended his children and he agreed to help. Clearly a police officer couldn't spend years on the beat without developing friendships with judges. Mr. Vachon went to the courthouse and met a friend he hadn't seen since his retirement. He explained the difficulties his son was experiencing, and the friend said he would talk it over with the judge assigned to the case.

Once Maurice came back to court, the judge said, "I was ready to give you six months in jail, but since that time, I have learned on good authority that you come from a good family. Suspended sentence."

In those years, the administration of justice depended much more on personal influence and interventions than it does today. A person like Ferdinand Vachon carried a lot of weight.

Maurice was increasingly aware his job was complicating his life. True, he was doing a good thing, ridding bars of bandits, criminals, and troublemakers. And this should have meant he was staying on the right side of the law. But he put so much intensity into beating up troublemakers that it was creating more trouble for him than he wanted. He didn't mind skipping a meal for a good fight, and that was the whole problem.

Ironically, the person who gave Maurice the best advice was actually a leading member of the Montreal Mafia.

Vincenzo Cotroni arrived in Montreal from Italy in 1924. He joined the Club Saint-Paul de Ville-Émard, where professional wrestler Armand Courville gave lessons. Cotroni and Courville were the same age, and they became fast friends. Courville initiated the young Calabrian into professional wrestling. They both wrestled in the 1930s, Cotroni taking on the ring name of Vic Vincent. The main venues for their bouts were stadiums located around the city, even the ones where Paul Lortie, one of Maurice's favorite wrestlers, used to perform.

In the early 1940s, Cotroni (now called Vic) went into business with Courville, opening several popular bars, cafés, and cabarets in Montreal, including Au Faisan Doré, whose opening reflected the economic prowess of the underworld at the time. Successful cabarets gave a boost to Montreal's economy, but they were actually front operations. Cotroni was considered by many to have been the founding father of the Mafia in Montreal: he opened not only cabarets but also brothels, illegal betting operations, and gambling dens in the heart of the city, near Saint-Laurent Boulevard, in Montreal's red-light district.

Maurice was widely known as a bouncer, and it made sense for Cotroni to hire him. He worked for Cotroni in several illegal establishments. Maurice had already learned how the decisions of a judge could be influenced. In just the same way, the Mafia now set out to influence Montreal decision-makers, especially the police force. By 1946, the police were so corrupt that crime-fighting lawyer Pacifique Plante was appointed head of the city's vice squad.

At the time, Montreal would have benefitted from having someone rigorous on the force like Ferdinand Vachon. Organized crime worked out a strategy of mobile gambling dens: this was how they managed to dart out of the way whenever the lightning raids of Plante and the vice squad were coming. Cotroni, Courville, and the others would get wind of a raid about to take place, then quickly move their gambling operations to another address.

"One day, the gambling den was in Montreal; the next day it was across the river in Longueuil. Often a den would spend a few months in the same place, but other times, it would be here one day, and a mile away the next day," Maurice later recalled.

Maurice liked Cotroni. "He was an extremely nice man, friendly, very friendly. He was a very fine man. I was several times at his home."

Cotroni's right-hand man, Courville, liked the young Vachon in return. He had a lot in common with Maurice: they were both from large families, they had grown up in modest neighborhoods, they both had boundless admiration for their fathers. Courville had also been a wrestler for fifteen years, so he understood what Maurice had achieved during his amateur career and he could see the huge potential of the young man. He had heard all about Maurice's escapades as a bouncer, and he knew probably better than anyone in Montreal the type of people hanging out in clubs, cabarets, and gambling dens. Courville could peer into Maurice's foreseeable future as if he were looking into a crystal ball. So he had something specific to tell Maurice when he invited him to dinner at an Italian restaurant at the corner of Sainte-Catherine and Saint-Denis.

Maurice long remembered the conversation.

"Maurice," Courville said, "the way things are going, you have to be one of the best men of the city of Montreal. Nobody can beat you in a fight. But one day someone's going to come along with a gun and blow your brains out. My advice to you is drop all this bouncer business, because it's too risky for you. You were good at amateur wrestling. Why don't you take up professional wrestling? At first you won't be making any money, but you're going to end up making a living. Most importantly, you're going to live longer."

Maurice then recalled an encounter with one of Montreal's leading gangsters of the time, Eddie Sauvageau. He witnessed Sauvageau beating up a poor defenseless butcher. Then Maurice jumped him. Sauvageau didn't appreciate the way Vachon was getting involved so he pulled out a revolver. Maurice slugged him with his left fist, challenging him to pull the trigger if he had the guts. Maurice considered himself a fighting machine, but he also knew he didn't take the time to evaluate his opponents. Sauvageau was a good illustration of this. Some of Maurice's coworkers, the experienced bouncers René Trudeau and Gerry Turenne, got shot because of their work. He knew that situations like this could arise again, and one day someone totally ruthless was going to pull the trigger. Years later, in 1957, after Maurice had settled in Texas, Sauvageau was murdered in his sleep.

Courville's advice didn't fall on deaf ears. A few days later, Maurice left the world of bars and cabarets with the hope of becoming a professional wrestler.

Once more, wrestling came to Maurice's rescue. Unwittingly, he had gotten himself into a trap, placing his future — and his life — at risk. He was even more plagued by the world of violence than he had been when he was just a kid. And even if he didn't actually die from the violence, there was always a shadow looming — the shadow of the penitentiary, which threatened anyone working for the criminal underworld. As fate would have it, years later, some of his children found themselves behind bars. They could have done with some of Maurice's luck.

Maurice's father always told him never to stray too far from the straight and narrow, because it was too easy to take the wrong path. Frank Saxon, and then Courville, had helped Maurice choose the right way. Maurice would always remain grateful to Courville, expressing his gratitude to him even after the man died in 1991. Courville had warned him that professional wrestling would not be easy at first. But in 1951, Maurice had no idea how right Courville was.

NO MAN IS A PROPHET IN HIS OWN COUNTRY

In 1950, there had already been rumors in Auckland, New Zealand, that Maurice was thinking of going professional. So when Courville met him, the young French Canadian had already been toying with the idea for some time, which made it easier for him to make an informed decision.

But where was he to start? How did an amateur go professional? In the 1950s, the transition was much easier than it is today. Pro wrestling was more like Olympic freestyle wrestling than the kind of shows put on by today's WWE Superstars. But pro wrestlers had their own code of silence and they jealously guarded the secrets of their sport. When a neophyte entered pro wrestling, he wasn't taught all the tricks of the trade right away. The reason was simple. He might ultimately decide he wasn't cut out for the sport, so longtime pros thought it was better if the new guys weren't able to take the whole pro knowledge base with them when they left. At a time when the vast majority of fans thought pro wrestling was a sport, not a choreographed performance, the movers and shakers of the business believed this law of silence, called kayfabe, was vital to ensure the success of the discipline, with only a small number of people let in on the secrets of pro wrestling.

Maurice eventually got back into shape after Auckland. He still weighed more than 200 pounds, but he now walked around at 215 pounds of muscle and sheer strength. He didn't have the physique of a bodybuilder, but his muscle mass was so great that people almost forgot how short he was — 5 feet 8 inches. Maurice's buddy Fernand Payette decided to go pro at the same time. That was all promoter Gerry Legault needed to hear to become interested.

Legault was a local journeyman who had trained with the brothers Paul and Bob Lortie, then started his career in the 1940s. His peak as a wrestler was when he wrestled at Madison Square Garden in New York. He was just thirty-one, and he continued wrestling from time to time. But he was now first and foremost a promoter. In wintertime, he would organize light heavyweight matches at a venue next to the Saint-Jacques Market, at the corner of Amherst and Ontario Streets, in South-Central Montreal. In summertime, he would organize matches at the Exchange Stadium, an open stadium at the corner of Mont-Royal Avenue and Iberville Street.

Legault hoped to have signed Quebec's two upcoming wrestling stars, banking on their Olympic credentials.

Payette started wrestling at the Exchange in July. But Maurice Vachon had his first professional match on May 14, 1951, against Al Tucker, a rough-and-tumble veteran. Maurice quickly realized it wasn't exactly a high-paid job to wrestle outside the Montreal Forum where the highest-profile matches were held. Courville had been right to say it wouldn't pay that well at first. Actually, Maurice earned between $10 and $30 per fight. Even when he took part in several matches each week, he was still earning a fraction of his previous salary as a bouncer. Wrestling took place at the Exchange on

Monday and Thursday evenings. But there were so many people promoting small shows in town that it was relatively easy for a wrestler to wrestle more than once a week. Moreover, especially in the summer, Montreal was not the only city in Quebec where wrestling matches were held. The pro wrestling circuit included stops in Quebec City, Trois-Rivières, Shawinigan, Chicoutimi, and Hull, in particular. Unfortunately, wrestlers had to pay their travel expenses and meals, the way they do nowadays, which reduced their take-home pay.

Maurice wrestled against Hank Pardi, who would later become known as Tony Angelo. Then he faced Harry Madison in a match of former Olympians. At first, Legault protected Maurice, getting him matches that often went to the time limit, or what wrestling lingo calls a Broadway, as a way of showing how long he could wrestle. Legault understood one thing about Maurice: the best way for him to develop was to spend time in the ring and to face more experienced wrestlers.

Then, a little over a month after his debut, Maurice was finally called to the Montreal Forum. This was like moving from a farm team up to the major leagues. Promoter Eddie Quinn kept an eye on young wrestling talent being developed by promoters Gerry Legault and Sylvio Samson in small stadiums around town. Maurice acquired experience in his first bouts, and in return, veteran wrestlers were occasionally sent to different stadiums across the city.

Maurice's first match at the Montreal Forum took place on June 20, 1951, against George Mann. But he didn't get as much media attention as he might have expected, because this was pro wrestling and he had turned pro only a month earlier. By comparison, the newspapers devoted a lot more space to the pro boxing career of Armand Savoie, who had gone to the Olympics with Maurice, because boxing was considered the "noble art." Of course, the papers would also provide much more coverage of a young Quebecer signing a contract to play hockey for the Montreal Canadiens, or football for the Montreal Alouettes, or baseball for the Montreal Royals. Young sportsmen knocking on the door of the big leagues practically monopolized the sports pages in Montreal, whether it was Tommy Lasorda pitching for the Royals or Jacques Plante, Jean Béliveau, and Dickie Moore playing for the Canadiens. Professional wrestling was undeniably popular, but it didn't reach the same level of popularity as other pro sports, which, when you consider the examples of native Quebecers like Kevin Owens and Sami Zayn in the WWE, is still the case today.

Still, Maurice got some notice in the newspapers the day before his match at the Forum. The papers recalled he had represented Canada well at the London Olympics and was considered a good prospect. But they made no mention of his gold medal in Auckland, which only went to show the British Empire Games were considered a second-tier event. But that didn't really matter: Maurice had finally made it to the major leagues.

Wrestling in the Montreal Forum was like playing hockey in the National Hockey League. The main event pitted the champion of the National Wrestling Alliance (NWA), Lou Thesz, against one of the most popular wrestlers in Montreal, Bobby Managoff. The semi-main event pitted the duo of Yvon Robert and Larry Moquin against Buddy Rogers and Fred Atkins. Maurice was finally joining the stars he had admired in his younger years — the men whose pictures he had pinned to his wall. Two days earlier, while awaiting confirmation of the match, the fact that Maurice had been an amateur wrestler meant he was allowed to be Managoff's training partner. He wrestled in the prelims and won in eleven minutes sixteen seconds. Like Legault before them, Quinn, Robert (a shareholder in the company), and Moquin (Quinn's assistant) decided to have Maurice wrestle as a babyface. What else could they do otherwise with a former Olympian who had represented his country so successfully? Maurice was paid

$200 for his match, for a show that drew 9,000 fans. This was nothing compared to the earnings Robert and the other big-name finalists raked in, but it was much more than Maurice had earned with Legault, and more than he brought in as a bouncer.

The match went so well that Maurice was back the following week, once again wrestling Al Tucker, who was often paired with young wrestlers just starting out. Maurice pulled off another victory. Although his pro career was just getting under way, the promoters were still protecting him by practically handing him victories in his first two matches. He was definitely a crowd-pleaser, with his good physique, dark hair, and manly look setting many a female heart aflutter. The promoters wanted to give him every chance to become a star, which meant winning his first two matches at the Forum. Once again, Maurice pocketed the tidy sum of $200. He felt he had finally succeeded, and he was in wrestling heaven.

Between matches at the Forum, Maurice continued wrestling for Legault, where everything was different: the pay, the crowd, and the quality of the wrestlers. However, he still had to learn his craft, so maturing in the minor leagues was a necessary evil. But he had fought in the major leagues and hoped to return there as soon as possible. Autumn came, and still there was no return to the Forum for Maurice. Legault was announcing with great fanfare that he had signed Payette and Vachon for the winter season in the Saint-Jacques Market, and even planned to have them wrestling as a team. Winter came, and Maurice was still waiting to head back to the Forum. To his dismay, it was a full ten months before he was called back to the Mecca of wrestling in Montreal.

Yet Maurice was one of the most popular wrestlers in Montreal and was clearly showing an aura of a star to be.

In 1952 he fought only five times at the Forum. When the Forum was fully booked, Quinn sent him to Ottawa to gain experience. As in the previous year, he protected Maurice by booking him to win or to do a double count-out finish, the latter in order to get a feud going with the other wrestler. Ultimately, 1952 had been disappointing, but 1953 was even worse: Quinn and his cronies ignored Maurice, who wrestled only one match at the Forum that year.

It wasn't surprising that a young athlete should have to prove himself before becoming a "regular." The difference was that there wasn't that much space for new wrestlers compared to players for a professional sports team. At the time, a show consisted of four matches on average, sometimes including a tag team match. That came to an average of eight to ten wrestlers per card. This was a far cry from *WrestleMania III* in 1987, which featured twelve matches involving thirty-eight wrestlers. Maurice was discovering that in wrestling, it didn't really matter who you were: what really mattered was who you knew. No one was willing to go to bat for him.

Besides, his amateur wrestling experience wasn't as big a plus as it might have seemed. In fact, Maurice was considered one of the best young "scientific" wrestlers around — this was the term applied to wrestlers who specialize in ground wrestling holds, don't get violent or go in for cheap shots, and don't cheat. But even if the discipline was more "scientific" then than it is today, the fact remains that this was professional wrestling, sports entertainment, where stars have to be good wrestlers while getting the public to come back week after week.

"When I turned pro, it was as if my past had simply never existed," Maurice later recalled. However, this statement doesn't tell the whole story. His past experience as an amateur wrestler was a double-edged sword. It allowed him to carve out a place for himself more quickly than other wrestlers, and it gave the media a reason to talk about him. On the other hand, Maurice's words did him a disservice. He always told anyone ready to listen that he was an Olympic wrestler and he could beat anyone in the ring. In wrestling terms, this made him a "shooter" — someone who could really defend himself in the ring when a situation started getting out of hand. But a shooter was also a wrestler who could take liberties and depart at will from the script agreed upon in advance. He didn't help himself by making such statements: he was only twenty-two or twenty-three, he didn't have the reputation of a Lou Thesz, and people in Montreal hadn't forgotten about his street fighting. His bravado turned other wrestlers off, and some were afraid to face him. Besides, Maurice occasionally took on a wrestler he disliked in the locker room. Everyone was afraid.

"When I worked for Sylvio Samson, Maurice was on the cards around Montreal. I was really afraid of him," says wrestler Pat Patterson. "But he watched me at work. One time, he told me with his loud voice: 'You're going to be a good wrestler!' I didn't say a fucking word back to him — not thank you or anything else. I was too afraid of him."

The former wrestler Gino Brito goes even further: "My father, the former promoter Jack Britton, was told it wasn't Maurice's size Quinn disliked, but his past as a street brawler."

Straight wrestling ability wasn't everything. Wrestlers like Robert and Managoff were very charismatic, Thesz was in a class of his own because he took wrestling to a whole other level, and Moquin was a born entertainer. These wrestlers all had their own personal characteristics, and fans identified with them. By comparison, Maurice, with his simple wrestling outfit and wrestling style, came across as lacking color.

In the early 1950s, there were plenty of wrestlers in Quebec, and Quinn had an endless supply of French Canadians to put on his cards. Veterans like Madison, Bob Langevin, and Eddy Auger were often featured at these shows. Madison and Langevin had been trained by Émile Maupas, the famous French coach who had also trained Robert and Moquin. Among the younger wrestlers, Guy Larose, Sammy Berg, and Tony Angelo were all in their twenties and were featured more often than Maurice was.

Somehow, Quinn and Robert were in a position to decide which French Canadian would be part of the show. They could make you a hero or a zero. Robert, in particular, was determined to maintain his position, even so late in his career. Over the past decade, Moquin alone had kept an enviable place in the organization. He understood the industry, and was used by Quinn as booker. There could be no doubt about the fact: Maurice simply didn't figure in Quinn and Robert's plans. For example, when they organized a show to raise funds to send Canadian amateur wrestlers to the national championships in Winnipeg and then the 1952 Olympics in Finland, they didn't call on Maurice, even though he had the ideal profile to promote amateur wrestling. Robert was in his early forties and knew his wrestling career was nearing its end. Clearly, he would get to choose who would take his place. Unfortunately, this wasn't going to be Maurice, Larose, Berg, or Angelo. He called on his brother, Maurice Robert, for some preliminary matches, but even he wasn't destined to bring Quebec wrestling into a whole new era.

Yvon Robert ultimately chose Jean Rougeau, a young wrestler just three months older than Maurice. Rougeau was the nephew of the much-liked veteran Eddy Auger and had been wrestling for some time, making his debut at the Forum in February 1952. This wasn't the first time Maurice's path crossed with Jean's, and it wouldn't be the last. Not only did Quinn prefer the charismatic Jean Rougeau to Maurice, Legault had him wrestling in several main events at the Exchange, whereas Maurice could only hope to occasionally take part in preliminary matches.

Indeed, in the summer of 1952 the honeymoon between Legault and Maurice was over. Maurice hardly wrestled at all in Montreal, and had to wrestle for smaller promoters. He was ignored for shows in Lachine, Montreal-Est, Saint-Eustache, and Verdun — shows promoted by the Lortie brothers, the Dufresne brothers, and Sylvio Samson in the greater metropolitan area. On top of it all, television was coming in Quebec in the fall, and the Lortie brothers, with promoter Paul Roberge, would get the first broadcast. They called on several wrestlers who were wrestling at the Forum, but Maurice was not invited to take part. And when Quinn started broadcasting his shows on Channel 2 live from the Forum, Maurice again wasn't involved. Legault called on him to wrestle outside of Montreal and sporadically in the city. In the fall of 1953, as Rougeau was quietly rising in the wrestling hierarchy, Maurice realized he had to leave Quebec if he wanted to make the sport his career.

"When you start in professional wrestling, you think you're better than you really are," he recalled. "Promoters have other plans in mind for the wrestlers, and, besides, Montreal already had one big star, Yvon Robert."

Maurice was discouraged by this turn of events. He now had to leave the country he loved and try to discover something special within himself that would interest promoters. The young Olympian would return to his hometown only after finding that something special, and he would only find it by listening to his dark side . . .

6

MAKE LOVE, NOT WAR

Because of the disappointment he was experiencing in his home province, Maurice knew he had to look elsewhere for wrestling opportunities. And that meant the United States. He had had his first break in 1952 thanks to Paul Bowser, the head honcho of wrestling in Boston, who had handed Eddie Quinn the Montreal territory in 1939. Since Quinn had no place for Maurice in Montreal, or at least he didn't want to have a place for him, he sent him to work a few weeks in Boston for his former boss. South of the border, Maurice was still too much of a babyface for things to change. The fact that he was an Olympian meant nothing. He just didn't have what it took to get a rise out of the crowd. He didn't have the moves or the presence that would get people rooting for him. So it was in Boston that Maurice got his first crack at wrestling as a bad guy, as a heel. He worked there for a few weeks in a row, earning just $20 per match, which made him make some very questionable decisions.

"I was staying with the wrestler Claude Saint-Jean [who would become Yvon Robert's son-in-law] in Boston, and on the last night we didn't pay for our hotel room," Maurice later recalled.

A few weeks in Boston wasn't enough to earn him a regular spot at the Montreal Forum, and it didn't help him with promoters Samson or Legault either. By the end of the summer of 1953, Maurice had become a rougher and more aggressive wrestler, and he finally hit the road that fall. But this time, he wasn't getting short-term experience in another city: apart from a few summer matches, he wouldn't return to wrestle regularly in Montreal before 1956.

This was a road trip with no final destination. His first stop was Detroit. "When I started wrestling pro, Eddy Auger suggested I go wrestle in Detroit, Michigan. He told me there wasn't much money there, but I would get to wrestle every night of the week and I was going to learn my trade."

During summers in Quebec, it wasn't difficult to wrestle on a regular basis, but during winters things were tough. Maurice didn't earn much in Quebec, and he also didn't wrestle often enough. So Detroit was a golden opportunity. The Detroit wrestling territory was controlled by three men, Harry Light, Bert Ruby, and the Quebecer Jack Britton, the first promoter to popularize midget wrestlers. Auger himself regularly performed there, so it didn't come as a surprise he should recommend that Maurice pursue his career in Detroit.

Maurice started making a name for himself in Detroit by capitalizing on his rivalry with one of the crowd favorites, the Flying Frenchman Larry Chene, a Franco-American. Chene was one of the good guys, and Maurice played his bad-guy role with flair. He was beginning to make his reputation. His new character was also beginning to emerge.

On reaching Motor City, Maurice moved to the Park Avenue Hotel, in the heart of Detroit. The city was the site of Henry Ford's first automobile assembly plant in the early twentieth century, but by the early 1950s things were changing: the plant workers became unionized, resulting in an exodus of Ford plants to other markets. The economic situation wasn't as dire as it became fifty years later, but it still wasn't exactly rosy. Maurice could afford to rent a hotel room for just $22.50 a week, which is what he got for one match.

"Ruby would quietly hand us $22.50, saying, 'Don't tell anyone, because the others are just getting $20,'" Maurice said. "Then he would pay the next wrestler $22.50, saying exactly the same thing."

In those days, hotels of this type employed an elevator operator, whose job was to deal with the operations of the elevator (the choice of floor, closing and opening the doors). At the Park Avenue Hotel, the elevator operator was a young woman named Dorothy Thomas. Born September 9, 1926, in the Detroit area, she was also a waitress at the hotel bar. It was love at first sight: Maurice fell under the spell of the beautiful redhead, who stood 5 feet 2 inches tall. Dorothy already had a four-year-old daughter, Linda Sue, but Maurice had always loved children, and he didn't see any problem with her being a single mom.

Maurice was wrestling on a much more regular basis, but the work wasn't exactly making him rich. With Detroit as his home base he could also get matches in the Canadian city of Windsor, Ontario, across the Detroit River, and in several other Michigan cities, which were considered small regional markets. He wrestled against Chene and also Lou Klein and The Sheik of Araby, whose real name was Edward Farhat, and who would later be better known by the Montreal public under the name of The Sheik.

Because of his relationship with Dorothy, Maurice spent his holidays in Detroit. Apart from a match at the Montreal Forum in February 1954, where he wrestled Jean "Johnny" Rougeau, he continued wrestling in Detroit until spring. Then he returned to Canada.

He spent a few weeks in Quebec, just long enough to help another young Quebecer make his professional debut. Some years before, when Maurice was still an amateur wrestler, he had met Jacques Bernard Prud'homme, a thirteen-year-old wrestler. Prud'homme was now a stocky twenty-year-old, raring to go. Brute Bernard trained at the Palestre Nationale on Cherrier Street.

"I was the one to open the doors of wrestling for him," Maurice recalled. "I've never seen a guy work as hard in my life. I got him started in places like Chicoutimi and Rimouski." Bernard subsequently wrestled all over the world, becoming a star in the New York territory.

Quebec was no longer big enough for Maurice. During his brief Montreal visit in February, he met wrestler and promoter Larry Kasaboski, better known in Montreal under the ring name of Larry Raymond. In 1945, Kasaboski had started promoting summertime wrestling cards, primarily in Ontario cities like Renfrew, Pembroke, North Bay, Sudbury, and Timmins, as well as in Rouyn-Noranda, Quebec. Thanks to his promotions, young wrestlers who weren't ready for the Montreal Forum or Toronto's Maple Leaf Gardens got valuable in-ring experience. Kasaboski had a good relationship with Quinn, who would send him well-known wrestlers from time to time, and in exchange, Kasaboski would give young wrestlers a chance to wrestle if Quinn was unable to have them on the Forum cards. So Kasaboski had a thing for Quebecers and regularly booked wrestlers like the Lortie brothers, Bob Langevin, and Eddy Auger. Kasaboski could guarantee Maurice earnings of $350 per week, a sum he had never before come close to earning.

In the summer of 1954, Maurice started working for Kasaboski. Things were finally going smoothly for him, both professionally and personally. Upon arriving, he was immediately placed in main events against the more experienced wrestlers, and he took part in a tournament whose top prize was a championship belt sponsored by Labatt Breweries. Shades of things to come on so many levels, Maurice won that title. He was having success, and not just in the ring. He had no trouble making friends, thanks to his usual good humor and his love of alcohol and partying. Besides Kasaboski, he also made friends with Roy Shire and Dory Funk Sr., who was living in Ontario for the season with his two sons, Dory Jr. and Terry, who were just thirteen and ten years old at the time.

Years later, the Funk brothers would both become NWA world champions. It was also during the summer of 1954 that Maurice got his first nickname. It filled out his identity and became an essential asset in the ring.

He had been a heel for almost a year now, and his style of wrestling was much rougher and more aggressive than before. He had started wrestling this way in Detroit and was now pushing it even further in Kasaboski's territory. He kicked, he punched, he used illegal tactics, he threw his opponent out of the ring, he did everything possible to generate a hostile crowd reaction to the character he was portraying. He was given the nickname of "Madman Vachon." The name was like a prototype version of the ring name that would one day make him famous. He was still a "scientific" wrestler, but he was using this approach more as a way of humiliating his opponent than of affirming his own talent.

"Madman Vachon" went nuts in the ring, berserk, out of control, and for the first time in his career, he was getting the crowd boiling. He joined Dory Funk Sr. to create a great villain tag team.

"I was happy in the role of villain because I was the one running the show. My opponents weren't doing much, so I decided I was going to be the big boss once I got into the ring. I would use any means at my disposal, any methods. I would do everything I needed to raise the ire of the fans. So kicks below the belt, punches in the face, pulling hair, sticking my fingers in the eyes of my opponents, scratching them, biting them, stuff like that. I went crazy because I wanted to. I wanted to pretend to be completely insane. But I wasn't crazy — I've never been crazy . . ." Maurice said.

In the ring, the heel is the one who controls the match, because most of the time he's the one getting the better of his opponent, who is always struggling to regain the advantage. The heel dictates the pace of the match; he listens to the crowd to decide when to let his opponent back into the game and when to stop. In those days, very little about a match was preplanned. And Maurice, in particular, was one wrestler who brought a lot of spontaneity to his matches. The start and finish of a match were often decided in advance, but the rest was played out in the ring. Which is why the heel was so important — he was like the conductor of an orchestra. Maurice was gaining experience and he felt more comfortable in his new role.

Outside of the ring, Maurice was getting even greater satisfaction. He and Dorothy had been together for several months now, and at the end of winter she told him she was pregnant. Maurice wasn't the kind of man to follow all Church laws to the letter, but in the 1950s it was important for every Catholic to marry before the baby was born. Otherwise, a child born out of wedlock would be considered a bastard. Maurice planned to leave Michigan and settle in Ontario soon, and he liked the idea of marrying on Canadian soil. Dorothy abandoned her native Detroit and followed him. As a matter of fact, it is unfair to say she "followed" him because she was the one driving the car. Maurice hadn't learned how to drive yet — and he would never turn out to be a good driver. Dorothy had already been married, so they couldn't marry in a church and had to settle for a wedding at the North Bay courthouse.

Summer never lasts long enough in Ontario and Quebec, and all good things eventually come to an end. With September looming, Maurice had to find a new place to wrestle. Over the summer, some wrestlers had suggested he go west. But Dorothy still had to give birth: the due date was late October, and it was important for Maurice that his first child see the light of day in Montreal. So the couple spent a few weeks in Quebec, and their first child, Maurice Michael Vachon Jr., was born October 30, 1954.

Within a few years, the amateur wrestler who had dreamed of traveling overseas had become a pro wrestler with a career, an American wife, and a child. During the past year, both the wrestler and the man went through a process of emancipation. Maurice was now twenty-five years old, he was facing new challenges and responsibilities, he had a family to support, and he couldn't do whatever he pleased. He had to look out for his future. And for him, that future lay in the great state of Texas.

MAURICE CHEATS DEATH, PART ONE

7

J.R. Ewing, the legendary character on the TV series *Dallas*, used to say, "All that matters is winning." And that catchphrase summed up why Maurice moved to Texas in 1954: he wanted to win. Naturally he wanted to win matches, but above all he wanted to win financially, something he had been struggling with ever since becoming a professional. As the saying goes, everything is bigger and better in Texas. It's currently the biggest state in the U.S. after Alaska. It's also a state where openly carrying a handgun is legal, and it has huge oil and gas production, a high number of death-row inmates, and arguably the biggest steaks in America.

In 1954, Texas was one of the biggest and busiest wrestling territories. The Guerrero family from El Paso in Far West Texas dominated the western and northern parts of the territory; Amarillo, in the Texas Panhandle, would become the fortress of the Funk family. There were more cities in North, Central-South, and Southeast Texas, such as Dallas, San Antonio, and Houston, as well as smaller markets such as Galveston, Corpus Christi, and Waco.

Morris Siegel controlled the cities of Southeast Texas. Originally a New Yorker, he had been promoting wrestling since the 1920s and ran his territory from Houston. Between the 1930s and 1960s, he was famous for having the most stable wrestling territory in the United States. By the time Maurice reached Texas, Siegel was a member of the NWA. He used talent from all over and put on events in all the cities in his territory with ten thousand or more inhabitants.

Siegel's territory was enormous. A normal week for a wrestler started with Monday in Fort Worth, then a 40-mile drive; Tuesday in Dallas, then a 300-mile drive; Wednesday in Victoria or San Antonio, then a 90-mile drive; Thursday in Corpus Christi, then a 210-mile drive; Friday in Houston, then a 45-mile drive; Saturday in Angleton, then a final 305-mile drive back to Fort Worth again on Monday. And since the promotion was sometimes doing more than one show per night, it involved driving 250 miles between Wednesday night and Thursday to reach Galveston (not Corpus Christi) before evening so they were closer to Houston.

On this circuit, there were one thousand miles of driving per week. But in the years before the interstate highway system was inaugurated, road conditions weren't that great. Gas went for 21¢ a gallon, so a week of crisscrossing Texas by car cost between $10 and $15 worth of gas — a tidy sum considering the salaries of wrestlers at the time. However, wrestlers often shared costs by traveling in groups.

Once Maurice and Dorothy's baby was born, they took a few weeks to let her recover from the birth, then got ready to leave Quebec. Before hitting the road, Maurice bought a brand-new Ford from a dealer in the Montreal suburb of La Prairie for $2,050, the average price for a new car at the time.

The Vachon family — Maurice, Dorothy, Linda Sue, and Mike — headed out on the longest journey Maurice had undertaken since returning from the British Empire Games. They left behind Quebec's typical winter temperatures of 5°F for the milder winter temperatures of 60°F in Texas. Maurice's first match in Texas was scheduled for Monday, December 20, 1954, in Fort Worth, a mere 1,740 miles from Quebec. Maurice didn't have a driver's license so Dorothy was behind the wheel for the entire trip. After passing by their future home in Houston, Dorothy had a hard time driving the final thirty miles from Dallas to Fort Worth; she kept dozing off, and it took her an entire afternoon to cover the short distance between the two cities. Maurice started his first week of wrestling in Fort Worth. He headed on Tuesday to Dallas, and on Wednesday to San Antonio, then on Thursday, December 23, he was in Corpus Christi. The next destination was Houston, several hours away.

On Friday morning, the family headed out from Corpus Christi, taking the road for Houston. Between the two cities, there were several lakes, the largest of them Green Lake, a little to the north of Corpus Christi, plus other bodies of water. After traveling sixty miles, they reached a region where several bridges crossed bayous, snake-like bodies of water between Tivoli and Port Lavaca. It was 1:00 p.m. on a bright and sunny Christmas Eve. An oncoming pickup truck crossed the bridge heading towards them, hitting the Vachon family car on the side, then missing the car immediately behind them but smashing head-on into the third car. Dorothy slammed on the brakes and the car immediately behind — the one that had barely escaped being hit by the pickup, rear-ended the Vachon family car. This was a serious accident.

Cars and the highway code weren't the same then as they are today. The whole family was sitting in the front: Dorothy was at the wheel, Linda Sue was in the middle, and Maurice was in the passenger seat holding little Mike in his arms. He was even trying to bottle-feed the baby, who was just seven weeks old. Miraculously, the Vachons walked away practically unscathed, although they had really been shaken up. Maurice and Mike didn't have a scratch. Linda — now five years old — had only a few bruises on her face. Dorothy was hurt, however. The pickup had hit her side of the car. She had a cut on her mouth, another on her buttocks, and various bruises, especially on the legs.

The pickup driver was thirty-nine years old and worked in the dredging industry. Authorities detained him at the scene of the accident and eventually charged him with drunk driving.

But that wasn't the end of the story for the Vachon family.

Little Mike was allergic to milk, orange juice, and tomato juice. He drank only soy milk, mixed with corn syrup. The family therefore had to keep a gallon bottle of corn syrup handy when they were on the road — a glass bottle that broke under the impact of the collision, spilling its sticky contents all over the couple's suitcases. The car had sustained damage. Dorothy was taken to hospital where she was treated for injuries including a six-inch cut on her buttocks, and Maurice was left wondering what to do. That's when a middle-aged couple, caught in the traffic jam caused by the accident, decided to help. They were driving from Houston to Mexico. Even though they were halfway to Mexico, they took Maurice, his two children, and clothes dripping with corn syrup back to Houston so he could get changed and get soy milk for his son. Then they dropped the young family off at the hospital to be with Dorothy. This amounted to a round-trip of five hours of extra driving!

Maurice would remember these Texans all his life. "I regret today that I never took their name, address, or phone number, because it always touched my heart and inspired me to have met such deeply generous people as them."

It was the first time Maurice cheated death in a car accident — but it wouldn't be the last.

Maurice had come to Texas to gain experience and get into the ring practically every day, and that's exactly what he did. Sometimes he wrestled in singles, sometimes in tag teams. He did the rounds of the entire wrestling circuit of Texas every week. Some nights, he even wrestled twice: a warm-up preliminary match, then a semi-final or sometimes even a main event.

Vachon perfected his heel character while fighting most of the babyface wrestlers of the territory. Texan newspapers described him as a nasty, crazy, and rude wrestler, which meant he had taken on just the right attributes to appeal to Texan fans. It also meant he could try some techniques mastered by the Polish-Canadian heel Killer Kowalski, like the diving knee drop (when Maurice's opponent was caught in the middle ropes in the corner, he would drop two knees into the opponent's abdomen). Larry Chene, the very man he had so often fought in Detroit, was his most frequent opponent in Texas, and for good reason. Chene was five years older than Maurice and had the same build: not very tall but compact. He could be spectacular in the ring, where he pulled off interesting new moves. Above all, he got the crowd so fired up they were desperate to help him defeat his opponents. All his contemporaries agreed on Chene's reputation. In other words, Larry was the perfect opponent to Maurice's new aggressive style. In the world of professional wrestling, a heel is as good as his opponent: if the blows he's raining down don't seem to hurt, the fans will simply lose interest. The wrestler who simulates pain has to give fans the impression he needs their support to win, which means he has to be a good actor as well.

Maurice sometimes teamed up with "Professor" Roy Shire. In the early 1960s, Shire would become the promoter who controlled the San Francisco territory, and would be widely considered a genius in the realm of pro wrestling. For Maurice, however, wrestling in Texas meant spending time with an old acquaintance.

Eddy Auger was in his early thirties when he settled in Texas, and he already had a solid reputation as an amazing wrestler with great in-ring abilities. Actually, whatever he did, he did well. In Quebec, he wrestled under his real name, but in the United States he used the ring name of Pierre LaSalle, which was easier for Americans to pronounce. He was more experienced than Maurice, but the two wrestled together in Texas, and for Maurice it was a great opportunity to learn the craft. Dorothy and their two youngsters didn't join him on the weekly circuit, so sometimes Maurice would travel with Auger and other wrestlers — always with the heels — because the babyfaces weren't allowed to travel with the heels. This was to preserve the kayfabe from the fans. Long road trips crisscrossing Texas were also conducive to discussions, questions, and advice of many kinds. It was a nice way for young performers to learn from veterans and educate themselves about their profession.

"Eddy Auger was the greatest guy in the world," Maurice later recalled. "He helped everyone. He sent guys to Texas and Ohio."

Auger teamed with Maurice several times in 1955, and together they won the NWA Texas Tag Team Title, the first title Maurice won in the United States.

Several other Quebec wrestlers were also in Texas at this time: Tony Baillargeon from the famous family of strongmen, the Mohawk wrestler Don Eagle and his younger Mohawk protégé Billy Two Rivers, and Johnny Rougeau.

The fates of Maurice Vachon and Johnny Rougeau crossed again, and it wouldn't be the last time. They had met at the Montreal Forum and also working for other promoters, so it wasn't that surprising they should meet up again in Texas. In the wrestling world in those years, relationships were developed and referrals were given by word of mouth. Auger had been wrestling in the United States for close to a decade, and his opinion was respected by American promoters. By dropping a word about Maurice to the Detroit promoter or about Johnny to a Texas promoter, he was improving their chances of getting further on the wrestling circuit.

Maurice had spent long years in Montreal, a city where nobody seemed to be rooting for him, so he saw Eddy Auger as a good man who could really help him become somebody in the business. In later years, Maurice followed Eddy's example and did his best to help other wrestlers, especially those from Quebec.

Maurice and Johnny wrestled a few times, but Johnny was not as well protected in Texas as he had been in Quebec, so Maurice ended up winning many of their matches.

Overall, Maurice's first experience in Texas was positive. He got the opportunity to refine his heel character, gain experience, and make new contacts. He didn't wrestle in front of large crowds — there were often only a few hundred fans in the stands — but the matches were televised, which was becoming an important part of the wrestling business. When he finally decided to leave Texas, Maurice looked somewhat worn compared to a few years earlier. There could have been many reasons for this, whether marriage, the birth of his son, traveling, fatigue, or inheriting family traits. He didn't know it at the time, but he was beginning to go bald, and one day he would turn this into an advantage. Things had gone well in Texas but it was now time for Maurice to head back home.

8
ANOTHER VACHON ENTERS THE FRAY

It was almost summer, and that meant Larry Kasaboski's territory in the Ottawa Valley was about to kick into high gear. For a second summer in a row, Maurice headed to eastern Ontario, the place where he'd been married the year before, and where he had experienced some initial in-ring success.

Maurice was now flourishing as a heel, and it could be disadvantageous for a heel to overstay his welcome in a territory. People bought tickets in the hopes of seeing the babyface overcome the heel — most good feuds could be played out over a number of matches. But at a certain point the feud would go stale: the babyface had to beat the heel. Promoters then needed to get a new rivalry brewing, by matching the babyface against a new heel. The end of a long-standing feud was often a heel's swan song — his final match before moving out to the next territory. Wrestling constantly needed new faces and new feuds to keep the story going. When a heel left a territory, it was to wrestle somewhere else, returning stronger than ever after a few months. This was a way for heels to stay fresh. It also meant fans would have forgotten a heel just long enough to be willing to buy tickets to see him get beaten again. At least that's how the system roughly worked in Maurice's day.

After spending six months in Texas, Maurice brought his family back to North Bay. Two things highlighted his return to Canada: his feud with Dory Funk Sr. and the wrestling debut of one of his brothers.

Funk was ten years older than Vachon but not much more experienced. He began his career as a professional wrestler after serving in the Marines during World War II. At 5 feet 11 inches, weighing 230 pounds and already beginning to lose his hair, Funk was built much the same way as Maurice, and in the summer of 1955 the two men got a really good rivalry going. They competed in numerous matches that went right to the time limit of sixty minutes — a rare occurrence in Maurice's career. Maurice had worked hard in 1954 to win the North American heavyweight title against Rocco Colombo in Sudbury, Ontario, but then he lost it to Funk. But the rivalry with Funk also marked the entry of Maurice's brother Paul into professional wrestling.

Born October 7, 1937, Paul Vachon was the seventh child in the family. In the summer of 1955, he was just seventeen years old. He worked on the family farm in the Eastern Townships and had taken part a few months earlier in the Canadian amateur wrestling championships in Regina, Saskatchewan, in the 191-pound class. Paul was trying to follow in the footsteps of his older brother, and he won the silver medal in Regina, with the gold going to another Montrealer, Bernadin Hornblower. While passing through Chicago on his way home, Paul phoned his brother in Texas to announce the good news. Maurice also had good news to share.

"Good Lord! You've done enough amateur wrestling," Maurice told his kid brother, who was planning to go on to the 1956 Olympic

Games in Melbourne. "You'll never make any money doing that. When I come back this summer, you're going to go professional."

Maurice kept his word, and Paul became the first of many wrestlers Maurice would take under his wing. He brought Paul to North Bay and quietly introduced him to professional wrestling. He made Paul his manager, the person accompanying him and ensuring that Maurice won each fight. Paul learned quickly, and he understood his role. Sometimes he got physically involved in the match. Other times he rang the timekeeper's bell to sow confusion and give Maurice a chance to recover. The duo worked so well together that Paul often had to fight his way back to the locker room, and eventually Maurice would have to do this too.

Paul recalls: "In those years, Maurice believed that if the match didn't end in a riot, or if we didn't have to fight our way back to the locker room, then we hadn't done our job properly; we had failed in our mission."

Sometimes, after the match, Maurice would jump back into the ring to set the crowd on fire. Then he would throw his opponent out of the ring, smash a chair on his head, and fight with anyone getting in his way before finally returning to the locker room. This meant infuriating a few thousand fans, often making them dangerous. What was Paul's role in all this? Protecting his brother, of course. "At the time, I wondered who was protecting me," Paul said.

Larry Kasaboski didn't like this kind of chaos. But Maurice got him to understand that even more fans would come back the following week, and sure enough, the crowds increased. Any promoter could see how successful this formula was proving. Maurice had been a heel for over a year. He was now starting to get comfortable in the role and he knew what worked best with the fans. His behavior was increasingly demented, disproportionate, unreasonable . . . He really looked like a "mad man." These riots became his calling card, the little something that had been missing when he had wrestled in Quebec, and he knew it. He was beginning to build a solid name for himself.

During one of these riots, Funk challenged the Vachon clan, but not specifically Maurice. Instead, the challenge was intended for Paul, who was poking his nose into other people's business. Maurice came to his brother's defense, retorting that Funk should go out and find a partner: then they could settle things with a tag match. This was an ideal turn of events for young Paul's debut, because at more than six feet in height and with a very strong build, he could handle himself in the ring.

The match was scheduled for July 1 in North Bay against Dory Funk and Dinty Parks. This was the first time the Vachon brothers teamed up, but by no means would it be the last. Maurice started the match against Funk, then after a while handed things over to Paul. But there was a big difference between fighting one's way through a crowd and fighting in the ring. Paul froze up. He didn't know what to do, so he froze and decided not to move. Maurice gave him some good brotherly advice: "Get into the ring now, or tomorrow you'll be back shoveling manure on the farm!" That was enough to get Paul into the ring, his brother's words scaring him even more than the taunts of the crowd.

At the end of the summer, despite this first experience, Paul headed back to the farm while Maurice went with his family to Montreal. Maurice renewed with Eddie Quinn and the Montreal Forum, the temple of wrestling he had been dreaming about since childhood. Maurice had been away from the Montreal scene for a year and from the Forum for eighteen months; he wasn't the same wrestler he had once been.

He came back to Montreal with quite the reputation, although he hadn't yet reached the star status he would enjoy in later years. Quinn used him both in Montreal and Ottawa. But there wasn't any question of protecting him anymore, as Quinn had done in his debut. Within a few weeks he wrestled — and lost — against Bobby Managoff, Larry Moquin, and Yvon Robert. Maurice took things in stride and happily worked against his childhood heroes. It's actually a big step in a wrestling career when your heroes become your opponents. Maurice knew this and he made a good impression, which would serve him well later on. Meanwhile, once autumn came to Quebec, it was time for Maurice to head back to Texas.

However, this time around, he wouldn't have to wait another eighteen months before he was asked to return to the Montreal Forum.

BETWEEN TEXAS AND QUEBEC: A FAMILY AFFAIR

On returning to Texas in the fall of 1955, Maurice wouldn't be wrestling for Siegel's promotion. Dory Funk had just bought the West Texas territory from Dory Detton, along with "Doc" Karl Sarpolis. They brought Maurice in to wrestle that fall in the cities of Lubbock, Abilene, and especially El Paso and Amarillo.

"My father just adored Maurice," Terry Funk says. "He made more money wrestling against Mad Dog than against anyone else there. When my father opened the territory in Amarillo, the first thing he did was to call 'the Dog.' Both men were fearless and they respected each other."

The Texas promoters first set him up in a rivalry with Gory Guerrero, who would later enter the Wrestling Observer Newsletter Hall of Fame and become himself the patriarch of a great family of wrestlers. Guerrero had begun his career in Mexico in the late 1930s and is best known by fans nowadays as the father of Eddie Guerrero and the grandfather of Chavo Jr. Of Mexican origin, Gory was actually born in Arizona and had spent most of his life in the United

States. Gory was 5 feet 9 inches tall and weighed 209 pounds, so he had much the same build as Maurice. He had wrestled against the biggest names in *lucha libre* and brought a lot of experience to pro wrestling in Texas. He also invented the camel clutch, which became one of his signature moves. In later years, he coached his four sons and became the local promoter in El Paso.

The rivalry between Maurice and Guerrero ran from October to December. The high point of their series of matches was a Texas death match, where the wrestler had to pin his opponent or force him to submit while the referee completed a ten-count. Obviously, as the crowd favorite, Guerrero defeated Maurice in this final confrontation. After a loss of this magnitude, Vachon couldn't remain in the territory — and that's exactly what Guerrero's win had been scripted to facilitate.

In fact, Maurice had received an interesting call from Montreal. Eddie Quinn was on the line. Maurice's performance a few months earlier had convinced Quinn and his partners there was a place for Maurice at the Forum, so Quinn wanted Maurice back. Quinn was not interested in Maurice the "scientific" fighter: he wanted the rude and aggressive bad guy the former Olympian had become.

Maurice was back at the Forum on December 28, wrestling none other than his longstanding nemesis Johnny Rougeau. This time around, things were different. The office was protecting Maurice again, pretty much like in his debut. He would win matches, draw some, do time-limits, lose by disqualification, or, like in this match with Johnny, do a double-disqualification.

Between late December 1955 and November 1956, Maurice wrestled all over the province, in towns like Quebec City, Shawinigan, Ottawa, and Montreal. He faced many veterans, opponents like Ovila Asselin, Eddy Auger, and Larry Moquin, as well as up-and-coming wrestlers like Sammy Berg, Rougeau, and Camille "Tarzan"

Tourville, who would later be known as Tarzan "the Boot" Tyler.

However, Maurice's return to Quebec was no picnic. True, he was wrestling more often at the Forum than at any previous time in his career, but he was still only getting onto the undercards. While the venues in Quebec weren't as far apart as in Texas, he had to take other factors into consideration. He was no longer single the way he had been in 1951. He now had a family to support, and that took money. Quinn had him wrestling on a regular basis, but cities like Ottawa and Shawinigan didn't pay well. The Forum was still the place where wrestlers made the most money. In other territories, wrestlers made less money when the matches were televised. Promoters justified this by saying TV was good for them, since it made them more well-known. But in Montreal, TV cameras filmed wrestling live at the Forum rather than in a studio, and TV brought in more revenue. Meanwhile, Maurice faced two problems. On the one hand, he didn't wrestle every week at the Forum. On the other hand, from January 1956 onwards, he was restricted to preliminary matches. The fact that he hadn't been able to rise up the ranks after ten months meant that Quinn — or someone else in the promoter's organization — didn't want him to rise.

Moreover, Quinn didn't use Maurice or other recruits during what could be called "the Summer of Carpentier." Édouard Carpentier was three years older than Maurice and made a stunning debut in Quebec, bringing in over 75,000 fans while main-eventing four big wrestling cards in July and August 1956. If Maurice had been able to wrestle in these events, he could have made good money, but Quinn preferred rewarding local veterans at his big shows. In any case, the destinies of Maurice and "the Flying Frenchman" would cross at a later date.

The Saguenay region, north of Quebec City, was the only place where things were going well for Maurice. Television was in its infancy, and he was already using it to his best advantage. TV coverage of wrestling included interview segments. Maurice didn't simply answer the interviewer's questions. He wanted to do something more original, so he would grab the microphone and speak directly to the camera, more or less making the interviewer obsolete to his act.

"At a certain point, I think I started to shake up the announcers," Maurice later recalled. "Sometimes I would yank the mike out of the announcer's hand and say a few words that literally set the crowd on fire. After that, I would hand the mike back."

Wrestling fans were astounded by the new media and the effect of such a strange character entering their living room. Maurice did his best to provoke people in the Saguenay region, whether in the cities of Chicoutimi or Jonquière. He would grab the microphone and howl that the Saguenay was *his* territory. This would drive the crowd wild. Like a comedian on the road, he was already honing his character and refining interviews into a style that would eventually become legendary.

Maurice's matches in the Saguenay region were successful, but he reached an agreement with Quinn and decided to pack up and head back to Texas, which he figured was the best place to get the respect he deserved. Dorothy was the happiest of all about this, because it meant she could finally return to the United States. Maurice may have been close friends with Funk, but Funk's territory was West Texas, and there was more money to be made in the large cities on Siegel's territory in the Southeast of the state.

A few weeks later, in December 1956, Siegel gave Maurice a break by lining things up so he could win the Texas junior heavyweight title. During this run, Maurice developed rivalries with wrestlers like Pepper Gomez, Amazing Zuma, and Luis Martínez (Luis won the junior heavyweight title back the following February). Siegel also had Maurice reviving familiar feuds from the past, wrestling

Larry Chene and Rocco Colombo. This meant Maurice could wrestle more often in the main-event spot. But the most notorious episode of this period of his career was his association with Joe Christie, a wrestler nearly as rough and belligerent as he was.

Christie was a native of Buffalo, New York, but had been raised in Brantford, Ontario. By the time he began teaming with Maurice, Christie had just reached the age of forty. He was nicknamed "Killer." Coming in at 6 feet 3 inches tall and weighing 235 pounds, Christie had begun his professional career in the mid-1940s and was now mentoring Vachon. The two men developed a real bond: they were both aggressive during wrestling matches, and they were both just as charming outside of the ring.

Together they won the "Roughest and Toughest" trophy. At the time, tag teams often vied for a trophy rather than a pair of belts, and the trophy was defended just the way title belts are nowadays. Two months later, Vachon and Christie lost out to Martínez and Gomez in a barbed-wire match, some forty years before this kind of match became popular in Japan and in Extreme Championship Wrestling (ECW). Texas was one of the few states where barbed-wire matches were held, and it perfectly suited the style of the two northerners. When Christie was wrestling in singles competitions, Maurice also helped him by doing outrageous things to heat up feuds. In fact, both men did just about anything to get disqualified, like repeatedly smashing the heads of their opponents on the ring posts.

By the time he was ready to leave the territory once again, Maurice had been given many nicknames: "Mad" Maurice Vachon, "the Bad Man," "the Mad Man from Canada," "the Mad Man of Wrestling." All of them were derived from the original nickname he was tagged with in North Bay. They stressed the irrepressibly crazy style Maurice was developing for his character as he made his way to stardom.

This time, Maurice returned to Quebec for the summer. It was a departure from his first years on the road, but it turned into a kind of ritual he followed for the rest of his career. It also meant returning to Quinn's booking.

Things still hadn't changed at home in Quebec. The promoter protected him so he could win or lose by disqualification. He was rarely defeated. But this still wasn't enough to get him into main events in Montreal. Maurice wrestled extensively against Larry Moquin who, in addition to being one of his childhood idols, was well positioned in the organization to assess Maurice's potential, reporting directly to Quinn and Robert. Even though Robert's career was rapidly nearing its final stage, and Moquin was in his mid-thirties, Maurice still hadn't gotten to the top rung of wrestling in his hometown. In those years, other wrestlers like Hans Schmidt and Tarzan Tyler tried to carve out a place for themselves in Montreal, but they also had to go to the United States to get work. In the years following, a whole new generation of wrestlers, straight out of Loisirs Saint-Jean-Baptiste, would have to do the same. Meanwhile, Yvon Robert became Rougeau's manager and officially protected him, even to the point of getting him into a title match during this period.

In Montreal, the good guys were Carpentier, Rougeau, and Moquin, and the heels were Killer Kowalski, Gene Kiniski, and Buddy Rogers. This meant there was only room for Maurice in the prelims, and he was getting fed up with the situation.

Wrestling-wise, 1958 didn't seem to offer anything new to Maurice, who divided his time between Texas and Quebec. He regularly informed his family on the farm about his exploits by mailing them the wrestling programs showing the matches he was in.

But 1958 was important for the Vachon household for a completely different reason: on December 4, Dorothy gave birth to a second son, Denis. So when Maurice hit the road shortly after the

New Year, he had four mouths to feed, including nine-year-old Linda Sue and four-year-old Mike. Maurice needed more than ever to make a good living, and he came to the same conclusion as before: staying in Montreal would not provide his family with financial security.

They say that family is even more important when times are difficult, and this was true in his case. He left with his wife and children for Alberta, an even colder and snowier province than Quebec, but for the first time he took along his brother Paul. He was determined to establish a real place in wrestling, but reaching the top rung of the profession he loved was even more difficult than he had ever imagined.

"To become good at anything, you have to be willing to do it for nothing," Maurice would often say. But he was beginning to lose patience. Armand Courville had told him wrestling wouldn't pay at first. But Maurice could never have imagined it still wouldn't be paying eight years later. The Calgary territory, teaming with his little brother Paul, might just have been the solution he was looking for.

10

THE WARM BREATH OF MABEL AND THE FREEZING AIR OF CALGARY

After wrestling two matches in the summer of 1955, Paul Vachon returned to the family farm in the Eastern Townships of Quebec. Later, he joined his brother Guy in Montreal to work as a doorman — a popular job with members of the Vachon family. Six months later, he worked for a promoter who put on wrestling matches in carnivals, and after a few months he headed for Detroit. Paul, now eighteen, had blue eyes and blond hair, and although he stood 6 foot 1 and weighed 240 pounds, he looked more like a teenager than an adult. It didn't seem like he would last long in Michigan. But with Detroit promoter Bert Ruby he developed a Russian character, Nikita Zolotoff, shaving his head and growing a long beard. Playing this character helped him lose the teenager look. He worked in Detroit and Minnesota for a year and then returned to Montreal, where he took up again as a bouncer. Thanks to this job he started going out with the French-Canadian popular singer Alys Robi, who also performed in New York City and England, and whose father, Napoleon Robitaille, was also a wrestler.

In the fall of 1958, Maurice told Paul that Stu Hart, the promoter of the Calgary territory, was looking for a team of Quebec lumberjacks.

By this time, Maurice had decided against another return to Texas. He learned from his friend George Scott that George and his brother Sandy were headed for Calgary. Maurice realized there was a lot of potential in a rivalry between two teams made up of brothers. This meant he needed his "little" brother.

"Back in the late '50s, and even before that, there was always a little rivalry between French Canadians and English-speaking people," Stu Hart said. "If you fanned it a little bit, it was a fertile field to work and the Vachon boys as French-Canadian lumberjacks sort of fit into a situation." Stu Hart is best known by an entire generation of wrestling fans as the father of Owen and Bret "The Hitman" Hart. Like Maurice, Stu was a well-known old-school shooter. At the end of the 1940s, Hart turned professional, and since he needed to support his family, he opened his own company, which would become Stampede Wrestling.

The Vachon brothers were expected to arrive in Calgary at the beginning of 1959, but Stu wanted to get photos of them wearing lumberjack outfits as soon as possible so he could get an advertising campaign under way. The only problem was that Paul had just shaved off the beard he had needed to play Nikita Zolotoff, and Maurice, as crazy as it sounds now, was also beardless.

"So we went to a costume shop that supplied theaters props in Montreal," Paul remembers. "We got ourselves some lumberjack costumes — trousers, boots, shirts, everything we needed. Then they fitted us with fake beards, which looked more real than if we had our own.

Once the publicity photos were taken, the Vachon brothers had two months to grow real beards before taking the train out to Western Canada.

Wrestlers from all over the world visited Stu Hart's territory, and he took a certain malevolent delight in inviting them to his Calgary home — an enormous house that was almost like a mansion. He took his guests down to the basement, to the so-called dungeon, and he had fun "wrestling" with them — usually until they begged him to stop.

Maurice didn't have the profile of the typical wrestler visiting Stu: he was preceded by his reputation. Paul had taken part in national amateur wrestling competitions too but wasn't as well-known as his older brother. Stu would often ask Paul to come down to the "dungeon," and each time, Paul would refuse. But Stu never asked Maurice.

Then, one day, when the Vachon brothers visited Hart to get their paycheck, Maurice asked Paul to come down to the "dungeon" and train. Stu finally saw his prey descending to the torture chamber: he was practically drooling when he followed the two men downstairs. Maurice told his brother to get on all fours on the mattress and he would try to reverse him, which is a classic move in amateur wrestling. Stu wanted Maurice to leave him with Paul for a few minutes, long enough to warm up, but Maurice refused, saying he needed to train. So Maurice and Paul began wrestling, and Paul managed very well. Too well, in fact: he found his way out of each of Maurice's holds. After a few minutes they switched roles: now Paul had to try to reverse his brother, and although Paul didn't manage to pin his shoulders to the mat, Maurice was having trouble getting out of his younger brother's holds. Stu the patriarch watched the scene in amazement; he simply couldn't believe what he was seeing! After about fifteen minutes, Maurice interrupted the session, looked at Stu, and said: "OK, he's warmed up enough now. He's all yours. I can't do anything against him."

"No. Not now," Stu answered. "I can hear Helen [his wife] calling me upstairs."

Maurice's trick worked. Stu never again asked Paul to go "train" with him. Maurice had succeeded in persuading the veteran that Paul was better than he actually was. The key to professional wrestling lies in making your opponent look good. The two brothers headed back, jogging to their hotel about ten miles away. On the way back, they discussed what had just happened.

"Thanks, Maurice, for making me look good in front of Stu."

"What are you talking about? You did it on your own, kid. You're good and solid."

"So you say I'm good? Then why did you let me do anything except beat you?"

"You're good, kid, but not *that* good."

If Maurice had managed to fool Stu, at least Stu could console himself with the thought he wasn't the only guy getting fooled.

Antonio Barichievich, a Yugoslav by birth who became known as "the Great Antonio," was in his early twenties when he arrived in Montreal in the mid-1940s. He became a folk hero in Quebec for performing strongman stunts like pulling a single bus with his hair, and for journeying in the Rosemont neighborhood of Montreal like a homeless person for years and years. But Antonio was also a wrestler and even worked as a promoter between the 1950s and 1970s.

The Great Antonio had tried to make a name for himself in Hollywood, but since things were not going well for him in California, he called Maurice in Calgary, begging him for work. Maurice spontaneously invited him up north. As a wrestler, Antonio was limited because of his incredible size — he was 6 feet 4 inches tall and weighed close to 450 pounds. On the flip side, his size made him a huge attraction. In a "battle royal," it was always possible to hide his shortcomings. Besides, his prodigious feats of strength were a great way to draw new fans to the matches.

Stu Hart's territory was no easier than the Texas territories.

Stu produced events not just in Calgary but also in Edmonton and Lethbridge, and even in Saskatchewan. A workweek started in Edmonton, then continued on to Saskatoon and Regina, ending finally in Calgary — doing the whole circuit involved 1,125 miles of driving every week.

After doing a few loops, Antonio got a phone call one winter day from a woman named Mabel. A few wrestlers knew about her already, but Antonio had never heard of her. Over the phone, she turned him on with her sexy voice, inviting him to join her and her friends while her husband, a pilot, was away working. She asked Antonio to bring Dave Ruhl, a well-established wrestler in the territory, and Maurice Vachon. Antonio tried to convince her he preferred to come alone, since he would certainly be able to take care of her and her friends. Mabel said Antonio didn't know where she lived, but Ruhl knew the way. She also asked him to bring some beer.

Antonio and Maurice got into Ruhl's Cadillac, and the three men cheerfully drove to Mabel's place. She lived in a renovated house a few miles outside downtown Calgary. Actually, that's a nice way of putting things: the house was located in a forest in the middle of nowhere, and the only way to get there was by taking a series of dirt roads. Finally, just as evening fell, the three buddies reached their destination, taking their beer and sandwiches with them.

At that exact moment, a man dressed as a pilot burst out of the woods holding a pistol and shouting: "So you are the disgusting bums who have come to fuck my wife!" He fired in Antonio's direction, but Maurice sacrificed himself by moving in between the shooter and Antonio. Maurice was hit in the stomach and fell to the ground. Then the husband started shooting at Ruhl, who yelled to Antonio to run for his life — but the Yugoslav had already begun running when the gunfire started. Antonio fled at full speed, dropping the booze and food, having already his own considerable weight to carry.

Hidden behind the house were Paul Vachon and a small group of people, including Stu Hart, George Scott, and four or five other wrestlers. Once they were sure Antonio was out of sight, they came out of hiding to join Ruhl and Maurice, who were very much alive! The bullets had been blanks! Antonio was the victim of a practical joke or rib — the specialty of professional wrestlers.

The prank involving Mabel had been tried out more than a few times in the Calgary territory. The pranksters needed to find the right person to work their mischief on. Antonio was not the first victim and would not be the last. At the time, the prank had already become famous, but it reached legendary status when Antonio was taken in. Mabel was played by none other than the prankster-in-chief, Ruhl himself, who knew how to put on a sexy female voice to get things going. Antonio fled back to his hotel, while the practical jokers gathered up the beer and sandwiches he had dropped during his escape and partied until the wee hours.

About four in the morning, Dorothy got a call from Antonio. She was in on the prank and said Maurice hadn't come home yet. Then Mabel phoned Antonio to say Maurice was dead, Ruhl was seriously injured, and her husband was out looking for him. This sent Antonio into a panic: he called the police and asked them to pick him up at his hotel room, saying he had witnessed a murder, and maybe even a double murder. The police arrived at the scene of the alleged crime but found nothing but an abandoned house. While investigating the matter further, they called Maurice and Dorothy; it was part of the prank that Dorothy would tell them Maurice hadn't come home, so they should call Paul instead. That's when Paul realized things had gone too far, so he told the police what had really happened. They asked him for advance warning next time, which shows they were already familiar with "the Mabel Rib."

Antonio was distraught — he was still convinced that Maurice was dead. After all, he had seen him take a bullet, and "Mabel" had confirmed the death. Paul and Maurice had to meet Antonio in person to bring everything back to normal and convince him it had all been just a practical joke between wrestlers.

But Maurice wasn't always so cruel to Antonio.

While Maurice was still working with Antonio in Calgary, Gorgeous George arrived in the territory. With the advent of television, George had become a major star in the United States a decade earlier, and for good reason: with his glamor-boy blond hair and effeminate manner, he always came into the ring wearing a long bathrobe and holding a mirror, accompanied by his wife.

George had developed his wrestling character well — he was haughty, arrogant and prudish. He was also deeply and genuinely disgusted by Antonio's body odor. In fairness to George, Antonio didn't exactly have the best personal hygiene of wrestlers on the circuit. George ridiculed Antonio on every occasion, but never to Antonio's face.

One night in Saskatoon, the wrestlers gathered in the arena for a meeting. Maurice spoke. He said one of them liked to talk about one of their colleagues behind his back, without ever having the guts to say things straight to his face. He then pointed at George and calmly laid out for him what was going to happen.

Maurice gave "the Gorgeous One" two choices: either get into the ring and wrestle Antonio or get into the ring and fight Maurice. He added that the second option was going to be very unpleasant. In other words, he wanted George to take back his words, otherwise Maurice would personally make sure to stretch every single limb in George's body to the extreme, until he cried for mercy.

George knew Maurice by reputation, so he chose the first option. This was a good choice, even if it meant rubbing against his opponent's stinking body for a few long minutes. He would never again speak ill of Antonio — at least not within earshot of Maurice.

However, Calgary was not just about fun and pranks. Maurice took his training very seriously. He ran a few miles a day, on a fairly regular basis, braving the cold and snows of Alberta. He even got his brother Paul to join him running, although Paul hadn't developed the same passion for running as Maurice.

In the ring, the matches pitting the Vachons against the Scotts quickly became classics. George Scott would later become a major player behind the scenes, including as booker for the World Wrestling Federation (WWF) and the NWA. George and his brother Sandy were good-looking wrestlers, were comfortable in the ring, and were definitely crowd-pleasers. Their good-guy characters were in marked contrast to the heels played by the Vachon boys, whose beards, bald heads, and lumberjack getups made them seem like two hideous and insidious French Canadians.

Maurice and Paul also wrestled against other teams, including Shag Thomas and Mighty Ursus, as well as the Millers, although these matches didn't fire up the crowds quite like their matches with the Scott brothers. With all of these tags, the Vachon brothers became champions of the territory several times.

Maurice continued playing the intimidating character he had been developing over the last few years. Stu Hart knew a good "scientific" fighter when he saw one. But he was a promoter who liked best of all to have well-drawn characters, and Maurice played an incredible and unique one. When Maurice wasn't wrestling in tag teams, he would go up against a host of very different wrestlers. He fought against a former boxing champion, the defending champion of the NWA, and even . . . a spectator.

On February 26, 1959, Maurice got into his first world championship fight, for the NWA title, the most prestigious professional championship at the time. Pat O'Connor was the defending champion. During his career, Maurice didn't have many opportunities like this, probably because his style didn't match expectations of what an NWA champion should be: the organization seemingly always wanted a scientific wrestler who could regularly wrestle a full sixty minutes to be its flag bearer.

O'Connor was on his way to becoming one of the biggest wrestling stars of his era. He had also taken part in the British Empire Games in 1950 as a representative of the host country, New Zealand. Maurice had won the gold in his class, while O'Connor had picked up the silver as a heavyweight. Then O'Connor had gone professional, winning the NWA world title the month before against Dick Hutton, a former Olympian from 1948.

Hutton was on the undercard of that show, and it goes without saying that the publicity surrounding the card emphasized the amateur wrestling past of these three athletes. This kind of publicity was rarely used in Maurice's case — he was better known as a heel than an Olympian. But that evening Maurice was just expected to make O'Connor look good. He lasted thirty-five minutes before Paul intervened. Then Maurice was thrown out of the ring and simply never returned. He lost by count-out. This kind of booking was and still is frequently used to protect the heel and give the win to the babyface.

Alberta was full of surprises for Maurice: on April 3, 1959, after a tag team match with Paul in Calgary's Victoria Pavilion, a fan named Abel Gunther sucker punched him. Maurice was taken by surprise and fell onto a row of spectators. He filed a complaint against Gunther for assault, winning his case on April 27: his aggressor had to pay a fine of $20 or do thirty days in jail. It was only fair that Maurice finally had justice on his side — and it was ironically in English Canada.

Just before leaving the West, Maurice fought Jersey Joe Walcott, a former world heavyweight boxing champion who had become famous in the 1940s and 1950s fighting against Joe Louis, Ezzard Charles, and Rocky Marciano. He was also one of the former boxers Eddie Quinn liked to bring to Montreal as a special referee.

The match between Maurice and Walcott was planned a week before. Walcott was the special referee during Paul's match against "Whipper" Billy Watson. Ever the good teammate, Maurice came into the ring to help his brother, but Walcott, wanting to keep order, tried to get Maurice to leave. Maurice then challenged Walcott to a match the following week. Walcott agreed on the condition the two men wear boxing gloves. This was the special attraction of the biggest card of the year in Regina, and it was shaping up right before the eyes of the stunned spectators.

The match between Maurice and Walcott was one of three main events on the evening of July 14. The other two were a championship match between O'Connor and Lou Thesz, and a British Empire championship title match between Whipper Billy Watson from Toronto and Gene Kiniski, a former member of the Edmonton Eskimos football team.

The next day, the *Regina Leader-Post* devoted an article to the spectacle under the heading "Walcott Flattens Wrestler." Despite the level of championship fights on the program, reporters were dazzled by this boxing match between Walcott and Maurice, which was supposed to go to fifteen rounds, but the boxer knocked Maurice off his feet three times, winning in the second round. Of course, this match, just like all the other ones of the evening, was scripted, and Maurice's defeat was mapped out in advance, not because he was about to leave the territory, but because he was one of the wrestlers the crowd hated the most. Then again, despite appearances, Maurice was still protected: he could always justify his performance, saying he was a wrestler, not a boxer, whereas Walcott wouldn't have had a chance against him in a wrestling match.

This is what Maurice might have said if there had been a rematch, but he left the territory a few days later and never returned. "My father would have loved to have Maurice back, but the timing was never right," says Ross Hart, one of Stu's son. "He had great respect for Maurice, both for his record as an amateur and his reputation as a street fighter."

This would also be the last time Maurice and Paul would wrestle as a team for such a long time in one territory: it would take another full decade before they would do that again.

The brothers returned to Eastern Canada for the summer, wrestling in Toronto, Ottawa, and Quebec on the way home. But Maurice had other commitments. In fact, he had already agreed to go back to his first love, the place that had treated him so well when he needed it the most, Texas.

The 1960s had to be decisive for Maurice. He had just celebrated his thirtieth birthday and his career was not going as well as he wanted. By returning to Texas, he could gain even more experience, and maybe acquire a certain something that he was still lacking — something that would enable him to become a superstar. Not for the sake of being famous, but to make it easier on him to assume his family responsibilities.

As the saying goes, sometimes you need to take a step backward in order to move forward. It's with this philosophy in mind that Maurice and his family returned to spend another winter in Texas . . . hoping to finally move forward.

STRONG AS A BEAR!

Winter began and Maurice was back in Texas. He had always been well-treated in the territory, although the paychecks could have been more generous. Apart from a brief interlude during the summer, he would remain there until the end of 1960. The big difference this time was that his reputation was now well established. He was doing main events and semi-main events, and he even appeared in a main event at the famous Sportatorium in Dallas, the territory's Mecca of pro wrestling.

Canadians who head south for warmer weather during the winter are sometimes called snowbirds. Every year, several Quebec wrestlers spent the winter in Texas — which essentially made them a subgroup of the snowbird species. These wrestlers included a few midgets as well as Maurice Lapointe, Robert Paré (the Marquis de Paré), and Ovila Asselin, who wrestled under the ring name of Guy Larose.

February 1960 saw the Texas debut of another French Canadian, Frank Valois, a veteran with several years of experience. Maurice and Valois began teaming up and achieved some success. Valois would later become a promoter in Montreal, but for now he was surfing on the wave of Maurice's "popularity" — a wave that was sweeping the territory. He quickly became Maurice's sidekick, something like a Robin to his Batman. But there was a slight difference: in April 1960, Maurice was considered the most hated wrestler in the territory. The local promoter in Corpus Christi even came out of retirement to face him.

Of all the opponents Maurice wrestled during the season, one stood out in particular. On February 16, 1960, Maurice lost a match, and losing that match meant that the following week, he would have to face not a giant or a champion, but a bear. A real, *live* bear.

"The Wrestling Bear," nicknamed "Terrible Ted," was a black bear from the Gaspé Peninsula in Quebec. Black bears are the most common bear species in North America. After a few wrestling matches for a carnival organizer, Terrible Ted was adopted by the Canadian wrestler Dave McKigney. The animal was seven feet tall and weighed six hundred pounds. He'd been declawed and had his teeth removed to keep things relatively safe. Terrible Ted had previously wrestled at Maple Leaf Gardens in Toronto, but it was in Calgary that he became the most famous bear in all of wrestling. Terrible Ted was the crowd favorite in Texas, so Maurice, true to form, managed to get disqualified. Between the man and the bear, Maurice was the one acting most like a beast!

It probably seems surreal today, but Ted would continue wrestling into the 1970s, and he was not the first or the last bear in wrestling. In fact, this Texas match wasn't even Maurice's first match against a bear.

A few weeks before that, in San Antonio, he had fought against a bear called Tokyo Rose, whose name was linked to World War II. That time as well, Maurice lost the match. In May 1959, Maurice and Paul had faced another wrestling bear — the eight-hundred-pound Gorgeous Gus. The Vachon boys actually won that match in Vancouver, which only goes to show that two Vachons are better than one . . . bear.

In the summer of 1960, Maurice returned to his northern roots — like a true snowbird — to his home province of Quebec so he could spend time with his parents and friends. Like the two previous summers, he also wrestled for the promoter Sylvio Samson. This time, however, it was as a babyface, something that he hadn't done in Quebec for several years. However, he wasn't exactly playing a conventional hero: instead he was playing a role more like the one "Stone Cold" Steve Austin would personify nearly forty years later — he was, in fact, the same wrestler, with the same aggressiveness, the same tactics, and the same antihero personality. The real difference was the roles his opponents were playing.

Samson set Maurice up in a rivalry with P.Y. Chong, described by newspaper reporters at the time as a "Chinese Communist." Maurice had met him in Texas the previous winter and had actually recommended Chong to Samson for the summer season. Later in his career, Chong would be better known as Tojo Yamamoto. He was a native of Hawaii and would go on to a phenomenal career in Memphis, Tennessee, and would later train wrestlers like Jerry Jarrett, Bobby Eaton, and Sid Vicious.

For good measure, Samson also had Maurice wrestling one of the pioneers of what is now called "hardcore wrestling": a wrestler of Lebanese origin called "Wild" Bull Curry, known for his thick and nasty eyebrows and his skill at triggering riots. Samson lined these wrestlers up as an explosive combination. He decided Maurice would team up with Antonio (Tony) Baillargeon, a member of the famous Quebec family of strongmen and wrestlers. Several tag team matches were planned, and they would take place inside a cage or spindle fence, which was still new for the time. Maurice became a babyface, even in Chicoutimi, where he was more hated even than in Montreal. This was the first time Samson was promoting shows at the Coliseum in Chicoutimi (now the Georges-Vézina Center), and he found just the right strategy to make Maurice a crowd favorite.

In his first match of the season, he took on Paul Bouchard, a local wrestler. Maurice was obviously the heel, but before the match ended, the two men were suddenly attacked by Chong and Curry. A series of matches would follow, as Maurice had to face two aggressive, foreign-looking contenders. The storyline wasn't that complicated. Maurice didn't have to change his characteristic style, because his job was to wrestle a wicked "Chinese Communist" and a frightening Lebanese wrestler with menacing eyebrows. The fans just loved it. Maurice was *their* heel. This was fighting fire with fire. His wrestling style was just as offensive as theirs, but he was French Canadian, so the crowd could identify with him because he somehow defended the interests of all Quebecers.

Like everything else, this summer run drew to a close and in September 1960, at the end of the Chicoutimi season, Maurice headed back to join the heels he had left just a few months earlier. In a tag team match in which Maurice teamed with local hero and well-known wrestler Ovila Asselin, Maurice was accidentally hit by Asselin. That's all that was needed for Maurice to retaliate in the ring, attacking his partner and finishing the season in a match against Asselin under a hail of abuse from the crowd. This is the essence of pro wrestling: creating situations that play on the crowd's emotions, getting them to become part of the story. It was a lesson Maurice would apply throughout his career.

Circumstances were such that Maurice was in Quebec when his better-known namesake, Maurice "Rocket" Richard, the most famous Maurice in the history of the province, retired from the Montreal

Canadiens on September 17, 1960. Richard was the first man to score fifty goals in one season, the first to score five hundred career goals, and a member of eight Stanley Cup championship teams. He played in the same Forum where Maurice Vachon loved to wrestle. Vachon was also in town almost a year tot he day before Richard's retirement, when another famous — or infamous — Quebecer named Maurice, the autocratic premier of Quebec, Maurice Duplessis, died and was succeeded by Paul Sauvé. Maurice Vachon couldn't have known it at the time, but he would end up being as known as the other two Maurices and, as fate would have it, would end up wrestling his last match in a venue called Paul Sauvé Arena!

Heading back to Texas once more in the fall of 1960, Maurice reunited with his brother Paul, who had been wrestling in the Lone Star State since the middle of the year. Logic was respected, and the two brothers were put together and won the NWA Texas Tag Team title in November.

For wrestling fans, Maurice was the man they simply hated, but he was liked by the wrestling promoters. They could see the fans kept coming out week after week. He knew how to fire up a crowd, applying the perfect mix of aggressive attitude, cunning strategies, and provocative interviews that would have them coming back for a chance to see him get the beating they felt he deserved. For promoters, a wrestler like this was a gold mine. Besides, Maurice sometimes teamed up with his kid brother Paul, who complemented him perfectly. Paul wasn't as belligerent as his older brother, but then he didn't need to be: he relied instead on his massive size.

On their way back to Montreal, the Vachon brothers wrestled in the Carolinas and Virginia. Beginning in January 1961, they fought in Charlotte, North Carolina, and Richmond, Virginia, where legendary promoter Jim Crockett had them in the main event of the first show he organized there. Many other Quebecers went to wrestle there in the winter of 1961, among them Bob Boyer, Eddy Auger, Terry Garvin, and Louie Tillet. Once again, the Vachon brothers won the Mid-Atlantic NWA Southern Tag Team Title in Charlotte before leaving in early April. Finally, this short stay in North Carolina enabled Maurice to help another Quebecer. Paul recalls: "My brother sent Louie Tillet to Don Owen, promoter of the Pacific Northwest wrestling territory in Portland, Oregon."

When Maurice headed back to Quebec for the summer, he couldn't know yet that he wouldn't be back in Texas until 1975. He had finally managed to make a name for himself in the American South, getting in the good books of new promoters like Crockett. This was the end of a chapter in Maurice's life. Breaking through in Texas hadn't been easy: he had been in a road accident that could have been more serious; he earned so little that he sometimes had to clear out of his hotel room without paying, to keep his earnings for the family. Ultimately, however, this six-year-long Texan adventure had proven more positive than negative: he had gained the experience he needed to grow professionally.

His return to Quebec marked his ten-year anniversary as a pro wrestler — ten years of ups, but also of downs. Things had improved for him in the United States, but he was still struggling to establish himself each summer back home.

Ten years earlier, Maurice had been a twenty-two-year-old dark-haired and almost slender greenhorn. A decade later, he was a young thirty-two-year-old veteran who had not yet reached stardom but had gained a lot of experience. He was going bald, he sported a long beard, and he had filled out to 235 pounds. He was also married with two children. Maurice's life had changed. And it would change again, because 1961 would bring something new: a daughter.

ALOHA, CHERYL

Maurice returned to Quebec in the spring of 1961. The previous year hadn't gone well for Eddie Quinn and his organization. It was so bad that in the summer of 1960, Quinn wasn't able to put on his weekly wrestling shows at the legendary Forum: instead he had to settle for the Mont-Saint-Louis gymnasium or Loisirs Saint-Jean-Baptiste, keeping the Delorimier Stadium, home to the Montreal Royals, for the big shows. Then, in November, things went from bad to worse when he lost his biggest sponsor, the Dow Brewery, which meant the plug was being pulled from his Wednesday night TV show. Quinn's show — *La Lutte* — was now prerecorded and broadcast on Friday nights. Worse, the show was broadcast in the late evening, from 11:30 p.m. to 12:30 a.m. — hardly a prime-time slot. In the summer of 1960, Sylvio Samson promoted cards at the Coliseum in Chicoutimi with Maurice billed as the main event. This not only effectively booted Quinn's organization out of the city, but Samson brought in far bigger crowds on a more regular basis in Jonquière than Quinn and his local promoter, Lucien Grégoire, had managed to do.

Samson was glad to see Maurice back for the summer of 1961. Then, as now, it was the only time of the year when Quebec arenas weren't fully booked with hockey games. In the summer of 1961, Maurice wrestled in Montreal and everywhere else in Quebec, but it was midway between Quebec and Montreal that he really made his name. Wrestling fans in the city of Trois-Rivières still remember the intense rivalry he got involved in at the time.

It all started in late June when the Vachon brothers opened the local wrestling season at the Trois-Rivières Coliseum. The referee for this inaugural match was a local wrestler named Glen Parks, a big guy over six feet tall and weighing 250 pounds. Parks wrestled locally, but generally settled for the role of referee when wrestlers from the Montreal territory turned up, whether they worked for Quinn or Samson. But the referee didn't always get the last word against the Vachon brothers. Escalating this conflict was a dream scenario for Samson, who added another, even better-known local wrestler in Trois-Rivières, Walter "Tarzan" Babin.

With his impressive physique, Babin was both a wrestling and football star in the region. Everybody knew him, from Trois-Rivières to Shawinigan, from Grand-Mère to La Tuque. He had been wrestling for a decade, and like Parks he served as referee when wrestlers turned up from Montreal. In the early 1950s, he hoped for a lucky break in the big city, but like many other wrestlers he realized Montreal was a tough place to make it big.

Once the match started, the Vachon brothers started bullying the ref, Parks. Babin jumped into the ring "dressed in civilian clothes," as the newspapers said, to make his intervention seem more justified. After two weeks of preparations, the natives of Trois-Rivières were finally getting to see the first of five matches pitting Babin against Vachon. But to the crowd's dismay, Vachon was getting some help from a controversial referee by the name of Eddy "The Brain"

Creatchman. Long before he became famous as one of Quebec's most hated wrestling managers, Creatchman was a referee, and fans didn't like him any more in that role than they did as manager. With the match descending into chaos, it was clearly time for a rematch, and what could be better than a "death match" to settle the score?

On the evening of July 24, Vachon skipped out of the death match, fleeing into the street, to the great dissatisfaction of the 3,500 fans in the Coliseum — the biggest crowd of the season. The match continued in the street, however: Babin chased after Vachon and the two men began fighting outside, damaging several cars in the process. Then it was announced with great fanfare that Babin was challenging Vachon to a match at the Coliseum, but inside a fence so Vachon couldn't run off the way he had just done.

But municipal authorities in Trois-Rivières wouldn't allow the kind of match Babin was proposing. At the time, only a municipal authority like an athletic commission or the police could make that kind of decision, even in the case of a staged match. Promoters often created scenarios involving local authorities to add some sizzle to the storyline, but this was one case where no municipal regulations could actually prevent Maurice from leaving the ring in the middle of the match. As a result, another "death match" was organized, but it only attracted three thousand fans, five hundred less than the first time. People were afraid Maurice could still run away from the match, even though Maurice and Babin staged a public confrontation at the popular tavern Chez Jack, which belonged to the former wrestling promoter and hockey player Jack Toupin.

Once again, the fans felt cheated because the match ended without a clear winner. Other wrestlers actually intervened to set up a tag team match for the following week. That idea didn't work any better: only 2,300 fans turned up. A week later, in a six-man tag with the Vachon brothers on one team and Babin on the other, only 2,000 people turned up. The same evening, Vachon and Babin took part in a boxing exhibition, which would lead to an "official" boxing match between the two men that would close the season in late August. But this match drew just 2,000 fans, even though Babin was awarded a knockout over Maurice in the fourth round, his win putting an end to their rivalry.

The summer of 1961 left a lasting impression on the imagination of people in Trois-Rivières. Promoters, wrestlers, and fans still remember the way Vachon and Babin "filled the Coliseum several times" that summer. Although the facts were entirely different, the people of the region have never forgotten Maurice and his legendary rivalry with Babin, the most colorful in the history of wrestling in Trois-Rivières. For people there, it was their version of the great rivalries that occurred in the province of Quebec, such as the Rougeaus and the Garvins, Kowalski and Yukon Eric, or the Leducs and the Vachons.

In the early 1960s, Maurice was still spending just a part of the year wrestling in Quebec, and there was ever more truth to that as insiders could see Quinn's empire gradually collapsing. Indeed, Radio-Canada canceled Quinn's TV show altogether in the summer of 1961. Eventually, Quinn and Samson would even share the brand-new Paul Sauvé Arena, at the corner of Beaubien Street and Pie-IX Boulevard in Montreal. Maurice also had the honor of taking part in the first main event to be held there: the match pitted the Vachon brothers against the popular Fortin brothers, drawing some 4,000 fans. This surprising performance convinced Quinn to use the new sports center, especially since the previous month Carpentier had managed to draw only 3,000 fans at the Forum.

Maurice's brother Guy actually made his professional debut — and only match — against the Fortin brothers. "That was in Jonquière in the late 1950s," says Guy. "It was a ten-hour round-trip

by car, and I made $40. I actually made more money as a doorman."
At the same time, Maurice also tried convincing Samson to team his
brother Régis, a good amateur wrestler, with Paul, but the promoter
refused. Samson claimed that if Paul and Régis ever succeeded as a
team, they would go over to Quinn. Samson clearly couldn't have
imagined that he would one day be competing with Quinn head-on.

The Quinn organization was still strong in the smaller regions
of the province of Quebec, but it was no longer the gold mine it
had once been. Maurice had gotten used to spending his winters
in warmer climes, and this year was no exception. He headed for
Hawaii, which had become the fiftieth state of the Union just two
years earlier. There was only one problem: Dorothy was expecting
their third child. Maurice knew his wife disliked traveling. Although
Maurice wrestled in the same territory for months at a stretch, he
was often away from home. Dorothy wanted a more settled family
life. The children were growing, and Linda Sue and Mike in particular needed stability, since they were going to school. Dorothy had
to take care of three children on her own, with a baby on the way.
The Vachons didn't have enough money to hire a tutor on the road
the way the wealthy Hollywood families do. It was hard for children
to switch schools during the year, but it was even harder when the
new school was located in another state. Maurice wanted to spend
summers in Quebec because it gave some stability to his children and
also exposed them to a French-speaking environment, at least for a
few months each year.

The lifestyle was very different in Hawaii. The children went to
school barefoot. The beach and the ocean were nearby. And on top
of it all, by wrestling in Honolulu three times a week, Maurice made
the same money as he earned anywhere else doing it every night. It
seemed like they were living the life of the rich and famous. Because
of that, Dorothy found it easier to accept the way her husband had

to keep on the move to make a living. She felt Hawaii marked a new beginning. It was here, on December 16, 1961, that she gave birth to their last child, a little girl named Cheryl.

"The best time we had was in Hawaii," Maurice later remembered, somewhat nostalgically.

In Honolulu, Maurice wrestled against guys like Lord James Blears (who would become the booker there), King Curtis Iaukea, a former football player Don Manoukian, a young Nick Bockwinkel, and another Quebecer, Luigi Macera.

In 1962, wrestler Ed Francis bought the Hawaii territory. He would hold onto it for another seventeen years. Don Owen, the promoter of the Portland territory in Oregon, went to Hawaii for a vacation and watched Maurice at work. He liked what he saw and asked, through Francis, whether Maurice would be interested in working for him. When Francis laid things out for Maurice, he praised Don as a man of his word, who generally paid well and loved offering wrestlers like Maurice, who were a bit smaller than average, a chance to shine. Don Owen wanted to make Maurice his main heel, and Maurice accepted the offer on the spot.

However, before leaving Texas, Maurice had committed to help wrestler Dick Raines set up his promotion in Australia. He liked Owen's offer better, but he didn't want to leave Raines high and dry. So he called his brother Paul, then in Western Canada, to see if he would take his place in Australia. Paul was always on the lookout for opportunities to gain experience in his brother's footsteps, and he accepted at once, leaving for Australia with his wife. Paul's wrestling tour down under was only supposed to last two and a half months. But things often took unexpected turns in the wrestling world. After Australia, Paul went to New Zealand, then he headed for India, Pakistan, and finally England. He began his overseas adventures in May 1962, and he wouldn't return to North America until February

1966. So much for the original plan! During this time, Paul got to add some impressive experience to his resume as a professional wrestler. All thanks to his older brother.

Maurice was excited to go to Portland. He trusted Owen, who seemed to want to give him a real break. In October 1961, Maurice had lost a match against Neff Maiava. The deal was, the wrestler who lost the match had to shave his head completely. Maurice was already losing a lot of hair, so by the time he met Owen he was bald, which didn't seem to bother the promoter much. Owen asked him to grow a new, but shorter, beard. (On arriving in Hawaii, Maurice had shaved off the beard he had kept for the last few years.) Owen had a clear idea of the unique character he wanted: a bald, bearded man with a few missing teeth.

For Maurice, a great opportunity seemed to await him on the U.S. mainland. For some time now, the tide had been turning in his favor. He no longer had to look for work; he got offers without having to make cold calls. He had no way of knowing, however, that moving into this new territory would change his career . . . and his life.

13
MAD DOG IS BORN

On May 2, 1962, Maurice wrestled for a last time in Hawaii. He made his debut in Portland two days later — and what a debut it was.

He arrived in Portland late in the day, as the card was about to begin, and quickly met with Owen. Maurice was expected to take part in the first match of the night, against Dick Garza, who years later would become known as the Mighty Igor. Owen told him to get into his wrestling gear and head out to the ring.

Garza was already in the ring when Maurice made his entrance. The announcer wasn't even there yet. At the time, wrestlers didn't make grand entrances with music the way they do nowadays. So Maurice made his way down the aisle without fanfare. Once in the ring, he started bouncing up and down like a kangaroo — which would become one of his trademarks — and then he violently body slammed Garza a few times before tossing him between the ropes and onto the concrete floor. Maurice continued his attack outside the ring, body slamming Garza on the floor. The referee finally arrived, but it didn't stop Maurice, who continued his attack, this time on the referee. Bear in mind that this all took place even before the match officially started! That's when a policeman actually intervened.

"He tried hitting me with his billy club. He thought I had really lost it," Maurice said. "So, I bent down, grabbed the constable, and threw him into the third row."

As Maurice told and retold this tale over the years, the drama took on ever greater proportions. The sequence of events also changed. But one thing was clear: the story involved Garza, a referee, and a cop. Maybe the policeman worked for Owen, but in the eyes of fans he was still a policeman. The referee was Shag Thomas, who was also one of the most popular wrestlers in the territory. He had no choice but to disqualify Maurice. At the time, it was more common for wrestlers to improvise and go off-script than it is today. Promoters relied on the referees to make the best possible call when things got out of hand. The Oregon Athletic Commission wasn't too happy about this turn of events, since it disapproved of a referee getting beaten up and bashed around, whether or not it was part of the script. And most other commissions across North America took a similar position

Once Maurice got back to the locker room, Owen confronted him.

"You've just arrived in town. We haven't even had the chance to shake hands," said the promoter. "And then you get into the ring and you get yourself in trouble with someone you don't even know? You looked like a god damn mad dog out there . . ."

Maurice acted and looked exactly like a "Mad Dog" — he was stocky, bald, bearded, covered with body hair, and missing a few teeth. A wrestler who had just attacked two other men he didn't even know. And so the legend of "Mad Dog" Vachon was born, and fans would simply love to hate Mad Dog for the rest of his career.

Maurice knew what he had just done would leave nobody

indifferent. He had followed the advice of Francis, the Hawaiian promoter: "The guys who succeed in Portland are a little crazy," Francis had told him. "If you want to be over, you have got to be wild!" People would remember him and his actions for a long time to come. And Maurice knew this recognition had a lot of value.

In fact, Garza and Thomas weren't mad at Maurice very long, if they were ever really mad at him at all. They simply played along with his craziness without asking too many questions because that meant return matches and better payoffs.

Even before Maurice reached Portland, Owen had started publicizing his imminent arrival, seizing on the nickname "Mad" that Maurice had earned in recent years, and deciding the character he portrayed was from Algeria.

From 1954 to 1962, war was raging between France and Algeria, one of the colonies France maintained in North Africa after World War II, along with Tunisia and Morocco. But the three North African colonies wanted their independence. When conflict broke out in Algeria, there were still about a million French citizens of European origin living there. The resulting war was horrific and dark. Newspaper photos of the many atrocities went round the world. Algerians were not well-liked in North America, since they were fighting France, one of the Allied powers from World War II. So when Owen promoted Maurice as a "Mad Frenchman" from Algeria, he was making sure Maurice got a knee-jerk reaction from Oregonians.

"Owen told me this was going to help my character, since people were going to think I was a maniac, the way Algerians were perceived at the time," Vachon recalled.

And his behavior on that first appearance in Portland threw gasoline on the fire.

Owen later said during an interview, "What he did that night was reason enough for me to call him a 'mad dog' because he didn't really look like a 'Maurice'…"

The story goes that Maurice took the nickname "Mad Dog" the very next day. But things didn't actually work out that way. It was only on May 27 that the nickname appeared for the first time in print, in a daily newspaper in Salem, Oregon. The biggest Portland newspaper, the *Oregonian*, only mentioned the nickname on June 22. The territory of Seattle in nearby Washington State shared many wrestlers with the Portland territory, and Seattle newspapers didn't use the nickname "Mad Dog" until September. Instead, they called Maurice "the French Buzz Saw." "Mad Dog" was used for the first time by the Portland television station KOIN-TV in June.

In retrospect, "Mad Dog" was the culmination of a natural progression. Nothing had been planned in advance. Over the years, Maurice was occasionally referred to as "Mad," "Madman," and "Mad Frenchman." "Mad Dog" was even more evocative, and it fit him like a glove.

But Maurice's last name, meanwhile, began creating some confusion, and this would long haunt Maurice and his brother, sister, and niece. There is a straightforward explanation. In the early 1960s, communications were not as instantaneous as they are now. When a newspaper published an article in the lead-up to a card, or when it reported the results afterwards, there wasn't always an eye-witness journalist reporting from the scene. Most of the time, the promoter or someone in his organization dictated news releases over the phone to someone on the news desk at the local paper. For this reason, many of these items weren't signed. Press releases were often taken down phonetically, because time was money, and reporters didn't pay much attention to spelling. Besides, of all wrestling territories in the United States, Don Owen's Pacific Northwest territory was probably the one featuring the most errors in the names of wrestlers.

In English, the family name "Vachon" is hard to pronounce, especially the last two letters "on": in French the vowel "o" is nasalized, and the final "n" is not pronounced because it only serves to mark the nasalization. But in English, the name often ended up being pronounced "Vachonne" — like the words "dawn" or "gone." So in newspaper articles, promotional posters, and photos, as well as in magazines, "Maurice Vachon" quickly became "Maurice Vachone." On top of it all, the family name "Vachon" was often confused in Seattle with Vashon Island in nearby Puget Sound. So, at a time when the kid from Ville-Émard was finally becoming a pro wrestling star, it was under a variety of names — from Maurice Vachone to Vashon and Vachon.

Owen quickly put Maurice in a program with Shag Thomas, who had refereed his first match. This matchup might have given the impression everything was staged, but that wasn't really the case. In any case, a wrestling promoter would be crazy to switch direction, with Mad Dog's ongoing antics being better than any scripted ideas. Thomas was five years older than Maurice, about as tall, but much larger and more muscular. By the end of his career, he would become one of the state's most popular wrestlers of all time. He was an African-American and stood as living proof that for Owen, what mattered most in the ring was performance and interaction with the crowd, not skin color or size. Maurice and Thomas worked together in many different combinations, whether in singles, in tags, or in six-man tags. Maurice also regularly teamed up with the Germans Fritz von Goering and Kurt von Poppenheim, while Thomas was associated with his usual partner, Luther Lindsay, another African-American, and a third partner who varied depending on the month, such as Pat O'Connor and Herb Freeman.

The rivalry between Maurice and the Germans, on the one hand, and Lindsay, Thomas, and Freeman, on the other hand, was the defining story of the territory for the rest of the year. Maurice was featured in the main events or the semi-mains, or was involved in them one way or the other. Owen trusted him completely. This was one of the few times in Maurice's career that he was called on to battle bigger and taller wrestlers on a regular basis and wasn't expected to lose after a few minutes.

Maurice settled in the Portland suburbs and was widely respected. Now that he was comfortably established, he reached out to help someone else.

The previous summers, when he wrestled for Sylvio Samson in Quebec, he studied and evaluated new talent coming along. He had noticed a young wrestler then making his debut. Maurice received a letter in Portland from René Méthode, manager of Terry Garvin, who had also wrestled for Samson. In the letter, Méthode let him know a certain wrestler Maurice had enjoyed watching a few summers earlier was now in Boston.

"I get a letter from Maurice who says I'm booked in Oregon in two weeks and he's waiting for me," said the wrestler in question. "But I have no car and no money. The Boston promoter [Tony Santos] calls me into his office and lays out the biggest map I have ever seen in my life, to show me how far it is from Portland to Boston. 'Coast to coast,' he says. So I didn't answer Maurice."

Maurice didn't give up, however.

"But Maurice sends me a second letter, for Christ's sake — worse than that, he gives me hell, and he gives a second start date on the territory, warning me I had better be there. So I borrowed money from my friend Louie and I headed out to Portland. I made the preliminary match on the first night, a nice little match. My pay was $300, whereas I've been earning $15 a night in Boston. I go to see Maurice and I tell him there must be a mistake, it's too much. And Maurice answers: Don't worry about it, you're still getting screwed!"

This young wrestler was none other than Pat Patterson, regarded today as one of the best wrestlers of his era and one of the top hundred wrestlers of all time. He also served as Vince McMahon Jr.'s right-hand man after his in-ring career ended during WWE national expansion.

Patterson made his debut in Portland on July 31, 1962. He was supposed to have debuted the week before, but he was a few days late in reaching Oregon. Santos was right: Portland is indeed 3,100 miles from Boston! He became known as "Pretty Boy" Patrick Patterson, and he and Maurice would team up together several times over the next two years. For his part, Maurice ensured that his young protégé learned the ropes. They became fast friends, and the Vachons invited Patterson to celebrate Christmas with them. The two buddies loved joking around, having a drink, and getting up to antics, even though Patterson infuriated Maurice one time by waking up the children on Christmas Eve to tell them Santa Claus had just delivered their presents in person.

The way things were turning out, 1962 was becoming Maurice's year, and Portland was becoming his territory. He won the Pacific Northwest heavyweight title twice against Lindsay — the most important single title he'd earned up till then, and he also won the tag titles with von Goering.

The following year was just as fulfilling. Maurice was building an increasingly strong reputation as a main-eventer and champion. And while wrestling championships didn't have the same weight as boxing championships, a wrestler billed as a champion was someone who enjoyed the promoter's confidence and who had status to represent the company.

Patterson says, "Maurice was fucking respected in Portland! I always traveled with Maurice and nobody ever gave me a hard time, and other wrestlers even encouraged me to get better."

What Patterson was always shy in sharing until recently with his own biography, *Accepted*, was that Maurice was actually quickly accepting the fact that his protégé was gay. He would even go as far as making sure Patterson's boyfriend, Louie Dondero, was accepted in their wrestling brotherhood, pretending he was first and foremost Maurice's friend. Years later, Maurice and others like Nick Bockwinkel made sure to let everyone in the business know that there was nothing to it and that Pat and Louie were just great guys. Even if he was a little wary of the situation at first, Maurice quickly struck a friendship with Louie that lasted for the rest of their lives. Maurice and his wife even spent weeks at Pat and Louie's place in Florida towards the end of his career. Maurice would judge you only by who you were and not by what you were.

Quite apart from the titles, Maurice's matches were increasingly creating a buzz. The very least one can say is he made good use of his nickname.

In Eugene, in a match against Billy White Wolf, he wrestled his opponent into the arena parking lot, where the men bashed each other's heads against cars until the blood-fest was stopped. When fans turned up for his match against Rocco Colombo, they were advised it wasn't part of the regular card. However, they were invited to stay on to witness a settling of the scores, adding that the two men would battle either with their bare hands or wearing boxing gloves. The veteran Haystacks Calhoun was asked in an interview where the promoter had found Vachon. He replied that in all his travels, he had never met a person like Mad Dog, who lacked any kind of personal ethics. Maurice was probably helped along and even motivated by his new nickname. He adopted an even more ferocious fighting style. The nickname added to his public persona, but fans wanted more: Maurice played his role so well they actually bought their tickets in the hopes of someone shutting the Mad Dog down.

But Maurice wasn't just a crazy brute; he could wrestle with style when he needed to. In a match against Luther Lindsay, both men wrestled for an entire hour. During the last ten minutes, the fans were on their feet, cheering on the two gladiators. The atmosphere in the arena was so emotion-charged and inspiring that some wrestlers watching that day said even they felt shivers going up and down their spine.

In the ring, Mad Dog was notorious for his bad temper, and in his everyday life, Maurice wasn't much different. He was an avid boxing fan, and in 1963, while he was wrestling in Seattle, he decided to go see a closed circuit display of the "noble art." He paid $25 for his ticket — a good sum at that time, considering that's what some wrestlers earned in an evening. But he barely had time to sit down and the fight was already over: Sonny Liston knocked Floyd Patterson out in two minutes. Maurice headed back to the arena for his own match in a foul mood: "I didn't see anything and it cost me twenty-five fucking dollars."

Another time, Maurice and Pat Patterson went out for a coffee after a show. Maurice came back from the bathroom and said, "We're going to have trouble, so be ready." Three teenagers had confronted him while he was in the washroom. Sure enough, the teenagers came to their table, calling them names. Maurice reacted quickly and instinctively, tossing some water in their faces. That was enough to scare them off, but just a few years later, Maurice wouldn't hesitate to use his fists in similar situations.

After over a year in Oregon, Maurice missed Quebec. He had lost the title in July, so nothing was holding him on the West Coast. True to form, he spent the summer at home. On reaching Montreal, he discovered the wrestling landscape had changed radically. While Maurice had been enjoying his new-won success in Portland, Quinn had tried to revive his wrestling TV show on a new station, Channel

10. Eventually he headed back to his native Boston, and he would die the following year.

In the summer of 1963, Yvon Robert took over the territory. But times were tough. Robert didn't manage to land a TV contract, and it was always harder to attract a big crowd when the product wasn't televised. What made things worse was Robert was using stars like Killer Kowalski, Édouard Carpentier, Larry Moquin, and Johnny Rougeau, who expected big fees.

These wrestlers were better known in Quebec than Maurice, who had yet to become "Mad Dog" in la belle province. Robert used him in main events, trying to capitalize on the rough style and emotions he brought to wrestling. Maurice teamed up with Kowalski, squaring off against his oldest foe, Johnny Rougeau. He also wrestled in singles competition against "the Flying Frenchman" Édouard Carpentier. It was as if Maurice had finally been accepted — for the first time he was featured prominently at the Montreal Forum. Unfortunately, Robert's promotion didn't last long enough to meet with much success, and this period in Maurice's career didn't leave a lasting mark in the collective memory of Quebecers. In late summer 1963, a lot of Quebecers were skeptical about whether anyone could resurrect the French-Canadian wrestling scene, because even the great Yvon Robert had failed. For Maurice, there was only one option — to return to Oregon. His children had to head back to school, and Montreal was no longer a place where he could make a living.

This episode was enough to discourage a man who had always maintained ties with his home province and badly wanted to succeed there. When Quebec had wanted him, Maurice hadn't been ready, but now that he was ready, Quebec couldn't offer him much. This would be the last time he wrestled for more than a month at a time in Quebec until 1967. Before leaving the province in 1963, Maurice once again helped a fellow Quebecer. Robert "Bob" Bédard was thirty-one years old and unable to gain a foothold in the wrestling world. Since going pro in 1957, he had worked here and there in the regions, for starvation wages, but he had failed to make a breakthrough. Over the summer, he hooked up with Maurice, as the two of them had become friends in recent years.

"Why don't you work in the United States?" Maurice asked.

"I don't speak English," answered Bédard, a native of Quebec City.

"Let me call Wally Karbo in Minneapolis. You're going to work there."

Maurice was a man of his word and called Karbo. So, like Maurice had promised, Bédard went to wrestle in Minnesota. Bédard says: "I told my wife if things didn't work in Minnesota, we would return to Quebec and I would give up wrestling. It was in Minnesota that I got the ring name René Goulet and I never left the United States." As Goulet, he would wrestle until the 1980s, after which he would become one of the leading agents behind the scenes in the WWF. He would also keep in touch with Maurice throughout his life.

Maurice returned to Portland, where he continued to wrestle for Owen. He continued wrestling against Freeman, Thomas, and Lindsay, whether in singles or with a new partner named Soldat Gorky. This would not be the last time those two wrestled as a team.

Apart from his regular opponents, Maurice began a new rivalry with Nick Bockwinkel. Then twenty-eight years old, Bockwinkel would one day be the American Wrestling Association (AWA) champion and would be inducted in the WWE Hall of Fame. He had been wrestling the last few years and was also trying to break through to stardom. He was a second-generation wrestler, known for his blond hair and tanned skin. He knew all about the psychology of wrestling, and in interviews he spoke with almost aristocratic eloquence.

Bockwinkel had been in Hawaii along with Maurice and was now part of Owen's organization.

In 1963, Bockwinkel was the crowd favorite and the very opposite of Maurice. On one side of the ring, the fans saw a technical wrestler, blond with blue eyes and a build that delighted female fans. On the other side was a shaggy little mad dog, a few pounds overweight, who could turn the world upside down! The contrast was striking.

Their rivalry came to a breaking point when they competed for the title. Bockwinkel won it on October 30, but a few weeks later Maurice got the title back, only to lose it on January 3, 1964, to another great wrestler, Dick "The Destroyer" Beyer.

This date was important in Maurice's career because it marked the end of his association with Don Owen. Mad Dog now left Portland, which had been so good for him, for another booming territory in Omaha, Nebraska. To his credit, he had fought against all the major wrestlers in the Pacific Northwest territory at least once, often in the main event. It was a good territory, but it was small. This wouldn't be the last time Maurice wrestled in Portland, nor even the last time he would lose the Pacific Northwest title. But it was the last time he wrestled there on a regular basis. He had become one of the biggest stars in the territory, one of those attracting the most fans, but it was time to move on.

Just the way he had done in Portland years earlier, Maurice now arrived in Omaha, his reputation greatly enhanced, and bearing a ring name that reflected the wrestler he had worked so hard to become. As things turned out, Omaha would only be one step towards an even greater territory. Nevertheless, it was the beginning of an extraordinary adventure. The adventure of a career. The adventure of a whole lifetime.

14
A NEW START
IN THE MIDWEST

By the early summer of 1963, Maurice felt he had experienced everything the West Coast had to offer, and he now needed to find a new territory. He knew Wally Karbo's promotion in Minneapolis had a good reputation and paid its wrestlers well. He decided to call the promoter. The world of professional wrestling was small and Karbo knew about Maurice's success in Portland and elsewhere. Maurice was on the point of heading back to Quebec for a few weeks, so Karbo asked him to make a stopover in Minneapolis. At that time, it was still common for wrestlers to make long road trips by car. Crossing the continent from west to east wasn't a problem for Maurice.

On July 9, 1963, Maurice made his official debut in Minneapolis. He lost to Don McLarty, but the result was irrelevant: Maurice made a great first impression, and Karbo extended an open invitation to him — to return any time he wanted.

Maurice stayed a few weeks in Quebec, wrestling for Yvon Robert. Then he got a date for his return to Minneapolis. However, in a sad twist of fate, his first bouts were canceled a week before he left Quebec, on the grounds there were already too many wrestlers in the promotion. But Karbo offered Maurice an interesting alternative.

The Omaha territory was a little south of Minnesota and controlled by former wrestler Joe Dusek, one of the famous Dusek brothers who had made such a big splash in Montreal in the 1940s and 1950s. Maurice had paid to see them at the Forum. Omaha was an independent territory associated with Minneapolis under the banner of the AWA.

Karbo warned Maurice that main-eventers earned only $200 a week in Omaha, but if he performed well, the territory would be his. In other words, Maurice would become the star attraction, which meant more money, better visibility, and new opportunities, such as entering the Minneapolis territory, where there was more money to be made.

Maurice loved a challenge, so he accepted Karbo's offer and gave notice to the Owen organization in Portland. After losing the title to the Destroyer, he made his debut in Omaha the very next day facing one of his old friends, the Quebecer Maurice Lapointe.

Mad Dog lived up to his reputation and became the biggest star in Omaha. Instead of the $200 per week he had been offered, he earned four times that much and proved he had what it took to bring in the fans. The highlight of his run occurred on May 2 when he defeated the champion, Verne Gagne, in the Omaha Auditorium. For the first time, Maurice became the world heavyweight champion of the AWA.

Gagne and Karbo had founded the AWA in 1960. The previous year, under the name of the Minneapolis Boxing and Wrestling Club, the two men had bought the rights to the territory from the Stecher family, who were well-known in the wrestling world for their strong presence in Minnesota.

Gagne and Maurice had known each other a long time, but they had only occasionally appeared on the same card. Of French ancestry, Gagne was a native of Robbinsdale, Minnesota. He had turned professional in 1949 and quickly rose in wrestling thanks to his television appearances in the early 1950s. This was the dawn of wrestling on television, the matches being broadcast on the DuMont Network, one of the first national networks in the United States. In the late 1950s, Gagne had become one of the most famous American wrestlers. However, he still hadn't won the NWA world heavyweight title.

In those years, the NWA promoters got together during the association's annual meetings to decide who would be the next champion: a list of candidates was suggested and they discussed the various possibilities. The champion would not only receive better pay, he would have to travel the country and even beyond to defend his title worldwide. If promoters felt a particular wrestler did not deserve a chance, then the options became limited for that candidate. Gagne saw several of his proposals shot down by key decision-makers. Frustrated with the situation, he decided to invest in the Minnesota territory. This meant joining forces with Karbo, who had already been promoting there for fifteen years. As a result, they created a new wrestling organization that ended up competing with the NWA for decades.

Over the years, their promotion extended its tentacles beyond Minnesota to include cities like Chicago, Denver, San Francisco, Las Vegas, Salt Lake City, Winnipeg, and, of course, Omaha.

But in 1964, Omaha still maintained a certain independence. Gagne and Karbo promoted wrestling talent from the AWA but also developed storylines that were specific to their respective area, and not necessarily recognized by the parent organization. Omaha also had its own TV show, distinct from the one produced in Minneapolis.

Maurice's situation is a perfect illustration of how separate these two territories were. Maurice was having a lot of success in Omaha, but Minneapolis fans never saw him on TV. Moreover, the title match he won on May 2 against Gagne wasn't even acknowledged on Minnesota television. The people who attended the show live remember it as one of the most physical defeats Gagne was ever handed in his career. Which only goes to show that Gagne intended to do everything he possibly could to ultimately give Maurice a real chance to become a star in Minneapolis. Eventually, Maurice became the new champion in the eyes of the people of Omaha, and in their eyes alone. In the eyes of fans in Minnesota or elsewhere, Gagne was still the defending champion.

Incredible as it may seem, this is the way things were at the time. This couldn't happen today because the outcomes of the shows spread like wildfire on social media in a matter of minutes. In 1964, it was still possible to reserve a championship match for local consumption only. The objective was to create local stars, and in years to come that objective would remain in force.

Maurice had the honor of being the first AWA champion to have won and lost the title in Omaha. But since the organization needed to provide a certain harmony to match results in Omaha and Minneapolis, Gagne got his title back two weeks later.

But it was enough to get Maurice over. He proved he deserved a place among the best wrestlers. Gagne was a good businessman and took notice.

Two months later, Maurice made his AWA television debut in Minnesota. He was still described as an Algerian, the way he had been in Portland — and the publicity machine made a big deal of his nickname. Newspapers called him Mad Dog and noted his style of wrestling, which included kicking, scratching, trampling, and biting his opponents. The year 1964 marked the start of a pivotal era for the AWA. Business was good and the promotion was becoming increasingly important in the world of professional wrestling. Maurice couldn't have chosen a better time to make his move.

Then, after a few TV tapings in Minneapolis, Maurice found validation in a way he'd never had yet. On October 20, 1964, he officially won the AWA world title, defeating Gagne in Minneapolis. This made him the fifth official champion of the territory, a champion recognized throughout the promotion, not just in one part of it.

"One of my great accomplishments is having defeated Verne Gagne for the title," Maurice later recalled.

He defended his title against several contenders, notably Gagne, who got several chances to regain the title. On November 26, during the first rematch in Minneapolis, over ten thousand fans turned up to watch the main event of the show. This was the first time Maurice had attracted a crowd of more than ten thousand. Having these two wrestlers face each other in the ring was a stroke of genius. Gagne was the opposite of Maurice, in terms of style, the way he presented himself, and the interviews he gave. That feud was gold for both of them from that point forward.

Maurice's favorite move at the time was the piledriver, and it brought him a lot of success. But it was dangerous, even when well executed. Today, WWE doesn't allow the move to be used by its wrestlers in order to protect their neck and head. The AWA even talked of "banning" the hold, which gave Maurice the chance to create more uproar in the arena whenever he used it. As a result, fans naturally believed that the Dog was the real deal.

From the time he won his first title onwards, Maurice generated a lot of heat. People kept wondering who would be able to stop him. He remained the champion until the middle of the following year. But when he lost the title, he didn't just lose it once, but twice. As he had with Gagne, Maurice began by losing his title in May in Omaha, against Mighty Igor (Dick Garza). Then he regained it against the same opponent the following week. But fans in Minneapolis knew nothing about these two matches.

Maurice then defended his title against wrestlers of the caliber of Blackjack Lanza, Danny Hodge, Pat O'Connor, Pampero Firpo, Reggie Parks, Ivan Kalmikoff, the Mongolian Stomper, and Wilbur Snyder. Then, on August 21, 1965, in Saint Paul, Minnesota, in front of twelve thousand delirious fans, Maurice officially lost to the man who would become one of his fiercest opponents, the Crusher.

An American from Milwaukee whose real name was Reginald Lisowski, he began wrestling in the late 1940s. And well before the era of Steve Austin or the Sandman, he was recognized as a tough beer-drinker kind of guy. Legend has it that he joined his father in bars, where he got a real education: from the age of seven or eight years old, he threw customers out into the street for drinking too much. He was a real man, always a cigar dangling from his mouth, and he quickly earned Maurice's respect in and out of the ring. After being a heel for years, this six-foot wrestler weighing 250 pounds had become a babyface a few months before the match, along with his partner Dick the Bruiser. So when he won his third and final AWA heavyweight title against Maurice, all hell broke loose in the arena. But the Crusher didn't keep the title for long: on November 12, he lost it again to Maurice in Denver, Colorado. The rivalry between the two men was only just beginning.

Between these two matches against the Crusher, Maurice returned to Oregon for a few weeks, where he won the territory's championship. He lost the title shortly after to a fellow Quebecer, George Stipich, better known as Stan Stasiak.

So in the years 1964 and 1965, Maurice earned a lot of credibility and renown in the wrestling world. As champion of the AWA, he enjoyed a status he had never before achieved. At a time when the great champions were wrestlers like Bruno Sammartino, Lou Thesz, and Cowboy Bob Ellis, Maurice was carving out a place not only in professional wrestling but also in its history.

"It took me twelve or fifteen years to become internationally famous and to make money for all my efforts. Once your name is made, you are in big demand," he said.

If things were going well for Maurice professionally, they weren't that good on a personal level. Maurice and Dorothy had been married for ten years, and their relationship was beginning to go sour. His brother Paul had already noticed signs Maurice wasn't getting along with Dorothy when the two brothers had wrestled together in Calgary. And when the family lived in the Portland suburbs a few years earlier, their arguments sometimes got so volatile that the police had to be called, and Maurice was ordered to leave home until the dust settled. When that happened, Maurice would take refuge on Pat Patterson's couch. That happened quite a few times back then. Though Patterson and Louie were happy to help and Maurice was happy to have such good friends, things with his wife had been going in the wrong direction for quite some time.

Dorothy regularly traveled with her husband, but she didn't like long road trips, especially since it meant bringing all their children in tow. She was like many women of her time. Her husband was often away. She was the one left looking after their children and making sure they were properly schooled and well cared for. Shortly after Cheryl's birth, Maurice had bought a house for Dorothy and the children in the Montreal suburb of Saint-Bruno. When Maurice debuted in Minneapolis, Dorothy stayed behind in Montreal with the kids. It should be noted that Maurice increasingly had to travel by plane and it was becoming hard for the family to follow him.

And that's when Maurice had an important encounter.

Wrestlers were treated like rock stars and were sometimes pursued by groupies and other adoring fans who idolized their favorite athletes. When Maurice began working in Omaha, a group of girls, including Kathie Jo Ustohal, her sister Sandra, and her friend Sheila, regularly attended the matches there. Kathie was born November 6, 1948, the year of the London Olympics, so she was only fifteen or sixteen when Maurice became a regular in Omaha. Obviously, women went for the babyfaces more than the heels: the bad guys were known for their atrocious behavior, and they could have disagreeable physical characteristics. Kathie had avowedly been a tomboy. She loved horse races, the New York Yankees, and their star right-fielder Roger Maris. At the age of thirteen, she began watching wrestling Monday nights on TV. Maurice was clearly not one of her favorite wrestlers when he arrived on the scene.

"I remember watching Maurice on TV and then seeing him outside the arena, with his custom-made clothes, and Frank Sinatra–style hat. He threw me a few naughty looks and I thought how dirty and disgusting he was!" she says. Photos of the leading wrestlers hung on a wall in the arena, and Kathie spat on the picture of Maurice in a sign of defiance and disapprobation of his actions.

Then, little by little, the charm, charisma, and masculinity of Maurice won her over. Maurice would invite Kathie (with Sheila chaperoning) for a root beer at A&W.

"I knew he was married because I had once met his daughter Linda in the arena bathroom, and she told me her parents were often getting into fights," she recalls. "At the time, Maurice was like a Hollywood star. We sat in the back seat of his Oldsmobile. There was even a mini bar in the back. I remember I loved his hairy arms and his watch."

Kathie insists, however, that nothing happened that evening or any other evening for a long time. Maurice was not only married, he was twenty years her senior. Customs may have been different in the 1960s, but as a gentleman Maurice didn't force things. But they kept in touch for years. Kathie even came to greet Maurice when he arrived at the airport, and she dropped him off on his departure. But still, nothing happened between them. Wrestlers at the time developed networks of contacts in each city they visited, so they could be driven around for free and learn about the best hotels and places to go out for a drink.

"We never talked about wrestling. He told me about his life, his family, his wife and his children. He must have felt I was mature for my age and I was a good listener," she recalls.

Kathie swears they didn't so much as exchange a kiss in all those years, but at the time she confided to a friend they were going to get married one day. It all might sound like a teenage girl's dream, but time would prove her right: Maurice would see Kathie and her hometown of Omaha again.

Meanwhile, Maurice kept busy with wrestling. In the fall of 1965, George Burrell Woodin, better known by the ring name Tim Woods, began wrestling in the AWA and benefited from Maurice's creative flair.

Woods had previously been an amateur wrestler at the college level in the United States. He was actually a late bloomer, having started his professional career just two years earlier at the age of twenty-nine. All he had was a wrestling outfit and experience in amateur wrestling. Woods was a babyface who made it to the mid-card level, where there was very little real chance of having a good future in the business. At the time, he even tried changing jobs because he was earning only $200 per week. He asked Maurice to help, and that's when he discovered Maurice had a magic touch.

Maurice later remembered: "I told him, people see good wrestling moves, but that's no good for us. If you want to follow my advice, go buy yourself a white mask, white boots, white socks, a white shirt, a bathrobe down to your knees, come running into the ring, just jump over the cables and start doing dropkicks and doing head scissors on your opponent. Combine that with the holds you are already using. When people start wondering who you are, you just tell them: 'I'm Mr. Wrestling — the man with a thousand holds.'"

Woods followed Maurice's advice and developed his new character in Omaha. Before long, he became the number one babyface in the territory. And as if that weren't enough, Maurice and Woods were paired in a program in Omaha, and Maurice was careful to make Woods look good. Woods's career took off after that and he would influence other wrestlers like Johnny Walker, Steve Corino, and the Quebecer Kevin Owens, who would also all use the ring name "Mr. Wrestling" at one time or another during their careers.

The year 1966 marked Maurice's brother Paul's return to North America. Actually, Paul had enjoyed traveling around the globe the last few years, but he hadn't made enough money to leave Europe — he was only just getting by with what he earned. Maurice sent Paul the money he needed to come home. Maurice's career and indeed his life had changed a lot since taking on the ring name Mad Dog. He now hatched a scheme so his young brother could make more money. "It wasn't really the ring name that turned Maurice into a star," Paul says, "but he believed it had made all the difference."

When Paul got back to North America, Maurice sent him to Kansas City, a territory run by Bob Geigel and Pat O'Connor, among others. "Promoters had asked Maurice what they should call me," says Paul. "And since a nickname had been so good for him, he found one for me too. I thought he would call me Paul 'The Fox' or Paul 'The Bull.' But he came up with Paul 'The Pig'! I told him I would never go by that name. We ended up laughing. But in hindsight, French Canadians might have liked me to be named after that animal — then they could have called me 'Vachon the pig'!" (The French word for pig, *cochon*, rhymes with Vachon.)

Playing on their French-Canadian roots, the brothers agreed on a nickname that was both French and bloody: "the Butcher of Paris." The nickname evolved over the years and Paul became known as Paul "The Butcher" Vachon. This ring name helped him win more money than any other nickname throughout his entire career.

For Maurice, 1966 looked a lot like the previous two years: he still dominated the Minneapolis territory. His biggest rivalry of the year pitted him against Dick the Bruiser, another physically imposing athlete. A native of Indiana, the Bruiser became a promoter in Indianapolis and would use Maurice several times. Maurice briefly exchanged the title with the Bruiser in Omaha in November, but otherwise remained champion all year. In fact, he was the greatest champion not named Verne Gagne in the short history of this young promotion. He still retains that distinction today.

Maurice's career as champion in Minneapolis was simple but very effective. After beating Verne Gagne in 1964, the two men started wrestling against one another less often. By 1966, the two former Olympians hardly worked together at all. Since Gagne wasn't "able" to wrestle for the main title of the promotion, he would be used in the tag team division, against then champions Harley Race and Larry Hennig.

However, on February 26, 1967, Gagne finally beat Maurice in Saint Paul, winning the title back. This defeat marked the end of an era: Maurice would never again win the AWA's biggest prize. Maurice had held the title for 776 days, which ranks him third in the history of the AWA, behind Gagne and Bockwinkel. Counting his two victories in Omaha, he had been a champion five times, only surpassed in this regard by the promoter Gagne.

There is a reason why Maurice lost his title. In early 1967, he entered the second half of his amazing career. In the space of three years, he had built up a reputation as one of the biggest stars of wrestling, as well as one of the most sought-after characters, especially in Nebraska, but also in the towns where the AWA was represented. That was when Maurice got a call from Montreal. At the other end of the phone was a man he knew well, even too well: none other than Johnny Rougeau . . . and Johnny made him an offer he couldn't refuse.

15
MAURICE CHEATS DEATH, PART TWO

Maurice didn't manage to get his annual trip back to Quebec in 1964, but he returned in both 1965 and 1966. Yvon Robert had failed to set Quebec fans on fire, but Johnny Rougeau invested great hope in his company to reinvigorate wrestling in the province. When Maurice came to town, Rougeau had just launched his new business with the help of Bob "Legs" Langevin. So it was under the banner of "Les Entreprises Sportives de l'Est" — better known as "All-Star Wrestling" — that Maurice returned home. His summer stays in Quebec in 1965 and 1966 were no more than interludes in Maurice's schedule. He hadn't yet seen how Montreal could possibly bring him more money and recognition than Minneapolis.

By 1967, however, the situation had changed. Rougeau now had *Sur le Matelas* (meaning "On the Mat" in English), a weekly television program, broadcast on the French-language station CFTM, also known as Channel 10, and now TVA). Moreover, he offered Maurice a schedule that allowed him to continue working for the AWA. So Maurice was returning to his home province of Quebec as champion of the AWA, and Rougeau made him the champion on his home turf as well. This was in Chicoutimi, a Quebec territory where he was well-known, during TV tapings on January 24. Maurice defeated Hans Schmidt, winning the heavyweight title recognized by the Montreal Athletic Commission. This title had previously been won by such stars as Killer Kowalski, Bobby Managoff, and the great Yvon Robert.

Then, the day after he lost his AWA title to Gagne, he was wrestling in the main event at the Montreal Forum before the largest crowd All-Star Wrestling had attracted since its debut (this was also the largest crowd of the year in Quebec). The Forum was packed with twelve thousand fans on hand to see the main event of Maurice and Sweet Daddy Siki against Édouard Carpentier and Johnny Rougeau. Maurice had virtually been ignored in his hometown ever since his professional debut in 1951. But now, finally, he had made it right to the top. And he was proving the naysayers wrong — all those people over the last sixteen years who had predicted his career would fizzle out. Unfortunately, circumstances didn't enable him to become a real star right away in the eyes of the Quebec fans — that was still a few years down the road.

It was also in early 1967 that he took Jim Raschke to Montreal and turned him into a German.

Born October 17, 1940, James Donald Raschke was actually not a native of East Germany, as people thought, but of Omaha, Nebraska. From 1958 to 1964 he had taken part in several university and national wrestling championships, winning the bronze medal in Greco-Roman wrestling in Halsingborg, Sweden, at the 1963 world championships there. And he would have gone on to represent the United States at the 1964 Olympics if he hadn't injured his knee. In the hospital, his neighbor on the next bed over was a big fan of professional wrestling, and the two men watched wrestling on TV while convalescing. Raschke started thinking about the pro wrestling business. He got in touch with Joe Dusek, who referred him to Verne Gagne. It was Gagne who took him to see his first show, pitting the Crusher in the main event against Maurice! Raschke remembers being impressed.

Gagne trained Raschke, who made his professional debut in September 1966 under his real name. Like many wrestlers before him, he tried to make a living out of sports entertainment, but his debut was slow and painful. Gagne wasn't completely satisfied with his young protégé's performance in the ring and continued to use him only as a referee. Meanwhile, whenever Maurice happened to meet Raschke, he pointed out the Nebraskan would make a great East German. Maurice didn't have the reputation of being nice to greenhorns in the ring, but outside of the ring he showed a whole other side of his personality. Raschke had never been formally introduced, he was naturally shy, and he was impressed by Maurice's reputation. Raschke ignored Maurice's comments until one day — out of the blue — he told him, "I am a German!" His parents were both American-born but of German origin.

Maurice had only been back in Montreal a short while, but his opinion already weighed heavily in the balance. He offered his friend Raschke the chance to make a name in a territory with which Maurice himself was only just coming to terms: he offered to become Raschke's partner and team with him, not for the AWA, but in Quebec. Maurice's brother Paul had left Quebec in the early 1960s, and since that time Maurice had been without a regular partner. He was a keen strategist and he knew there were a lot of advantages to working as a team: partners could recover more quickly, providing fans and promoters with much more exciting shows. Of course, having a teammate meant sharing the fruits of success, but Maurice didn't mind sharing because he knew there was nothing that worked in sports entertainment like an interesting character. And he knew, in this regard, that Jim Raschke, with his training in amateur wrestling and his lack of charisma, wasn't going to make a big splash, whether in Minneapolis or Montreal, unless some big changes were made.

So from Raschke's German-American origins Maurice transformed him into an East German. But a "German" wrestler couldn't simply go by the name of "Jim Raschke." Maurice proposed calling him "Baron Fritz von Pumpkin." Von Raschke wasn't particularly enthusiastic about the name and later said in an interview: "I didn't even know what a pumpkin was!" Von Raschke then suggested replacing Pumpkin with his own name, a real German name that would make his character seem more credible. Thus was born "Baron Fritz von Raschke."

For Canadians, World War II was still a fresh memory. German heel gimmicks worked with the fans, because they always saw them as enemies.

Von Raschke really hoped his career would take off, and he figured that Maurice's help could only help his odds. After shaving off the little hair he had left, he and his wife Bonnie loaded their belongings into their Mustang and drove to Quebec, where he made his debut in May 1967. Maurice was living in Saint-Bruno at the time and found a house for his friend. But it cost too much for von Raschke, who moved a few weeks later to the more affordable suburb of Saint-Hubert. It was there, on the South Shore of Montreal, that his wife gave birth to their first daughter, Heidi, on October 21, 1967, at the Charles LeMoyne Hospital in Greenfield Park. This happy event made their stay in Quebec even more memorable.

As a duo, Maurice and von Raschke met with resounding success in Montreal, Quebec City, and Trois-Rivières. Within a few weeks, the crowd at the Trois-Rivières Coliseum grew from 1,982 to 4,300 fans. In Quebec City, the duo's matches were held at La Tour.

Local newspapers predicted a revival of wrestling in the province. Maurice's instincts were still dead-on.

As a team, Maurice and von Raschke built up a raging rivalry with the brothers Johnny and Jacques Rougeau, to the point where one of Jacques Rougeau's sons was actually terrified of Maurice . . . or rather, of the character played by Maurice.

"I was twelve when I met him for the first time," says Raymond Rougeau. "My father took my brother and me to the Paul Sauvé Arena during the summer. I sat on the stairs and I still didn't know a thing about wrestling. Carpentier was nice to us and we chatted about fishing, but when I happened to see Maurice Vachon and the Baron turn up, I was super-scared. Maurice gave me a filthy look — playing his role to the hilt. I bet Maurice and my father laughed hard about it afterwards in the locker room. But you have to understand that at the time, they were protecting their business at all costs. My father continued working his story when driving us home later in the evening."

Maurice lost the title to Johnny on June 5 but then won it back again on August 14 before 7,000 fans at the Paul Sauvé Arena.

Just ten days later, Maurice's life took a tragic turn: he was in another car accident, thirteen years after the crash in Texas.

On Wednesday, August 23, Maurice wrestled in Rimouski, then departed 270 miles for Trois-Rivières, where he would be wrestling on Thursday evening. He was traveling with Larry Moquin and Mr. Haiti, a new wrestler who had just arrived in the territory; the latter was driving Moquin's Ford station wagon. In the early hours of Thursday, August 24, a tire burst on Highway 20 in Saint-Nicolas, west of the Quebec Bridge. The car skidded seventy-five feet, plowing about one hundred feet into a ditch before coming to a stop. According to reports, the car may have flipped at least four times.

Maurice was thrown from the vehicle. He tried to get up and give a hand to Moquin, who was trapped in the twisted wreckage.

"Larry shouted, 'Maurice . . . Maurice . . .' with blood flowing from a big wound in his head," Maurice remembered. "I saw two midgets running toward me, but I felt like I was caught between two different worlds: it all seemed like a dream. One of the midgets took out a handkerchief to wipe blood off my face. It was both funny and sad. I couldn't even move six inches. That's when I realized it must have been serious."

Maurice was taken by ambulance to the Saint-Sacrement Hospital in Quebec. Moquin and Haiti were also driven there, but in private vehicles. Moquin was left with seventy-five stitches on his head and a few bruises. The driver, meanwhile, sustained only a minor injury to his hand, and he was the first to leave the hospital.

But the diagnosis was more serious for Maurice: he had a fractured pelvis and multiple contusions. People around him feared the worst — and the worst wasn't to die; it was never to be able to wrestle again, or even to walk.

"I won't be able to enter the ring for at least three months. I count myself lucky to get off with just a single fracture to my pelvis," Maurice told the daily newspaper *Montréal-Matin* in a phone interview. He sounded optimistic speaking to the journalist, but people around him didn't agree. Even so, the three wrestlers had reason to be grateful: the following weekend, there were a dozen road deaths in all of Quebec.

At the time, interest in wrestling by the media was momentarily waning and Maurice wasn't as popular as he would be a few years later. Some newspapers didn't even mention the accident, while others treated it as an ordinary news item. The newspapers did no follow-up reporting. This media coverage was a far cry from the blaze of attention he got after his next big accident.

At the time of the accident, Maurice was expected to become the star wrestler people were hoping he would turn into, but his injuries prevented him from reaching the summit of Quebec wrestling right away. His success surprised even Johnny Rougeau, who didn't believe Maurice would succeed that quickly. Montreal hosted the Universal Exposition that summer — Expo 67 — and very likely the party would have continued longer if Maurice had been able to wrestle longer. However, it's another Vachon — Rogatien — who was put in the media forefront, when he helped the Montreal Canadiens reach the Stanley Cup finals that year, and by winning the trophy awarded to the best goaltender the following season, all of that during his first two seasons in the NHL.

"In Quebec, people always asked me if I was related to Mad Dog," said Maurice's son Mike years later. "In Ontario, I was asked if I was related to the family that owned Vachon Cakes, but when I went to work in the U.S., I was often asked if I was related to Rogie." Contrary to rumors started by wrestling promoters, the Montreal Canadiens goaltender wasn't Mad Dog's cousin.

Maurice was sidelined, but life went on for other wrestlers. A new partner had to be found for von Raschke, which meant creating a new feud. Another "German" fit the bill — Hans Schmidt. Maurice had lined things up so well that the new team continued to generate as much fan rage as the previous one. One evening in Rimouski, the match degenerated suddenly into a riot and the two "Germans" got shoved around by fans. Some chairs were even thrown into the ring, creating a pyramid in the middle. The two new partners were slightly injured but they were above all happy to escape the riot without serious injury. They decided to stop at the hospital to see Maurice on the way back. Maurice was by now beginning to feel better. He took one look at their bandages and wounds, then exclaimed with his usual repartee: "What's going on? Whatever happened to you? You look worse off than I do!"

Maurice remained in the hospital for a total of forty-five days. But misfortunes never come one at a time, and the day after the accident he faced another devastating experience.

His relationship with Dorothy was rapidly deteriorating. With Maurice constantly traveling, she stayed at home caring for their children in a province that was foreign to her and where she didn't know the primary language. The couple quarreled regularly, which was heartbreaking for everyone: Dorothy, the children, and Maurice himself.

When Maurice returned to Quebec at the beginning of the year, he met Nicole Chaput, a beautiful twenty-year-old brunette who stood 5 feet 6 inches tall. She lived in Chicoutimi and was unemployed, but she took care of her brothers and sisters, since her mother had a total of thirteen children. One night, her boyfriend invited her to the matches and introduced her to Maurice backstage. She didn't attach much importance to this encounter, because she had no plans to make him her new boyfriend, and, besides, Maurice scared her. But it was just the opposite for Maurice: Nicole had really caught his eye. When she came back to the matches, Maurice invited her to a restaurant after the show. Maurice deployed all his charms and Nicole fell in love with him. But Maurice was still married to Dorothy, no matter how much they fought. Nicole and Maurice had to be discreet if they wanted to protect their relationship from the public eye. That's why she went to live with one of her cousins in Quebec City and subsequently with the wrestler Pat Lawrence, one of Maurice's close friends.

When the accident occurred, Dorothy wasn't even aware her husband was unfaithful. But on the morning of August 24, she learned Maurice was in the hospital, and he was not alone. She left Saint-Bruno, driving straight to the hospital, where she demanded an immediate divorce.

Maurice must have known his marriage wasn't going well, but the divorce affected him deeply, since he was already in a vulnerable state, convalescing. Dorothy was still his wife — he had shared thirteen years of his life with her, and she was the mother of his children. He cried a lot. In the months following, Maurice didn't see either Dorothy or their children. Nicole, meanwhile, took care of her lover the best she could, visiting him forty-three times in forty-five days during his hospital stay.

Later, the couple moved to Montreal, where they lived in the home of one of Maurice's friends. Nicole found work in a bar while Maurice recovered. Then Maurice decided to live with his brother Guy, while Nicole returned to Chicoutimi to be with her mother. People close to Maurice put pressure on him to end his relationship with Nicole, because they considered her too young. The same thing happened on Nicole's side: her family felt Maurice, then aged thirty-eight, was too old for her. Everything seemed to indicate they were headed for a separation, but the lovers continued meeting.

Meanwhile, Maurice made the acquaintance of a man who would become one of the fiercest ring opponents of his entire career.

Paul Leduc wasn't just a wrestler: he was also responsible for transporting money to the federal government during the Universal Exposition in Montreal. From April to October 1967, he worked with a big guy named Michel Pigeon who was in charge of official visits on the site.

"I remember we took Maurice on a visit. All the little corners where nobody was allowed to go — we showed them all to Maurice, while pushing him along in his wheelchair. He was so impressed. Especially the Circle-Vision 360° cinema of the Bell Canada Pavilion: he just stared at it and sobbed like a little kid."

Michel Pigeon would later become none other than pro wrestler Jos Leduc.

A few weeks went by, and Maurice gradually improved. He was planning to break up with Nicole when she found out she was pregnant. She phoned him in a panic: "You can't leave me like this, Maurice. I got pregnant for you. I did it because you can't see your own children!" Nicole was profoundly distressed and she was crying for help.

She knew she was naïve. Maurice was definitely the love of her life, the one great love. She was only twenty-one years old. But Maurice was a family man, and when he learned she was pregnant, he returned to Montreal and they settled together at a friend's place. It was at this time that Maurice also got the green light to resume his career. His years of training had paid off: his rehabilitation was shorter and certainly more complete than the doctors had expected.

Maurice knew his divorce would end up costing him money because he had to provide for his children, now aged from six to thirteen years. Linda Sue was now a teenager, and the separation of her parents marked the beginning of a period of twenty years during which she never saw the man she would continue calling "Dad" for the rest of her life. Besides his own biological children, Mike, Denis, and Cheryl, Maurice now had a new child on the way. He had to start wrestling again, and he had to do it in a place where he could make good money. Montreal was still too uncertain: Maurice was stripped of his title since he couldn't defend it, the accident putting a stop to everything. The year 1968 would therefore be important to him, in terms of his professional career, his personal life, and his family. Once more, his life would undergo profound change.

At the end of 1967, before turning the page on his past, he appeared in a wheelchair at a Montreal show, assuring fans he would soon be back, stronger than ever. He would be back, that was true, but not right away. In 1968, there was only one option left: to return and work full time in Minneapolis.

16
THE VACHON BROTHERS AT THE TOP OF THEIR GAME

In Minneapolis, people didn't pay much attention to Maurice's car accident because they didn't see his injuries. At the time, wrestlers commonly left a territory, only to return sometime later. Back in Gagne's territory, Maurice didn't get involved in the heavyweight title picture: with his fighting style and status as a former champion, he didn't really need to. He repeatedly wrestled against René Goulet and also teamed up with Dr. X, a.k.a. Dick "The Destroyer" Beyer.

Nicole joined him in Minneapolis, then they headed back to Quebec during the summer, where she gave birth to their first child. But from mid-May to mid-June, before making his way back to Quebec, Maurice returned to his old stomping ground, Oregon. Maurice and Nicole met Senator Robert F. Kennedy there during the U.S. primaries.

"When he finished his speech, he noticed I was pregnant, just like his own wife," Nicole recalls. "He told Maurice to take care of me."

Maurice was keenly interested in politics and kept up to date on political news. He would later become a fan of the all-news channel

CNN and Larry King. A few weeks after they met Robert F. Kennedy, the young senator was assassinated. Maurice and Nicole grieved his parting, along with the American people.

Maurice continued helping Quebecers debut in the United States when he brought to Portland Rolland Frenière, who wrestled under the name of Johnny War Eagle. He never really enjoyed a long run in the United States, but he remained in Oregon for more than a year before returning to Quebec.

On July 28, 1968, in Montreal, Nicole gave birth to a boy named Stéphan. They had been back for two weeks preparing for his arrival, and Maurice was still in the process of divorcing Dorothy. Maurice couldn't see his other children, and Nicole still hadn't met them. But Maurice's career came first, and the new little family left Quebec three weeks later for Los Angeles, where he would wrestle before heading to Japan. He was so well-known now that promoters handed him a win in his first match in the territory against Mil Máscaras, one of the greatest Mexican luchadores of all time, and the uncle of Alberto El Patron (Alberto Del Río). On September 6, before 11,153 screaming fans, he won by disqualification at the Olympic Auditorium in Los Angeles against the local champion Bobo Brazil. A few days later, Maurice left for the Land of the Rising Sun.

This was his first trip to Japan. In the 1950s, he had been in direct contact with the wrestler Charlie Iwamoto, better known under the ring name of Mr. Moto. Charlie was now organizing Japanese tours for American wrestlers. During his trip to Japan, Maurice sent Nicole and their baby, Stéphan, to Georgia to stay with his brother Paul, who had been wrestling there for some time.

The Japanese tour was scheduled to go from September 20 to November 6, 1968. At that time, the country had only one promotion, the Japan Wrestling Association (JWA), founded fifteen years earlier by the legendary Rikidōzan.

Maurice went there with other Americans like Killer Karl Kox and Red Bastien. Local media in Japan couldn't translate his ring name, Mad Dog, so they called him "the Crazy Fighter" instead. The concept of villains and heroes wasn't very clearly defined in Japan, but Maurice, as a North American, was considered a foreign villain. He wrestled against popular Japanese wrestlers including Antonio Inoki and Shōhei "Giant" Baba, the two biggest stars of the time. Both these men would create their own promotions a few years later, namely New Japan Pro-Wrestling and All Japan Pro Wrestling. Maurice and Kox beat Inoki and Baba, the tag team champions, in a non-title match, at a time when the Japanese team was practically invincible. Clearly, Maurice's stature combined with the popularity of his opponents saw him main-eventing throughout most of the tour, either in singles or teaming up with other North Americans.

Maurice then headed to Paul's place in Atlanta to be with Nicole and Stéphan. While there, of course, he got some more wrestling in.

Paul had been wrestling in Georgia since the summer of 1966. He then toured in Japan, returning to Atlanta in the summer of 1967. This time he teamed up with a new "Vachon." Leo Garibaldi, the booker of the territory, told Paul before his Japanese tour that he would have a much better place in the storylines if he got himself a partner. That was when Paul met Eric Pomeroy, a thirty-four-year-old wrestler from St. John's, Newfoundland. The two Canadians found themselves in Los Angeles: Paul was wrestling there before heading for Japan, while Pomeroy often fought there under the ring name of "the Mad Russian." Paul remembered Garibaldi's advice and called his brother Maurice for his blessing. The name "Vachon" belonged to everyone in the family, but its fame was due to Maurice's rise to stardom and it was important for Paul to make sure Maurice was aware and fine with it.

"I have this Canadian here and I would like to bring him to

Atlanta and make him my brother," Paul told Maurice.

"Do what you like, it's none of my business. Anyway, I can't go there myself."

So it was Pomeroy who teamed up with Paul as his new "brother" Stan Vachon. The two men were successful. They won the tag team title in the Georgia territory a few times. They especially got into a feud with the Torres brothers, which was why Maurice came to Atlanta in the first place.

The Torres brothers were three real brothers by the names of Alberto, Enrique, and Ramon. It stood to reason that they should get into a rivalry with the three Vachon brothers. Garibaldi mentioned to Paul that Maurice was doing really well in Minnesota and that it would be interesting to book them in a six-man tag program. Ray Gunkel, wrestler and also co-promoter of the Georgia territory, then asked Verne Gagne (whom he had known from their years in amateur wrestling) if he could use Maurice for a few weeks once he got back from Japan. Gagne agreed. As a result, Maurice, Paul, and Stan Vachon wrestled several matches in November and December 1968 against the Torres brothers.

But Verne Gagne then contacted Maurice again with a tempting new offer: wrestling alongside his brother in his territory. Gagne had just lost his best heel tag team, Larry Hennig and Harley Race, and needed to find replacements right away. This was an offer neither Maurice nor Paul could refuse: they remembered how much fun they had had a decade earlier in Calgary and they hoped to repeat the experience.

By January 1969, the two brothers began teaming in the AWA. In the first months of the year, the Vachon brothers faced teams like René Goulet and Bill Watts, as well as Pat O'Connor and Wilbur Snyder. Sometimes they even wrestled against Stan Pulaski, who, only a short while earlier, had teamed up with them as Stan Vachon!

However, it was only in the second quarter of the year that they really stood out, because of not one but two rivalries.

In Minnesota, the team they faced the most often consisted of the red-haired wrestlers Billy "Red" Lyons and Red Bastien, who worked under the name of "the Flying Redheads."

Originally from North Dakota, Bastien had been wrestling for several years. He was considered one of the best workers in the ring, and he would become one of the most successful wrestling trainers, launching the wrestling careers of the Ultimate Warrior and Sting. Maurice and Bastien would keep in close touch as long as their health permitted it. Bastien's teammate, Lyons, was a native of Hamilton, Ontario, with a few years of experience under his belt. Once his active career ended, he would long be associated with the Tunney brothers of Toronto and the WWE.

Both redheads were renowned for their skill in the ring and their athletic prowess, which is how they got the "Flying" part of their ring name. They were also considered the best babyface team in the country. Their style was in clear contrast to the Vachon brothers, and fans always found their matches exciting.

"We modeled this rivalry on the one we had with the Scott brothers in Calgary," says Paul.

In Chicago, Maurice and Paul often teamed up against another duo with a style similar to their own: the Crusher and Dick the Bruiser, two wrestlers Maurice had known from his debut with the AWA. By the time the Vachons got to Minneapolis, the Bruiser and the Crusher had just won the tag team titles for the fourth time.

The Vachon brothers wrestled against these two teams for more than half of the year before reaching their moment of glory. On August 30, 1969, before more than ten thousand spectators at the International Amphitheatre in Chicago, they defeated the defending champions and won the AWA tag team championship for the first time. This date marked the beginning of an incredible period for Maurice and Paul.

The heavyweight champion was Gagne, but his schedule was reduced, which created opportunities for the Vachons, enabling them to wrestle in the main events more often than not. During the year, they drew more than ten thousand fans to the same amphitheater in Chicago on four different occasions, which meant they came fifth in 1969 when ranked among North American wrestlers who drew the most. Their team was the only one ranked in the top ten, behind legendary wrestlers like the Sheik, Bruno Sammartino, Dory Funk Jr., and Ray Stevens.

At the beginning of the 1970s, Maurice got involved in two rivalries. With Paul, he continued the hard-slogging wrestling program against the Crusher and Bruiser, and in singles, Maurice was in a feud with the Crusher, which had already lasted several years and now intensified. In August 1969, the Crusher had gotten "injured" during their title match and hadn't wrestled since. Actually, Crusher just needed a break.

AWA wrestling fans still remember the legendary televised match on January 17, 1970, when Édouard Carpentier and Bruce Kirk worked against Mad Dog and the Butcher. Kirk, a jobber, was getting a beating from the Quebec duo. Then the Crusher did his big return by jumping into the ring to rescue Carpentier, successfully throwing Maurice onto the ring posts. Maurice slashed himself with a razor blade to make things look more dramatic, but just then the Crusher kicked him in the back. Maurice lost his balance and severed an artery: he began to bleed heavily, leaving pools of blood all over the studio. That moment remains ingrained in the minds of fans who saw the blood spurting. The Crusher didn't seem to realize the seriousness of the situation and continued beating Maurice up, unwittingly adding realism to the scene, but it is also quite possible that Maurice told him not to stop. Several wrestlers and referees finally came into the ring to end the carnage. Among them was a young Blackjack Mulligan (grandfather of Bo Dallas and Bray Wyatt of the WWE), who would later consider Maurice as a mentor. The referee, Bob Brunelle, better known in Quebec under the name of Yvon Robert Jr., was also present.

Maurice is remembered as one of the wrestlers who bled the most during his career, but he was in such bad condition that his scheduled match later that evening against the Crusher had to be canceled. "A policeman took me to the hospital in his car," he said. "Paul sat in the middle. I was sitting next to the door. I had both hands on the open wound. Paul pressed his hands over mine. The blood spilled through our hands."

The doctor couldn't understand how Maurice could lose that much blood without fainting: the cut was so deep it took twelve stitches. Of course, when the story was told and retold over the years, the number of stitches varied greatly. In Maurice's day, a wrestler only missed a main event if he was genuinely hurt. Public outrage was so strong that the TV studio considered banning wrestling from its premises, as wrestling fans deplored such displays of violence. Wrestling tradition holds that an unexpected injury like this should be incorporated directly into the story, as a way of setting the crowd's passions aflame. This would ensure a return match, with the fans hoping to see the Crusher finish the job against the dangerous and nasty Mad Dog.

Maurice himself told Paul: "Before going to the hospital, I want to make sure the cameras recorded everything right!"

The AWA realized this incident would have a major impact if handled properly, and that's exactly what they did. The Vachons and the Redheads had good chemistry, but the AWA decided to let the Vachons keep the titles. Lyons eventually left the Redheads and the AWA.

This rivalry attracted crowds all over the country and especially in Milwaukee, the Crusher's hometown. The most memorable match of this feud took place on June 13 in a cage at the Milwaukee Arena. There was something mythical and unsettling about the sight of a cage back then, since neither side was able to escape from it: so this was a match to the finish. The bout drew 12,076 fans and generated receipts of $58,270, a record that stood for a few years in Wisconsin. This bout remained etched in the collective memory of local fans, but not for the usual reasons. People vividly remember how a forty-year-old woman jumped over the barricade, literally climbing up the cage in a desperate attempt to help the Crusher. At that time, viewers were easily carried away by wrestling storylines and they literally believed what they saw. Maurice remained the undisputed champion to make the fans believe what was happening was real, and he didn't need a belt to prove it. Long after his career was over, the Crusher would do the rounds of Milwaukee bars, and he would often meet fans who remembered this match . . . but especially the lady who had climbed up the cage!

But the rivalry didn't stop there.

Like the previous year, the matches between the Vachon brothers and the Crusher and Bruiser continued and even intensified given the success of the program between Maurice and the Crusher.

The four wrestlers drew huge crowds throughout the territory, mainly in Milwaukee, Denver, Chicago, and Green Bay. The highlight of their feud was another cage match. On August 14, 1970, at Comiskey Park in Chicago, home of the Chicago White Sox, the Vachon brothers defended their tag titles against the Crusher and Dick the Bruiser in front of 21,000 spectators, the largest crowd of the year in all of wrestling. The gate was $148,000, a new record in the United States. Maurice's share of the purse came to $2,800, one of the best-paid matches of his career. Gagne was a hard promoter but he was fair: he paid the same amount to Paul, and Maurice wouldn't have wanted it any other way. This may seem a trifling payout compared to the millions of dollars in gates and payoffs that one can find in the WWE nowadays. It should be remembered, though, that tickets in 1970 cost an average of $10 or less, so it is still a remarkable feat. The other main event of the evening saw heavyweight champion Verne Gagne facing off against Baron von Raschke. The influence that Maurice had over the years was making its presence felt with these two main events. The "marriage" between Maurice and Paul was a complete success and Gagne rubbed his hands with glee.

However, another marriage was about to be celebrated: Maurice and Nicole signed the official papers August 31, 1970, in Quebec City, just fifteen days after the divorce judgment that ended Maurice's marriage to Dorothy. Maurice and Nicole would know many ups and downs in their years together, but Maurice would change Nicole's life, and the years she spent with him would forever remain in her memory. Even if Nicole's family was initially opposed to the relationship, they had finally accepted the obvious: the couple was truly in love. Nicole's mother came to live with them in Minnesota — a great experience for her since she had never left Quebec until then.

The divorce from Dorothy was extremely painful for Maurice. He wanted his children to have everything they wanted, so he left the beautiful house with the in-ground pool in Saint-Bruno to Dorothy. She promptly sold everything and headed back to Michigan, taking the children with her.

Between this difficult divorce and his second marriage, Maurice's personal life was like a rollercoaster of emotions. Luckily, he could settle back into wrestling because things were going really well for him.

At the end of 1970, Maurice and Verne packed the arena in Minneapolis, and the Vachon brothers were still reigning champions and arguably the best tag team in the country. Thanks to the feuds

Maurice was involved in, whether in singles or in tags, he finished fifth in 1970 among wrestlers in North America who drew the most, tied with none other than . . . the Crusher!

Early in 1971, Maurice and Paul headed for Japan. This was the first time they had wrestled there together. They were the guests of a new Japanese promotion, the International Wrestling Enterprise (IWE), which would long be associated with the AWA. The tour lasted only a week, but Maurice found a way to have an impact even before arriving in Tokyo.

A few days before leaving North America, Maurice and Paul wrestled for Don Owen in Portland. Maurice wanted to make his opponents look good and he also wanted to give a helping hand to the promoter, so he decided to lose the AWA tag team titles to Kurt and Karl von Steiger. The Vachon brothers had to come through Oregon on the way back from Japan to Minnesota, so they could regain the titles back then.

When Gagne found out, he was furious, but Mad Dog wasn't fazed. "Fans will never know about it," he said. Well, "never" was a big word, but at the time it was true that only Oregon fans knew about it. Those were the days. Maurice's generosity won out over everything.

All good things come to an end. On May 15, 1971, Maurice and Paul lost the titles — for good, this time — against the team of Red Bastien and Hercules Cortez. The Vachons had been reigning champions for a total of 623 days, the second-longest reign in the entire history of the promotion. Why did the Vachon brothers have to lose their titles while they were at the top of their game and there seemed nothing and no one to stop them? The reason was simple. It wasn't Gagne who decided, any more than it was the AWA. The Vachon brothers simply told the promoter they were leaving the territory. They were coming back to Montreal!

GRAND PRIX WRESTLING: MAURICE'S TRIUMPHANT RETURN

What motivated Maurice's return to Quebec? A few weeks earlier, Yvon Robert Sr. had come calling in Minneapolis. He had wanted to see first-hand how his son was doing. But his real intent was to bring Maurice back to Quebec, to compete head-on with Johnny Rougeau and his wrestling promotion. The relationship between Robert and Rougeau had deteriorated over the years. The filial bond Rougeau had once had with Robert was now nothing but a distant memory. When Rougeau started his company and got a wrestling show on Channel 10, he excluded Robert from the whole plan, turning Robert into a hostile competitor in the process. Moreover, he used recordings Quinn had left to Robert to convince the station's management that the show had big potential. But Robert knew that competing directly with a well-established promotion like Johnny's wouldn't be easy, especially for someone starting out on his own. Robert knew Maurice had a lot of experience in the ring and contacts in the business. He was convinced Maurice could make a big difference in helping him launch a new promotion. So he offered

Maurice the chance to become his own boss.

Maurice and his brother enjoyed their star status within the AWA, so this was a monumental decision. They were well established, they were widely respected, and they were making more money than ever. Most wrestlers slaved away for a lifetime to achieve this level of success in a major territory. However, the brothers also knew success was "easy come, easy go." They might not get another opportunity like this one. Sometimes it's better to quit while you're ahead, instead of being shown the exit. The next step in their careers was for them to become owners of their own promotion, working as their own bosses.

Maurice's favorite song was "Un Canadien errant" — "The Wandering Canadian." This folk song had been composed by Antoine Gérin-Lajoie in 1848, a decade after the 1837–38 Rebellion in Lower Canada, when many rebels who aspired to more independence — "les Patriotes" — were forced by British colonial authorities into exile in the United States, some even being deported to Australia. The song had resonance for Maurice since he had to work abroad, in a sort of exile, even though his circumstances were not as dramatic as the Patriotes of 1837–38.

The English version of this song, translated by John Murray Gibbon, goes:

Once a Canadian lad,
Exiled from hearth and home,
Wandered, alone and sad,
Through alien lands unknown.

Down by a rushing stream,
Thoughtful and sad one day,
He watched the water pass
And to it he did say:

"If you should reach my land,
My most unhappy land,
Please speak to all my friends
So they will understand.

"Tell them how much I wish
That I could be once more
In my beloved land
That I will see no more."

Like the character in the song, Maurice saw himself as a wandering Canadian, exiled from hearth and home. He had long secretly dreamed of becoming a promoter. Eddie Quinn had never recognized Maurice's true potential, and the time he had worked for Rougeau had been cut short by the car accident. Maurice now had the chance to prove what he was made of. He was a wrestling star in several American states, and he was determined to become a star in Quebec. Robert's offer was therefore a golden opportunity.

Paul had also been present at the meeting, and Maurice asked him what he thought about the offer, but in fact Maurice had already made up his mind. At the initial meeting, the shareholder structure had been discussed. Paul's name didn't figure among the proposed shareholders, but Maurice made his brother an extremely generous offer: if Paul could overcome his problem with alcohol, then Maurice would give him half of his own share in the company.

Therefore, it was in June of 1971 that Maurice set out on a new adventure. For the first time since 1967 and for only the second time since he had started traveling, Maurice settled in Quebec on a long-term basis. He was forty-one years old and he had matured. He was now married to a young French-Canadian woman and he had no qualms about "getting settled" the way he might have had in younger years. Summer tours, and coming to wrestle a few months in Quebec, and being under-utilized by Quebec promoters were now a thing of the past. Maurice would be his own boss and he was ready for the challenge. He had met with success and happiness during his years wandering, but now Maurice was finally coming home. He had forgotten neither his beloved homeland nor his friends, like the wandering Canadian.

The new promotion was called Grand Prix Wrestling. Its shareholders were Maurice, Yvon Robert Sr., Édouard Carpentier, lawyer Michel Awada, and promoters Gerry Legault and Lucien Grégoire. Each shareholder put up $4,000 to get the venture going. Unfortunately, Maurice didn't get the chance to work alongside his childhood idol, because on July 12, 1971, Yvon Robert Sr. died at the age of fifty-six. Yvon Sr.'s shares then went to his son, Yvon Jr. Legault lost interest before the promotion really got going and looked around for a buyer. Seeing a great opportunity, Paul bought up Legault's shares, which meant Maurice could keep all of his own shares, even the ones he had planned to hand over to Paul. Nowadays, Paul has been sober for over thirty years. He still wonders, given Maurice's own problems with alcohol, why his brother had insisted on him taking the pledge to go alcohol-free. Maurice drank about as much as Paul in those years and only addressed his personal problem with alcohol some two decades later.

Maurice saw Grand Prix as an excellent opportunity to give a chance to young wrestlers who wanted to break through and make a career in pro wrestling. Many Quebecers benefited from their association with Grand Prix, such as Gilles Poisson, Denis Gauthier, Dino Bravo, and Zarinoff Leboeuf. The promotion also offered opportunities to wrestlers from outside Quebec, like Angelo Mosca, Tokyo Joe, and the Hollywood Blonds and their manager Oliver Humperdink. Quebec wrestling fans hadn't often seen Maurice wrestle since 1967.

He had the reputation of being an aggressive wrestler — even too aggressive — but was well established in wrestling circles, including among the next generation of stars.

"On my first night as manager," Humperdink later recalled, "I had to hit Maurice with a cane so we could win the tag titles. Before the match, I told him I didn't know how to hit someone with a cane, but I also knew he could twist me out of shape and stretch me flat if I didn't hit him properly. Mad Dog then told me with his unique growling voice: 'If you don't hit me the right way with the cane, I'm going to rip it out of your hands and waste you!' To which I replied: 'Yes, Sir!'"

Denis Gauthier, the bodybuilder and former Mr. Canada, was recruited by Lucien Grégoire to become a wrestler in this new venture. He quickly learned the trade. In his first fifteen matches, he wrestled Maurice and Paul with partners ranging from André the Giant to Édouard Carpentier, Yvon Robert Jr., and Reggie Parks. It was a baptism by fire for a wrestling novice.

"With Maurice, you never knew what was going to happen in the ring," Gauthier explains. "It was rough. He scared people and he took everything so much to heart. But he was a good teacher — he always tried to help, giving us advice. I was a good boxer, so once, we had a boxing match to liven up the program. That's when he told me I was hitting too hard, whereas when we wrestled, he never lowered his intensity by hitting less hard."

Maurice then offered to help Denis Gauthier develop his career outside of Quebec, but Gauthier was one of the few to turn down the proposal: he preferred using wrestling to make himself better known within Quebec since it would help him grow his business, which included a training gym.

Gauthier wasn't the only one who chose to stay in Quebec rather than follow Maurice's advice. "When I got the chance to leave for the

WWWF, the Mongols told me they would take care of me," remembers Jackie Wiecz, Édouard Carpentier's nephew. "Maurice Vachon told me I should go. This is the only regret of my career."

Thanks to Grand Prix Wrestling, Maurice could now spend most of the year at home with his family. Nicole got pregnant at the beginning of the year, giving birth on October 4, 1971, to Jean-Pierre, the couple's second and last child. Maurice and Nicole wanted their children to grow up in Quebec City. They had several happy years together in their home in Sainte-Thérèse-de-Lisieux, twenty minutes from Quebec City. Maurice loved children and he was good at communicating with them when they were little. He cooked breakfast for them, often getting their friends and cousins to join in the fun. Maurice would then take them to the woods to play, winter storm or not. Throughout his life, the presence of children would have a positive impact on him. Once the children reached adolescence, however, like a lot of parents, Maurice found it harder to communicate with them. By now, Maurice had re-established contact with the children from his first marriage, and they would come to Quebec, particularly in the summer, to spend several months a year with Maurice and Nicole.

Mike resembled his father in several respects and he got into a lot of hot water after his parents' divorce. As he got older he realized how much he missed his father, and he gave his mother cause for worry. Maurice tried channeling Mike's energy into wrestling, the way his own father, Ferdinand, had done with him, but Mike wouldn't listen.

Maurice went on to help other young men interested in taking up wrestling. For example, he lined things up so Gilles Poisson, the "Strongman from Lac Saint-Jean," could wrestle in Calgary.

"Promoters listened to Maurice and they really respected him, because he had been there," says Poisson. "He had a lot of influence on other promoters: he would send them wrestlers, and his word was good. He could help you find a promoter, but after that you were on your own." Maurice offered him a chance to wrestle for Grand Prix, and Poisson leapt at the opportunity.

Richard Charland also benefited from Maurice's mentoring. A native of Ville-Émard like Maurice, Charland was friends with Maurice's sons Mike and Denis. He was a teenager practicing judo when Maurice suggested he take up amateur wrestling at the Palestre Nationale, where he was coached by Maurice's friend Ray Ricci, a former Canadian champion. Then, at fifteen, Charland began his professional training at the Grand Prix wrestling school. Maurice saw so much potential in Charland that he paid him $50 a week just to train. He went pro at the age of 16. He would go on to a great career for the time, wrestling for Lutte Internationale in Montreal and for quite a few shots in the WWF. His loyalty to Maurice may have cost him the only major opportunity he was ever offered: "I had an offer from the WWF in 1986. But I had promised to do Maurice Vachon's farewell tour. I was hoping I would get another opportunity to wrestle for the WWF," recalls Charland. However, that new opportunity never came.

For her part, Nicole did everything she could to get close to Maurice and Dorothy's children. She also had a great relationship with Maurice's mother Marguerite, treating her as if she were Nicole's own mother, and even played Scrabble with Ferdinand. In short, she did everything to become part of the Vachon family, and they made her feel welcome. She understood Maurice well, and despite his impulsive temperament, she always defended his actions and reactions. She wasn't completely wrong to defend him. Maurice wasn't the only one with a sometimes explosive character.

During a wrestling show at the Quebec City Coliseum in 1971, hundreds of fans got so angry with Mad Dog they began throwing rocks at him. To make matters worse, they also threw rocks at Nicole, who was pregnant at the time. The other wrestlers had to come out of the locker room to protect the couple. In defending his family, Maurice even had to punch a fan, and he probably hit him harder than he needed to. This was not an easy time for the Vachon couple, given how much the crowd hated Maurice. In fact, it wasn't easy for anyone called Maurice Vachon. Another man from Quebec City named Maurice Vachon began getting insulting and threatening phone calls from people who called him a fucking prick, thinking he was the wrestler Maurice Vachon! Another challenge was Maurice's long absences crisscrossing the province of Quebec and not being able to get home every night. This wandering life would have a big impact on the children in years to come, something that Nicole regrets to this day.

What hurt her most was that the wrestling world created problems for her children. Stéphan found it easy to adapt, but Jean-Pierre didn't. He liked being with his father, but unfortunately this wasn't always possible. Nothing can really make up for the absence of a parent, even if there are good reasons for that absence. But Maurice was more present at home than he had ever been at any other time in his career, and despite everything, his return to Quebec full time was generally a festive period for the family. The Vachon couple put on huge parties, and it was one of the rare times that Maurice enjoyed the little pleasures in life, such as mowing the lawn and ending the day with a cold beer with his stepmother, who lived in the guest house.

From December 1971 to February 1972, Maurice went to Hawaii with Nicole and Stéphan. This was just before Grand Prix became the terrific success everybody remembers. Being able to have a paid holiday on the beautiful beaches of Hawaii in exchange for a few matches per week was one of the perks star wrestlers could have at the time. During this tour, a feud started up over the name "Mad Dog." Lonnie Mayne, who had worked a program with Maurice in Portland, had borrowed his nickname to become "Mad Dog" Lonnie Mayne. A few years later, Vince McMahon Sr. transformed "Mad Dog" Mayne into "Moondog" Mayne. There were quite a few "Mad Dogs" in pro wrestling but there were also a few "Moondogs" directly derived from the nickname Maurice made so popular.

Grand Prix Wrestling definitely cemented the legend of Maurice as a wrestler. When he got back to Quebec, the promotion was in full gear. People in the community believed in the project because he was involved. "Wrestlers all came to work for us and people were convinced Montreal was going to become a major wrestling town," recalls Paul.

Grand Prix had such a presence in Quebec and was getting so powerful that in operational terms, it was practically split in two. On the one hand, Paul and Maurice were main-eventing all over the province, especially in Quebec City, where they drew record-setting crowds, stunning fans with the ongoing feud against the Leduc brothers. On the other hand, André the Giant and Édouard Carpentier were the big stars in Montreal, working against arch-rivals like Don Leo Jonathan and Killer Kowalski, including the "match of the century" when André faced Jonathan at the Forum. With the Vachon brothers, Carpentier, and Yvon Jr. all equal partners in the promotion, there were too many chiefs and not enough Indians. But Maurice never played boss with the locker room, and he could always be counted on to help, in and out of the ring.

Internal competition became so intense that each side was starting to wish for the other side to fail. The partners were all pro wrestling stars with big egos and an unshakable faith in themselves, so a clash of egos was to be expected. Even Maurice went in for this unhealthy rivalry. He gloated over the fact that Sherbrooke — one of his cities — brought in more revenue than Verdun, run by Carpentier and Robert Jr. Legend has it that Maurice's heat with Carpentier was so intense that he would wake up at night just to be able to hate him a little more.

"Édouard could be upbeat and positive one day, but the next day, quite suddenly, nothing was to his liking," explains Paul Vachon. "Then he set Yvon Robert Jr. against us, which prevented the company from moving forward, because no one had the final authority to decide things. We always ended up making compromise decisions."

The Montreal Athletic Commission didn't allow the promoter on record to wrestle in the city, so it was out of the question that either of the two biggest stars — Maurice or Carpentier — would run the promotion on paper. The company's daily management therefore fell to Paul Vachon, who developed a real business talent. He had been the last man to become a shareholder in Grand Prix wrestling, but he took the bull by the horns. Not only did he negotiate a TV contract, but he also lined up dates at the Forum, the Mecca of wrestling in Montreal, with the help of Jean Béliveau, the former captain of the Montreal Canadiens. A couple of years before, Maurice and Paul happened to be on the same flight as the Canadiens. "Maurice came to our section of the plane joking, 'Hey, where's my cousin?'" remembers former Canadiens player and general manager Serge Savard, talking about Rogatien Vachon, who was the Canadiens' main goaltender. "We often went to the matches. It was a lot of fun. We knew all the wrestlers. We spent pretty much the whole trip with them."

The coach, Claude Ruel, was a big fan of Maurice, and Paul offered to trade seats with him. On that same flight, the Vachon brothers, never too far from a good prank, did their best to stress out even more the Canadiens' backup goalie, Lorne "Gump" Worsley, who was afraid of flying.

Like the rest of the team, Jean Béliveau was on this memorable flight. Once he retired, he took on the job of vice-president and director of public relations for the Canadiens, and that's how he was able to get the dates at the Forum that Paul wanted for Grand Prix Wrestling. The Montreal Athletic Commission didn't want to give Grand Prix Wrestling a promotions license until they were able to secure dates at the Forum. In some kind of a catch-22, the Forum didn't want to give any dates to Grand Prix before it got its license. But after Béliveau helped Paul, the MAC, who were protecting Johnny Rougeau's promotion, had no other choice but to allow Paul to promote shows in Montreal.

Besides Paul in Montreal, other promoters for the group were Dick Marshall in Quebec City, who became a good friend of the Vachon couple, Michel Nordella in Sherbrooke, and Tony Mulé, who took care of regional tours. Maurice didn't really get involved in the daily operations of Grand Prix, but he sometimes got angry about things without necessarily confronting his partners. The situation wasn't easy: discussions between the shareholders often turned into shouting matches, right there in the Grand Prix office.

"It was hard to manage ourselves in the office, because nobody knows wrestling the way my brother and I do," Maurice later confessed. Besides which, the Vachon brothers were bringing several outside wrestlers into the promotion.

The least that can be said is that "communication" — a word not yet in fashion — was poor inside the company. Yvon Robert Jr. was always clear about one thing though: no matter what conflicts he had with the man, he always respected the image Maurice created for Grand Prix, the symbol he embodied: wherever Maurice went, he did a brilliant job representing the company.

As a matter of fact, for wrestling fans in the province of Quebec, Grand Prix Wrestling was closely associated with Maurice Vachon, and it remains so to this day. The reason is straightforward: it comes down to the legendary rivalry between the Vachon brothers and the Leduc brothers. The success of this rivalry helped build up the legend of Mad Dog Vachon throughout Quebec. But what made these events so memorable and inimitable was how locally focused they were: these four Quebecers would fight for the honor and prestige of being champions in their home province.

In 1967, Jack Britton thought of developing a team of Quebec lumberjack wrestlers, comprising Léodard Mimeault and Michel Pigeon. The idea wasn't entirely unprecedented because almost a decade earlier Maurice and Paul had wrestled in lumberjack outfits. But the Vachon brothers had never exploited their lumberjack characters in Quebec. Eight years later, the idea still seemed promising. So it was how Mimeault and Pigeon became Paul and Jos Leduc: not only were they known in the ring as the Leduc brothers, but Paul Leduc and Jos Leduc became their real names once their career was over. At the time, Britton was Johnny Rougeau's partner, so the two men made their Quebec debut for All-Star Wrestling. They instantly became a hit.

Once Grand Prix set up shop in Montreal, war broke out with the Rougeau organization. Both promotions were competing for the same venues, the same fans, the same talents. Grand Prix actively courted the Leduc brothers, and putting money on the table made the difference.

"Paul Vachon came over. He put $5,000 on the table in front of Jos, another $5,000 in front of me. We had just finished wrestling at the Paul Sauvé Arena, but for a lot less. By the following week, we had started working for Grand Prix," said Paul Leduc.

But it was symptomatic of the problems at Grand Prix that the shareholders didn't all agree about Paul's deal with the Leduc brothers — and problems like this would eventually lead to the promotion's premature demise. Lucien Grégoire and Carpentier were opposed to signing the Leduc brothers and seeing them work with the Vachon brothers — even though rivalries between two teams of brothers often draw a lot of money. For example, both the feud between the Vachon brothers and the Scott brothers in Calgary and the one with the Torres brothers in Atlanta worked well. Then, suddenly, Maurice got fed up. Why bring the Leducs into the promotion at all unless it was to get them involved in a program that would draw? "I'll take them!" he said during one meeting. "Give me a city, bring them on, and I'll take them!"

The Leduc brothers started with Grand Prix in February 1972 but their feud with the Vachons only got underway later that summer. Until then, Maurice wrestled against the Leducs teaming with Rapapapotsky — actually, Maurice had already teamed up with him in the United States when he was known as Soldat Gorky. On July 5, these four wrestlers competed in a final bout at the Forum before a crowd of 12,485 fans. This gave a foretaste of what would happen in coming weeks.

The rivalry began during a television taping in Sherbrooke. It was like a scene from a horror movie. Maurice had worked out the story for the match, and he had always gone for simple effects to make it easier for fans to follow the action. During the match, the Vachons handcuffed Jos Leduc to the cables. Maurice delivered a pile-driver to Paul Leduc on the concrete, and the latter started bleeding from the forehead like crazy. Paul and Maurice headed off to the locker room and an usher came to uncuff Jos. Then a close-up of Jos appeared on the big screen, an image that would long haunt the imagination of Quebec wrestling fans: Jos, hands and knees in Paul's blood, was lifting up his badly bleeding "brother" Paul by the head, while Carpentier doing the color commentary said in a dramatic and disgusted tone of voice: "They bled him like a pig!"

The show ended with this frightening image. Every fan in Quebec wanted the rematch to be held in his hometown, and the desire to "get back" at Mad Dog Vachon spread like wildfire.

"I really bled a lot," remembers Paul Leduc. "Maurice told me not to miss myself!"

The first significant match between the Leduc and Vachon brothers took place on July 31, 1972, at the Quebec City Coliseum. A crowd of 15,000 spectators packed the arena, only to see the match end in a double disqualification. Each team hurled insults at the other. "We are going to kill them," Maurice told the daily tabloid *Le Journal de Québec*. "They can thank the great Maurice for the opportunity I am giving them." Paul Leduc, meanwhile, accused Maurice of having called his brother's wife, threatening to dispense with Jos once and for all at the Coliseum. Fans just loved it! Maurice threw oil onto the fire by claiming on TV that Jos and Paul were not real brothers, which was true, although the public didn't know about it. Maurice added their mother had found little red-headed Paul as a baby on their front porch, whereas Jos had black hair.

Two weeks later, the rematch at the Coliseum brought in 17,008 spectators, a record that remains unbeaten in Quebec City. At the time, the promoters didn't want to publicize the record, however, because they knew the size of the crowd surpassed the authorized capacity of the Coliseum. Fans were packed into the aisles and sat on all the staircases in between regular seats. In the third fall, the Leducs hurt Paul Vachon, and Maurice had to fight the Leducs alone. Now that Maurice was at a disadvantage, and even though he was a heel, the crowd began siding with him for the first time in this rivalry. The Leduc brothers finally won the match

"Maurice wanted [us] to continue beating him up, but Jos wasn't happy because he worried they were going to turn Maurice baby-face," recalls Paul Leduc.

After that, Maurice and Jos, definitely the most talented wrestlers on their respective teams, had two singles matches. On August 28, 15,000 fans packed the Coliseum — the largest arena in the province of Quebec after the Montreal Forum. This was a double disqualification match. Then on September 18, the same crowd witnessed Jos beating Maurice in a cage match. It was after seeing one of these cage matches pitting Jos against Maurice that Jean Gagné decided to make a living of wrestling; he would wrestle under the name of Frenchy Martin. Without even realizing it, Maurice was influencing a whole new generation of wrestlers.

At the same time, Grand Prix Wrestling was running a program in Montreal between Don Leo Jonathan and André the Giant, which drew big crowds at the Forum. Nevertheless, Maurice must have been enjoying a nasty chuckle or two about his sell-out crowds at the Coliseum.

Aside from Quebec, the Vachon–Leduc rivalry met with the greatest success in cities like Trois-Rivières, Sherbrooke (where it all started), and Ottawa. "The rivalry worked really well with the Leduc brothers," says Paul Vachon. "Once, we put on a show in the afternoon, but we had to put on another one the same evening, just to meet demand." Paul Leduc adds: "We were wrestling in Saint-Basile, New Brunswick, just past Rivière-du-Loup, and we had to start turning people away at 4:00 p.m. — they were coming in from Edmundston, actually coming in from everywhere."

Yet the story of this rivalry was so simple. Both teams had a big brother and a little brother: naturally, Jos and Paul Vachon played the role of the big brother. There were never any uncontrollable outbursts at the end of the matches, even though this was Maurice's trademark. He worked out the scenarios and they worked well. Tying up the big guy and letting the little guy get beaten up: that was how the crowd got drawn into the story. Paul Leduc knew his role inside and out: he had to get beaten up so that the crowd could then watch Jos settle the score with Vachon the traitor!

Paul and Jos Leduc enjoyed working with Maurice because the pay was always good. Wrestlers' salaries are based on sharing the evening's gate between the wrestlers and the promoter. Wrestlers taking part in the main events get a bigger share than wrestlers in the undercard. The Leduc brothers reached the height of their career working with the Vachon brothers. They could well have brought in far more revenue if Paul Vachon had been allowed to wrestle in Montreal, still the biggest town in the territory.

This was one more time where Maurice created new opportunities for other wrestlers, helping them break through and make good money. He could have decided that Grand Prix Wrestling didn't need the Leducs, as a way of protecting his own position within the company, the way Yvon Robert had done back in the day. But that wasn't Maurice's way. He always recognized the potential of other wrestlers and the prospect of making more money with them in the future.

Besides, Maurice could have a good match with just about anyone. If a match failed, it meant the other wrestler was sabotaging it on purpose or was under the influence of alcohol. This happened one evening when Jos was wrestling drunk. Maurice had to do all the work. The match got so intense that it sobered Jos up: he never again dared wrestle against Maurice under the influence. He learned the hard way that you could drink a beer after the match — but not before.

Still, wrestling Maurice wasn't always easy. "The worst thing about Maurice in the ring," said Paul Leduc, "was that he never remembered how things were supposed to finish. When there was a big crowd, he was pumping so much adrenaline he lost track of the booking. He asked where we were at, how much time was left.

Maurice listened to the crowd, and the crowd was dictating what he should do."

And of course, Maurice was not all sweetness and light in the ring. "First of all, you had to let him control the match and the crowd, then after that you could get on with your business," added Paul Leduc. "That way, you were sure it would turn out to be a great match, and the next day when you woke up you wouldn't be suffering from too many aches and pains. But if you didn't leave him in charge, you were going to have trouble. He could get nasty and unpredictable, digging his fingernails into your skin. He was 'stiff' — super stiff — worse than Hans Schmidt. He grabbed you by a limb and dug his nails into you. Once he gave such a big chop to Tony Baillargeon that Tony told his teammate: 'What the fuck, come and tag in, I am heading for the locker room!'"

According to former wrestler and promoter Gino Brito, Maurice may not have been stiff, but he was hardly gentle: "It wasn't that hard working with him, but you had to be careful. One time at Paul Sauvé Arena, he hit me with a camera. I needed twenty stitches on the top of my head. He sometimes lost his temper, but I loved working with him. He made matches look so realistic for the fans."

The rivalry running between the Leducs and Vachons actually led to a warm friendship between Paul Leduc and Maurice, a friendship that would continue for many years, and even outlive the time Leduc spent wrestling for Grand Prix. Maurice paid regular but secret visits to Paul Leduc in Quebec City — secret because Maurice had to respect kayfabe. So they would meet in the woods behind Paul's house, to talk about wrestling and their respective families. Maurice looked like a beast but deep down he was a sensitive man, and female fans regularly fell in love with him. His behavior on two hunting expeditions showed just how sensitive he was. Each time, he found himself standing in front of a moose that was so beautiful and majestic he simply couldn't pull the trigger. Another time, after a show in the Gaspé Peninsula along the St. Lawrence river, he asked his business manager, Michel Longtin, to please be quiet and listen to the murmuring of the river as it flowed past them.

"I believe in nature. I think nature is a secret or, if you prefer, a big question mark that no one has managed to decipher. I love nature and I love to watch it alone," Maurice later said. This poetic attitude was at odds with the provocative outbursts of words and actions that were his wrestling trademark.

In private, Maurice was a very different person from the defiant gladiator in the ring. For many wrestlers he was a father figure in a world where survival and success were hard to come by, not to mention finding a true mentor. And that's exactly what Maurice would be for the Leduc brothers.

Once Grand Prix got rolling, Maurice had no interest in paperwork, but in the ring he was the uncontested master. He even told his buddies to pack arenas full of fans, and he would take care of the rest! Maurice never acted like he was the boss: instead he was a leader in the locker room and he helped run the show overall. He also collected honors while with Grand Prix: one tag team title with Paul, two reigns as Grand Prix Wrestling champion, and many sell-outs.

He also quarreled with Carpentier but that never prevented them from wrestling against each other. For Maurice, business came first. In April and in June 1972, he lost the Grand Prix title to Carpentier in front of nearly 13,000 fans at the Forum. But in May that year, he won it back from Carpentier in Quebec City.

Maurice would later recall: "Becoming the Grand Prix champion was special for me. Looking back, I felt I had become like my idols Yvon Robert, Bobby Managoff, Gorgeous George, the French Angel, and Jumping Joe Savoldi." In fact, this title was more important to him than the one he had won back in 1967.

Quebec wrestling fans loved the ongoing rivalry with the Leduc brothers. But in 1973 a match was held that entered the history books, turning Maurice into a real legend in Quebec and earning him the enduring love of wrestling fans for generations to come.

On July 17, 1972, the rival promotion All-Star Wrestling had put on a show at Jarry Park, home of the Montreal Expos baseball team and the largest venue at the time in Montreal. The main event, pitting Johnny Rougeau against Abdullah the Butcher, drew a record crowd of 26,237 fans. The Grand Prix partners had only one thing on their mind: how to break that record, leaving their mark forever on the history of Quebec wrestling.

Grand Prix started off with the idea of banking on the rivalry between the Vachon and Leduc teams of brothers by holding a match in Montreal's Jarry Park between Maurice and Jos. If they were able to draw 15,000 fans in Quebec City, they would surely make a killing in Montreal, where fans were not able to see that feud live. But even before marketing of the event started, Jos and Paul Leduc suddenly switched promotions, heading back to All-Star Wrestling. Paul Leduc recalls: "The lawyer Fernand Lévesque [brother of Quebec premier René Lévesque] worked in the same building as Michel Awada, got wind of something, and told us: 'Hurry up and get out of there!' The shot with Mad Dog wasn't worth it in the long run, and we wanted to be able to line things up with another promotion before it was too late."

By switching promotions, Jos left a gaping hole behind him. Maurice and Paul were looking at all their options to find a replacement. Just then, Paul asked his brother who was the most hated wrestler in the history of the territory. Maurice replied without batting an eye that it was surely Killer Kowalski. Paul told him Kowalski would be the replacement. But Grand Prix was taking a huge risk by booking one heel against another during the main event of the biggest wrestling show they had ever held. Paul reassured his brother: Maurice was a Quebecer whereas Kowalski was of Polish origin and hailed from Windsor, Ontario. Maurice had discovered early in his career that when the crowd had to choose between two heels, it always came out in favor of the local. Besides, by facing Kowalski in the ring, Maurice would, just like in his youth, be able to beat up another English Canadian, but without fear of arrest this time!

The Grand Prix show was set for July 14, 1973, almost a year to the day after the previous one held by All-Star Wrestling.

However, things didn't get off to a very good start. Presale of tickets was slow. In the weeks leading up to the match, Michel Longtin, who was Grand Prix publicist before becoming Maurice's manager, stayed out of sight so he wouldn't have to tell the wrestlers how many tickets had been sold. That's when Maurice showed what he was made of. He got Longtin to find him a rope, hung it on the ropes in the ring, then gave an interview in French and English — an interview that has gone down in history (if that interview were given nowadays, it would have the opposite effect on the public).

"If I lose my match against Killer Kowalski, I am going to commit suicide!"

Then Maurice picked up Longtin's rope and tied it around his neck for an even greater visual effect. He succeeded in getting his message across: the upcoming card was going to be an event not to be missed.

In the 1970s, things were simpler and people were less aware of the impact of words, or perhaps they didn't really care. There weren't that many sensitive busybodies around, taking everything literally and asking who could be offended or influenced by the words of a wrestler who was just trying to be sure an upcoming wrestling show would sell out. The fact that Maurice mentioned suicide in the interview made all the more sense given that his opponent was

Kowalski, who had a reputation as a fierce brawler. Kowalski was famous, particularly in Montreal, for having accidentally torn Yukon Eric's ear off during a bout at the Forum in 1952. Eric committed suicide in 1965. Wrestling fans never learned the true cause of Eric's tragic demise — a divorce followed by a severe depression. In fact, Kowalski was not involved in any way. But the story of Yukon Eric's ear getting torn off got passed down from one generation to the next, and by the 1970s fans were well aware of it and of Eric's suicide.

Newspapers wrote major news stories about the Grand Prix show, which even started thirty minutes behind schedule because so many fans rushed in to buy their tickets at the last minute. The temperature was perfect for a show under the stars. There were so many fans in the stands, Longtin no longer needed to hide: he proudly proclaimed it was a sell-out crowd.

The match between Kowalski and Vachon stands as one of the legendary bouts in the history of Quebec wrestling. The match ended in the third fall. Kowalski manhandled Maurice throughout the match, but in the end Maurice came from behind to win. He was greatly helped in this win by all the illegal tactics he used, even if he was the crowd favorite, and he won the last fall by pressing his feet against the ropes, without the referee, Omer Marchessault, noticing. Maurice didn't change his style, and in fact he didn't need to. Whatever he did, the crowd was behind him 100%, even when he tried yanking Kowalski's ear off.

"That night, Mad Dog became the people's champion for real, because Kowalski didn't take it easy on him in there," Marchessault recalled years later.

Kowalski rained unfair attacks down on Maurice, but the referee did his job and eventually caught Kowalski red-handed, which gave the crowd hopes that their "Mad Dog" — now suddenly transformed from a heel into a French Canadian hero like Yvon Robert had been for Maurice in his youth — could turn things around. The crowd exploded with joy when Maurice defeated his opponent, and that feverish moment is still remembered to this day. Forty years on, Longtin still has shivers up and down his spine when he thinks about it.

Attendance at the Grand Prix extravaganza established a record in Quebec and across Canada: a total of 29,129 spectators watched it in person. This record still holds in Quebec and will probably never be beaten. In the rest of Canada it held for thirteen more years, until a WWF main event between Paul Orndorff and Hulk Hogan drew 64,100 spectators at Exhibition Stadium in Toronto. The Grand Prix show would also be the biggest crowd of that year in the world of professional wrestling.

In the late 1990s, Maurice and Kowalski rekindled their rivalry during an interview conducted for a documentary, *Mad Dog Vachon: Wrestling with the Past*. It proved to be a very entertaining exchange.

"I became famous when I pulled off Yukon Eric's ear. You, Maurice Vachon, you tried to become famous by tearing off my ear at Jarry Park. I've never forgotten."

"Kowalski, you have a face only a mother could love," Maurice replied in a mischievous, caustic tone, but with disarming simplicity.

Kowalski was no longer as heavy as he once had been, but the fact remained he was about a foot taller than Maurice. Actually, Maurice had always had to deal with being shorter than his opponents. And that explains why the particular wrestling style he developed was so important for his career. Maurice didn't wrestle like a man 5 feet 8 inches tall.

According to Gino Brito, Maurice "didn't go in for pirouettes the way other wrestlers did, but people believed what he was doing." And if the crowd believed in him, then Maurice at 5 feet 8 inches could face Kowalski at 6 feet 7 inches in the ring, and the crowd truly believed Maurice could give Kowalski a regular thrashing. And he could.

"Here was a guy who was a horrible worker, and no matter who you were, you had to adapt to his style, and you never knew what the hell he was going to do," said "Cowboy" Bill Watts, a longtime friend of Maurice's, in the book *Pro Wrestling Hall of Fame: The Heels*. "But did Mad Dog draw money? You're damn right he drew money. Why'd he draw money if he was such a bad worker? He drew money because of the intensity of who he was. His interviews were so dominant because he believed that he was the toughest son of a bitch that walked. And he may have been."

Thanks to his character and the way TV commentators presented him, he was never considered a small man. On the contrary, Mad Dog was dangerous, someone to treat with kid gloves. He could face more than one opponent at a time, but he wasn't considered a small man because he had never fought as one. Bobby Heenan, the legendary former manager, said that "nobody ever told Maurice he was small. On the other hand, they told him how mean he was." Maurice often quoted Mark Twain, saying, "It's not the size of the dog in the fight that matters, but the size of the fight in the dog!"

All in all, the match between Maurice and Kowalski that evening at Jarry Park was a beautiful moment for the Vachon family. Paul was the promoter, Maurice was in the main event, and in the corner for him was his sister Diane, better known as Vivian Vachon, who proudly sported a beautiful evening dress.

Diane had been wrestling since 1969, and Maurice was the one opening doors for her, as he had done for so many others. She hated working as a receptionist, and one day she decided to hit a fan on the street who insulted Maurice. Her brother asked her if she was interested in becoming a wrestler, and she answered she definitely would.

Maurice sent her to Lillian Ellison, better known as Fabulous Moolah, who had been training women wrestlers for years, managing the flow of lady wrestlers between the different territories. Maurice gave her the ring name of Vivian. He felt she should have a first and last name starting with the same letter, like Marilyn Monroe.

Vivian enjoyed a great career and became one of the most famous female wrestlers of the time. In 1973, she was featured in the documentary film *Wrestling Queen*. Maurice, Paul, and their father Ferdinand also appeared in the film. In Quebec, she joined her brothers during the Grand Prix Wrestling period, sometimes teaming up with them in mixed matches, and also facing other wrestlers in singles matches. In the summer of 1973, Gerry Brown of the Hollywood Blonds smacked her in a match in Quebec City, which triggered a series of matches with Maurice, who naturally wanted to avenge his sister. Vivian didn't wrestle at the Forum any more than Paul, but it was for a different reason: the Montreal Athletic Commission banned any matches involving women. But Grand Prix Wrestling used her in other parts of Quebec. For a publicity stunt, they even had Vivian wearing a very short dress picketing in front of Montreal City Hall, demanding the right for women to wrestle. In the U.S., Vivian often worked for Verne Gagne, and wrestling magazines liked covering this unusual wrestling family with two brothers and a sister.

Despite everything Maurice had done to make the promotion a success, the Grand Prix adventure couldn't go on forever.

Yvon Robert Jr., Édouard Carpentier, and Michel Awada took advantage of the fact that Paul was outside the country and took control of the company. The trust between the Vachon brothers and the other shareholders had always been fairly tenuous but now it was broken. Shortly after, in December 1973, the Vachon brothers turned the page, selling their shares to Tony Mulé for $25,000 each.

"Just as Maurice and I had been happy to get Grand Prix going, now we were happy to put it behind us. A lot of things must have happened very quickly for us to change our mind about Grand Prix like this," says Paul.

It was the end of a glorious era for Maurice and for Quebec wrestling. Grand Prix Wrestling would never be the same without the Vachon brothers and it would take close to a decade for a comparable resurgence of popularity among fans.

Grand Prix Wrestling finally enabled Maurice to make peace with his native Quebec, but once again he was forced into exile in order to earn a decent living. For many, the 1970s were still a time of peace and love, but for Maurice things would work out differently, both as a wrestler and as a man.

A young Maurice Vachon.

| © Tony Lanza

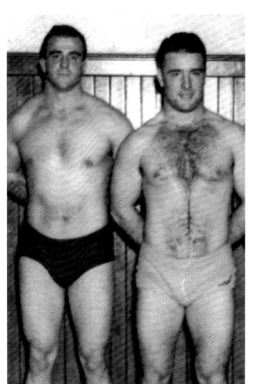

Fernand Payette and Maurice when they were amateur wrestlers [left]. The Vachon Gang core of Marcel, Maurice, and Guy [right]. | Kathie Vachon Collection

Ferdinand and Marguerite Vachon with their children Marcel, Maurice, Guy, and Jeannine. | Kathie Vachon Collection

It took Maurice quite some time to find all the right elements for his character [left]. Maurice and his wrestling teacher Frank Saxon at the British Empire Games [right]. | Kathie Vachon Collection

Maurice is about to win the gold medal at the British Empire Games against Bruce Arthur. | Dave Cameron Collection

Maurice wasn't too fond of authority. He handled quite a few referees very roughly, like Omer Marchessault [top left]. Maurice and Paul Vachon with their lumberjack beards, while teaming together in Calgary in 1956 [top right]. The beard, the teeth, a look that could kill: Mad Dog Vachon was born [bottom left]. | Kathie Vachon Collection   The Vachon Brothers at the top of the wrestling world as the AWA tag team champions [bottom right]. | © Tony Lanza

The piledriver, Mad Dog's signature move, on one of his favorite opponents, Red Bastien [top left]. It was another story when he was against André the Giant. Maurice was the one in trouble [top right]. As the world champion, Mad Dog was now a legitimate superstar in his chosen profession [bottom left]. Japan appreciates a real tough wrestler. Maurice had a lot of success there [bottom right]. | Kathie Vachon Collection

Maurice always had good tips for his brother Paul. He even found his nickname, the Butcher [top left]. One of Maurice's best friends was Baron von Raschke, who got his first break because of Maurice [top right]. Verne Gagne might just be Maurice's most famous rival. The two men knew each other since the 1948 Olympics [bottom left]. | George Schire Collection   Jos Leduc and Mad Dog: an epic rivalry in their native Quebec [bottom right]. | Kathie Vachon Collection

Pop star Maurice Vachon had a hit rap single to celebrate his retirement tour with Paul and Diane (Viviane) [top]. | © Linda Boucher   In 1988, WWE had a special night for Maurice at the Montreal Forum with Gino Brito, Raymond Berthelet, Raymond Rougeau, Édouard Carpentier, Randy Savage, and Miss Elizabeth [bottom]. | Kathie Vachon Collection

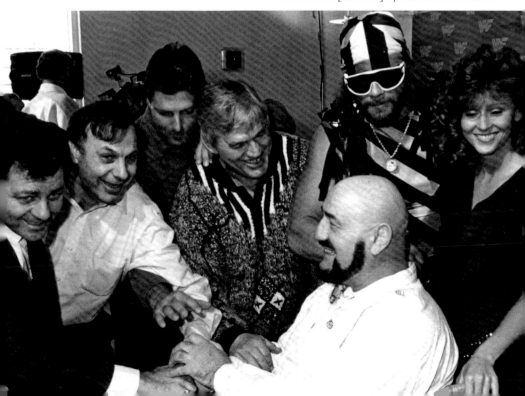

Hulk Hogan is definitely Mad Dog's most famous tag team partner [top left]. | Kathie Vachon Collection   Maurice was even welcomed in the Montreal Expos locker room. Here he is with Hall of Famer Tim Raines [top right]. | © Linda Boucher   Luna Vachon and her uncle Maurice, enjoying good time together [bottom left]. | Kathie Vachon Collection Maurice always had his way with women. In 2009, 1996 Olympic bronze medalist in diving, Annie Pelletier, was the one falling under his spell [bottom right]. | © Pat Laprade

The battle of the Mad Dogs: one of his last major feuds in Montreal, with the other Mad Dog, Pierre Lefebvre [top left]. | © Linda Boucher   While in Winnipeg, Maurice wasn't above having a good time and even putting on the Winnipeg Jets hockey jersey [top right]. Maurice called her his angel, his better half: Kathie was the woman of his life [bottom]. | Kathie Vachon Collection

For his last match, Maurice wasn't going to let anyone down. That meant hard times for Eddie Creatchman [top]. Maurice with Michel Longtin, his sons Denis and Mike, René Goulet, and Jacques Rougeau Sr. and Jr. [bottom]. | © Linda Boucher

The crew from the retirement tour: Richard Charland, Raymond Berthelet, "Hangman" Neil Guay, Paul, Gustave the Giant, and Armand Rougeau [top]. | © Linda Boucher At the Cauliflower Alley Club, Maurice enjoyed the company of his niece Luna, his brother Paul, and an old friend, Terry Funk [bottom]. | Al Friend Collection

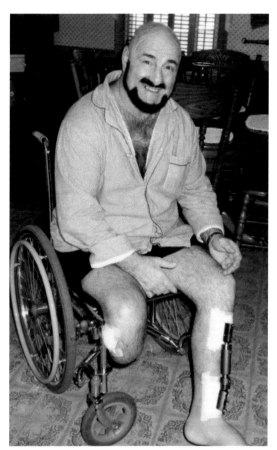

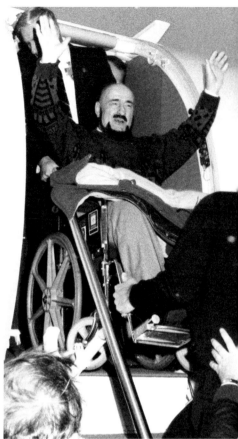

Even while fighting his toughest opponent, Maurice kept on smiling [top left]. A hero's welcome in Montreal, coming back from the October 1987 accident [top right]. Since winning a gold medal, Maurice dreamed of being the center of everyone's attention. Unfortunately, he had to lose a leg to get it [bottom]. | Kathie Vachon Collection

Who would not want to eat a Mad Dog burger? [top left] | Kathie Vachon Collection
Michel Jasmin was first and foremost his friend. But he was also the perfect tag
team partner for Maurice as he made his way into showbusiness [top right]. The
adventure of Mad Dog the Pirate was his last, and no puppets could change that
[bottom left]. | © Linda Boucher   By starring in an ad for Labatt Light beer,
Maurice changed his destiny [bottom right]. | Linda Boucher Collection

The crowd was mesmerized once again while Diesel (Kevin Nash) used Mad Dog's prosthetic leg as a weapon in Omaha in 1996 [top]. | Courtesy of WWE   Pat Patterson, Blackjack Lanza, Jim Cornette, and the Crusher, enjoying Mad Dog's stories [bottom].
| Charlie Thesz Collection

Quebec sports Hall of Fame: Maurice with his brothers Regis, Guy, André, and Paul and his sister Claire [top]. | © Pat Laprade Pat Patterson was proud to honor his mentor while inducting him into the WWE Hall of Fame [bottom]. | Courtesy of WWE

July 2013. Mad Dog had faded away, but Maurice still had that contagious smile.

| © Pat Laprade

18
FREE AGENT — IN WRESTLING AND IN LIFE

Throughout 1973, Grand Prix kept Maurice busy on the home front, but he found time to expand his wrestling horizons outside of Quebec as well. The Jarry Park show had been a huge success, but at heart Maurice was a nomad and there was really no way to keep him tied down, even at home in Quebec. In any case, trouble was brewing within the Grand Prix organization, and he may have considered the grass was becoming greener on the other side of the Canada–U.S. border.

That year he made his debut for the World Wide Wrestling Federation (WWWF) run by Vince McMahon Sr. Maurice also returned to Japan, then headed to the U.S. Midwest where he worked for Verne Gagne.

Mad Dog's first match in New York for the WWWF was actually the direct consequence of a screw-up at Grand Prix Wrestling. Promoter Abe Ford had proposed selling the Boston and New England wrestling territory to Grand Prix. This struck Paul Vachon as a great opportunity since he wanted to expand the organization outside of Quebec. He was all for striking a deal on the spot. Ford's asking price was $100,000 and Grand Prix had the cash in hand. But Yvon Robert Jr. countered there was no need to rush things. He wanted the Grand Prix partners to go over Ford's offer with a fine-tooth comb. As it turned out, he was right to be cautious: Ford didn't actually own the territory he was proposing to sell. Boston and New England actually belonged to Vince McMahon Sr. To smooth things out between WWWF and Grand Prix, McMahon invited the Vachon brothers down to New York to wrestle, and also to resolve the misunderstanding. While Maurice was used in the ring, Paul worked behind the scenes forging a strong connection with McMahon's organization, where in later years he would actually finish his career.

Maurice then embarked on two tours of Japan. In 1973, Maurice clearly reached his peak as a star attraction. During his second tour, he became IWE tag team champion alongside Ivan Koloff, a Franco-Ontarian wrestler whose real name was Oreal Perras, and who assumed the character of a Russian heel after a visit to Montreal in the 1960s. Koloff had drawn huge crowds to the Forum in 1968, where he wrestled Johnny Rougeau, and a few years later he would become WWWF world champion by defeating the legendary Bruno Sammartino—interestingly, that was the only world title Maurice himself never competed for. Thanks to his work in Japan, the business relationship between the IWE and AWA also opened the way to close ties between the Japanese promotion and Grand Prix Wrestling. Several other Grand Prix wrestlers would also travel to Japan, including Édouard Carpentier, Gilles Poisson, Jos Leduc, Don Leo Jonathan, and André the Giant.

The secret of Maurice's incredible longevity as a pro wrestler came down to one thing: training. Every morning in Japan, he put on heavy work boots and went running. His teammate Koloff would do the same in the 1980s, extending his own career. The ad campaign for Maurice's matches highlighted his Olympic past, which was important in Japanese culture, even though many people there realized pro wrestling was largely entertainment.

In Japan, interview skills carried less weight than in America. Wrestlers had first of all to perform well in the ring. Maurice was still the main attraction of the tour and got involved in several bloody battles where his "Crazy Fighter" nickname suited him perfectly. He always wrestled with great intensity in Japan because he was facing real athletes and he had to prove every night that he was going to wrestle on his own terms. In so doing, he taught Koloff that when you wrestle in a team, you need to have complete confidence in your partner, and also know how to defend him against hostile crowds. Maurice sure knew what he was talking about. He traveled by train from city to city, and his journeys were full of anecdotes and nights where alcohol was the real main event of the show.

"I went to a party and drank too much, and I started a huge brawl in a bar," recalled Koloff. "The brawl resulted in $2,000 or $3,000 in damages, but the next morning I had forgotten everything, even though my face was all swollen and my clothes were in shreds. Maurice was the one to get me back to my room, and when I tried to apologize, Maurice told me to forget it. He actually laughed it off, saying, 'That was fun — it looked just like a saloon brawl in the Wild West.' That's when I learned an important lesson: know your limit for alcohol and don't ever go beyond it."

Gilles Poisson was also on the same tour: "That brawl was the biggest fight I ever got into, outside the ring, during my entire wrestling career. We were in a village in northern Japan, the last stop on the railroad and a very boring place. But the whiskey was good, believe me. We had to pay all the damages because we had broken a lot of chairs and tables. But Maurice was right. It really was like a fight in a Wild West saloon — a unique experience."

For all these reasons, Koloff loved working with Maurice in Japan.

Getting up to mischief like this may sound funny long after the fact, but it nonetheless indicated the sometimes unhealthy relationship Maurice had with alcohol and violence. Fans often got involved in fistfights and Maurice was always around to dish out punishment. There was often some way of justifying fights outside the ring, but it was a dangerous game that could end badly.

One day he was wrestling in Minnesota, and a fan tried to punch him. While he was busy avoiding the man's fist, another fan landed a hard right. The police immediately apprehended the guy and led him to the exit, with Maurice raging after him. Once they were behind closed doors, Maurice gave the man a beating he would never forget. But before ejecting the violent fan from the arena, the police banged his head against a door and yelled he would go to jail if he ever came back. So Maurice wasn't the only one to exact revenge on aggressive fans who disrupted a wrestling card. And he actually took advantage of it when it happened, and his street fighter past clearly gave him the upper hand in this type of situation.

Beginning in the summer of 1973, Maurice played a babyface for the first time on his return to the AWA territory. His nemesis, the Crusher, wanted to find an ever more disgraceful wrestler to team up with in his feud against Billy Graham, followed by another one against Nick Bockwinkel and Ray Stevens. Maurice and the Crusher got over so well that they debuted as a tag team in 1974.

Leaving Grand Prix turned out be a great career move for Maurice because business was better than ever and he was practically a free agent. First he headed for Florida, a prime wrestling destination. Jos and Paul Leduc were well-established in the Sunshine State, and they convinced booker Louie Tillet, another Quebecer, to build up another Vachon–Leduc rivalry.

Paul Vachon was busy with other projects, and after trying different partners, Tillet asked Stan Vachon to team up with Maurice. But the story angle didn't work as well as expected because Maurice was so different from the wrestlers most Floridians were used to. He worked hard in the ring, but he had given up on scientific bouts many years earlier. Matches lasting thirty and sixty minutes, like the NWA title matches he had done against Jack Brisco, were difficult. And at this point in his career, Maurice wasn't about to change his style. Moreover, Floridians didn't care as much as Quebecers did about a rivalry between four Quebec gladiators.

If it didn't work in Florida, it would work elsewhere. Maurice decided to leave the territory and informed the Leducs of his decision. But Jos Leduc wanted a farewell party, one last time to celebrate together. The evening turned out to be expensive, especially for Paul Leduc, who estimates the attendees did $5,000 of damage to his kitchen. Then there was the collateral damage — the many bottles of whiskey the guests consumed. When Maurice partied, he never did things by halves!

After Florida, Maurice returned to his old stomping grounds of Minneapolis, Oregon, and Texas. In June, the Vachon brothers returned to Quebec, launching a new wrestling promotion called Celebrity Wrestling. They were convinced that it was shareholder disputes that had torn Grand Prix apart. Logic dictated that with just the two of them as sharcholders, Celebrity Wrestling stood a better chance of succeeding. Maurice felt enhancing his own visibility would help launch the new promotion, so he wrestled for everyone in Quebec, whether All-Star, Grand Prix, or Celebrity Wrestling. But Quebec media found his multiple affiliations confusing. Maurice was still so closely identified with Grand Prix that newspapers struggled to name the promotions presenting each of his matches. In any case, now that the rivalry between All-Star and Grand Prix was history, wrestling was going into a tailspin in Quebec. Maurice was trying to capitalize on his reputation, forging connections between Celebrity Wrestling and the two other Quebec promotions. The wrestling industry in Quebec was no longer at war: it was now in more of a survival mode, and the different players had to figure out how to work together. In this new venture, Maurice teamed up in the ring with one of his arch-enemies, Paul Leduc.

Maurice also took part in the most famous match of the time. On August 12, 1974, he faced Jacques Rougeau Sr. under the All-Star banner in a main event at Jarry Park. The two men had previously competed against one another, but this was their first match since the outbreak of hostilities between their respective promotions. It was also a match that Grand Prix and All-Star had been unable to put on earlier in the year, during the joint shows the two promotions organized. In fact, it was a match many fans had long been hoping to see, something like the rivalry between the WWF and World Championship Wrestling (WCW), which would reach a high point some thirty years later with Hulk Hogan vs. the Rock at *WrestleMania X8*.

To line things up for this stellar happening, Jacques Rougeau defeated Paul Vachon a few weeks beforehand. The promoters wanted a capacity crowd at Jarry Park for this dream match between two real tough guys with similar backgrounds. Indeed, Jacques had made a name for himself as an amateur boxer and then as a doorman in some Montreal nightclubs. But then, just ten days before the match, disaster struck: Jacques broke his fibula. But there was no stopping a gladiator like Rougeau — he was determined to go ahead with the match.

"We were at Cap-de-la-Madeleine, right near Trois-Rivières. The other wrestler fell on him and we heard the sound of the bone breaking in his leg," remembers Raymond Rougeau, Jacques's son. "They put his leg in a cast that evening. The morning of the show, we sawed the cast off and tied a sawed-off hockey pad onto his leg for the day. After the show, we went to the hospital and the doctors put his leg back into a cast. They were furious Jacques had taken such a risk. Maurice and my father wrestled like the dickens during the bout and they both ended up with swollen faces. But Maurice was extra careful to avoid hurting my father's leg."

The event attracted just ten thousand fans — well short of expectations. The joint shows from the beginning of the year had almost all drawn more fans, even though they had offered less compelling main events. By August 1974, wrestling in Quebec had seen better days. Making matters worse was the fact that a subway strike was making it difficult for fans to attend the show. But the real problem was that this match was a year too late.

With blood streaming down their faces, the two men fought to the very end, pushing their limits to give fans a real battle. Although Rougeau was concealing a serious injury, he won the decisive fall when the referee stopped the match because of all the blood Maurice was losing. After the fight, Maurice made a statement lining up a rematch.

"I may have lost the decision, but not the fight. I proved once again that I was the strongest. I lost a lot of blood and I'm proud of it. I've never been afraid of anyone, and especially not Rougeau."

The rematch took place on September 16 at the Quebec City Coliseum. The local promoter considered it a disaster. There should be no misunderstanding that the Vachon and Rougeau families were working together, but there was no love lost between them. Throughout this period, young Raymond Rougeau held a grudge against Maurice for being the symbol of a company that tried to put his out of business. This was quite a normal reaction considering the fact that All-Star Wrestling was a family business. It was founded originally by Johnny, and Jacques and Raymond were also shareholders of the company.

After that match, Maurice began touring the Maritimes. There was nothing special about the tour except the fact that he helped break in one of the biggest stars in the history of wrestling.

With Paul Vachon's assistance, the Winnipeg promoter Al Tomko sent a twenty-year-old named Roderick Toombs to Montreal. Using the ring name Roddy Piper, Toombs made his Quebec debut in July 1974, just when the Vachon brothers were launching Celebrity Wrestling. Maurice took Piper under his wing, taking him on a tour of the Maritimes. Piper lived in Moncton with Maurice and his children, who had joined him on the trip because they were on their summer holidays. Maurice wanted to show his young protégé the benefits of training.

"Maurice always called me cocksucker," remembered Piper. "He kept calling me that while trying to get me to train with him by putting big construction boot[s] on and running on the beach and in the ocean. I would get exhausted very fast but Maurice, he would do the running and full squat in the water like it was nothing. He was incredible. For Maurice, training was a way of life and he was constantly trying to initiate his peers."

According to Piper, Maurice tried to help wrestlers whenever he saw they had real potential. "If Maurice saw you had heart and give everything to the business, he would try to help you any way he could. Even if he was teasing you, in his mind he was really saying, 'He's a good kid. I need to help him out.' He was always helping someone. But he had no patience for people just passing by in our business," said Piper, who by the mid-1980s would become Hulk Hogan's number one enemy as the WWF was taking over the North American scene.

Maurice was so impressed by Piper that he called his friend Red Bastien and arranged for him to travel to Texas. It was the first time Piper would head south without going through Tomko and the AWA. Bastien then recommended him to the promoter in Los Angeles, where he really got noticed for the first time. The rest is history: Piper would become one of the biggest stars of all time.

"Maurice was very important in my career: he was my mentor. He taught me so much about wrestling, but also how a man should live his life. We had something very much in common: neither Mad Dog Vachon nor I were huge men in our business. So we had to make up for it with courage and not taking a back step; Mad Dog taught me that," said Piper, his voice choking with emotion.

The two men met up one last time in 2010 when Maurice was inducted into the WWE Hall of Fame. By then Maurice was already losing his memory, and he almost didn't recognize Piper — until suddenly his face lit up. "He didn't recognize me at first. Then something flashed and he said, 'Cocksucker, I remember you,' and he told me about the riot we were in together in Chicoutimi. That was a crazy night. He was fighting Leduc in a cage and people tried to attack the wrestlers. He had told me to go get the car ready because no one would recognize me since I was just a jobber. He was right — nobody cared about me. After the match, as things were falling apart, Gypsy Joe had to stop a kid from attacking Maurice with a tire iron as they were exiting the building. Maurice got to the car and told me: 'Start the car, cocksucker!'"

The episode mentioned by Piper took place during a Quebec tour where Maurice worked with Gypsy Joe, a Puerto Rican who wrestled until the age of seventy-three and had perfected the art of hardcore matches long before other wrestlers claimed to have invented this style of sports entertainment. The tour was going well for the wrestlers, but journalists at the time were turned off by the extreme violence and the way Maurice and his opponent sometimes exaggerated. In a match at the Verdun Auditorium, the two men leapt out of the ring and began battling outside.

"There was a bus stop in the little roundabout in front of the arena, and they fought there," says former Montreal Canadien great Serge Savard, an eyewitness to the fight. "We followed them outside. Just picture it: they actually got onto the bus. The driver and some old women quickly got off the bus via the rear exit. They actually fought on the bus! I witnessed that, I saw Maurice get on the bus . . ."

"This incident was not at all planned," Paul Leduc explains with obvious pleasure. "They went outside, the bus was idling there, and on the spur of the moment they got on board."

Maurice never minded heading off the beaten track when he was wrestling. In a match in Chicoutimi against Dick Beyer, the two men got out of the ring and fought all the way to the locker room. After a few minutes, Beyer said to Maurice, "Why are we still fighting here? There aren't any fans!" Another time, he wrestled against Bobby Heenan when the two men were working for the AWA. Right next to the arena were some railroad tracks. Maurice decided to go out and press his opponent's shoulders to the track. Young Heenan asked when he could get up, and Maurice answered: "When you hear the train coming!"

Meanwhile, Maurice's American career continued to thrive. Throughout the 1970s, just two wrestling matches were broadcast on a national television network in the U.S. The second took place in 1976 and saw the former heavyweight boxing champ Muhammad Ali getting a warm-up match as he was about to face Antonio Inoki in Japan. Maurice was lucky enough to be part of the first broadcast during that decade. In January 1974, Maurice wrestled former Olympic wrestler Chris Taylor in a match that aired on ABC's popular show *Wide World of Sports*, which was shown on Saturday afternoons and had a big following even in Quebec. The show covered sports events every week for close to forty years and its audience ran into the millions. Taylor was not a typical Olympian. The American wrestler was a 420-pound behemoth who had won a free-style wrestling bronze medal in the super heavyweight class at the Munich Games in 1972. Maurice held nothing back and literally made mincemeat of Taylor's nose.

According to René Goulet, an eyewitness, "Taylor was bleeding from the nose, and the poor guy was in the ring for several minutes. That's when Maurice decided to bite his nose! Taylor's blood was everywhere. Taylor won the match by disqualification, but Mad Dog definitely won the fight."

Taylor actually won the match by disqualification since Maurice was refusing to stop strangling him with the ropes. The commentator had little experience with pro wrestling and explained to viewers that Taylor's blood was real . . . but the strangling was staged!

But the confrontation between the two Olympians didn't stop there. Later in the show, they both were in a battle royal that spread between two rings. Taylor won the match alongside another Olympian from the Munich Games, weightlifter Ken Patera, after he threw Maurice over the top rope, right out of the ring. Maurice had clearly been chosen for this highly publicized match because he had fought at the London Olympics in 1948. Taylor generally faced opponents who were less intense, and he dispatched them in a few minutes.

Purists of the sport didn't care for this particular match, but the ABC broadcast increased Maurice's visibility at a key moment in his career. Taylor was never able to really get himself over, and he died just a few years later at the age of twenty-nine.

It was important for a wrestler like Maurice to command the respect of men new to the sport, even if their initiation was occasionally painful. He never hesitated to bully his opponents, like he did in Taylor's case. He liked instilling fear in the wrestlers facing him, and this fear only added to his legend. He often got his opponents to hit harder when he wasn't impressed by their shots. Jim Brunzell hit Maurice so hard when he debuted with the AWA that Maurice grabbed him by the mouth, stuck his fingers in his eyes and tossed him out of the ring. The message was "Hit hard, but not *that* hard," and Brunzell got the message.

Greg Gagne was the promoter's son, but even that didn't spare him from Maurice's initiation. "My father told me if I hit Maurice twice as hard as he hit me, I was going to be OK. But he hit me so hard my legs felt like wet spaghetti. We both gave it everything we got, and I returned from the match with blood running down my back because he had scratched me so much. Then he came to the locker room, kicking the door open. I picked up a chair to defend myself. And Maurice said, 'I respect you,' as if nothing had happened. The only way to earn his respect was to show as much determination in the ring as he did. Maurice was really unpredictable."

That same year, Maurice's son Mike decided to follow in his father's footsteps. The Grand Prix promotion no longer existed and Maurice didn't want to see his own son fighting for the Rougeaus, so there was no way for him to learn the trade in Quebec. Maurice sent his boy to Edmonton where his good friends Bud and Ray Osborne would train him. Apart from a tour of Japan in 1977, he used the ring name "Mike" — the nickname his family had given him years before. It is never easy for the son of a great wrestler to establish his own career, especially when he goes by the same name, as is shown by the case of Yvon Robert Jr. Anyway, Mike knew fans wanted to see Maurice "Mad Dog" Vachon, not "Maurice Vachon Jr.," which was his real name. After a first tour in the Maritimes, Maurice helped his son break into the U.S. They went to Texas together, where Mike used several different ring names, sometimes even wearing a mask.

This was a good way to learn the art of wrestling, and it was the only time his father intervened directly to help him get established. Maurice had helped many other wrestlers break into wrestling, and now he gave a hand to Mike, but it was up to his son to make his way after that initial intervention. Mike was the only one of Maurice's children to go in for a wrestling career. Denis attended the AWA training camp but didn't go any further than that.

In 1975, wrestling was still taken very seriously in Texas, so much so that promoters warned wrestlers to stay away from the barricades in case they were attacked by a knife-wielding fan. Maurice was an old hand at wrestling in Texas and it took more to impress him. In hockey, the saying goes that offense is the best form of defense, and that's exactly how he behaved. He would chase after fans and they would scatter like the wind. One evening, he even had to protect himself by slugging a spectator who was getting out of control. Maurice loved the fact Texas was more or less still the Wild West — which is why he kept going there to wrestle.

During his Texas tour, he was invited to Japan for a five-week tour in March and April. Towards the end of the tour, he won the IWE heavyweight title by defeating the Mighty Inoue, losing it again a week later to another Japanese wrestler. The IWE heavyweight title was unlike other major titles in Japan in that it was regularly given to North Americans, who usually kept it a short time before transferring it to a local wrestler. Maurice was the first Canadian to win it — an honor in itself.

It took Maurice a lot of moral strength to live on the road for several weeks in a foreign country where very few people spoke English, let alone French. He wrote poems, sending them to Nicole during his stay in Japan. He also sent her love letters she still treasures to this day. Throughout the 1970s, Nicole stayed in Hawaii while Maurice toured Japan, and he joined her for a vacation once each tour ended.

But the postman delivered other letters that weren't as fun to read. Maurice faced many temptations on tour, and letters started turning up from a passionate female admirer in Japan. Nicole never bothered to have them translated.

The couple would then spend a good part of the year in Texas with the entire family, including Maurice's three other children. Nicole had a heavy workload taking care of so many people during the family's time abroad. This would also be the last time she went on a road trip with Maurice. The following year, she refused to follow him to the Midwest. She was getting tired, and she had more doubts about whether he remained faithful.

Even so, she enjoyed the years she spent in wrestling. She often laughed along with him when he played ribs on her, like the time he put on André the Giant's boots before hugging her tight in a slow dance. Anything was fodder for a laugh — over the years, Maurice teased the Giant relentlessly without fear of reprisal. One of the most unusual pranks he played on André took place during a battle royal. Maurice scratched the Giant's back the way only he could do, then darted off into the group of wrestlers before André could identify him. In fact, when André turned around to face his assailant, he thought the real culprit was Buddy Wolfe, who was at the time Maurice's brother-in-law, married to his sister Vivian. This was how Maurice, always the joker, could pull two ribs at once without anyone except a few spectators realizing what was going on. Laughter was always part of the deal with Maurice, either on the road or working with him.

In Texas Maurice won the Brass Knuckle title (more or less the precursor of the hardcore title) in a match with Superstar Billy Graham, who would become WWWF world champion two years later. Graham was built like a Greek god. He was much bigger than Maurice — something of a prototype for Hulk Hogan a few years later. The fact Maurice won the match gives an idea of how much credibility and notoriety he enjoyed in a major U.S. wrestling territory. However Graham would not remember Maurice fondly in his memoirs. "Maurice 'Mad Dog' Vachon was a mark for his own gimmick. He'd rake his dirty fingernails across your back and deliberately scrape off skin."

Just as Maurice was planning to leave Texas, another Quebecer by the name of Rick Martel arrived in the territory. He would later become an AWA world champion just like Maurice. Rick's older brother Michel had brought him to see Maurice a few years earlier in Sainte-Thérèse-de-Lisieux. That same evening, Rick had watched Maurice wrestle at the Quebec City Coliseum before a raging crowd. At the time, Michel was just starting out in the wrestling business and helped Maurice out, for example, by serving as his regular driver. Maurice would also help establish Michel's career outside of Quebec, getting him to wrestle in the Kasaboski promotion in Ontario. So here was yet another novice wrestler getting a helping hand from Mad Dog. Michel worshipped Maurice, even to the point of later adopting the ring name "Mad Dog" in his honor. In 1978, Michel died after a match in Puerto Rico. Maurice turned up at the funeral in Quebec City, without fanfare, simply to convey his condolences to the family.

"That was a first-class thing for him to do," says Rick Martel. No offense to Billy Graham, but Maurice Vachon could also be a gentleman.

In October 1975 when Maurice met Rick in Texas, he made a point of contacting Red Bastien to sing Martel's praises, telling him the young wrestler was the future, that he had a good attitude, and that he was prepared to let the young man defeat him in the ring. At the time, victories and defeats meant more than they do today, even though wrestling was already a form of sports entertainment.

Rick remembers this special episode to this day: "Mad Dog felt the respect my brother and I had for the business. I was incredibly nervous. I was scared stiff, because of his reputation, that he was going to demolish me. This was a milestone for me. He didn't have to lose 1-2-3. This was the only time we ever wrestled. At the time, Maurice loved going down and putting you in holds where you could barely move your fingers. Maurice helped young wrestlers and he did more than his share in this respect."

But Maurice didn't lead Rick by the hand: just as he did with other young wrestlers, he gave Rick a little push in the right direction. He could be helpful on some occasions, but also ruthless on others.

A week before Martel fought Maurice, he got kicked in the face — his mouth was cut and he lost a tooth. The doctor was stitching Martel, and a bunch of other wrestlers were standing around him when Maurice came over after his own match, growling in his well-known voice: "It's just a tooth. Don't make this a big deal." Obviously for Maurice losing a tooth was pretty much a matter of indifference, but for Martel, with his good looks, things were different.

By the second half of the 1970s, Maurice had made the AWA his home territory. His age was beginning to catch up with him, and the AWA was the only place where he could count on being consistently on top of the card. In 1976, Maurice teamed up again with Baron von Raschke, his former partner in Trois-Rivières, and they got into a rivalry with Larry Hennig and Jos Leduc, then with the High Flyers, Jim Brunzell and Greg Gagne. The AWA tried to recreate the once-magical rivalry that had existed between Maurice and Jos Leduc, not learning from what happened in Florida. The two rivals wrestled in the main event of most shows during the summer, but they didn't draw very good attendance. In any case, the AWA had lost ground the last few years.

On the personal front, Maurice's marriage with Nicole fell apart. They agreed to live separately. They reconciled on a number of occasions, but by the summer of 1976 came the definitive break, and they finally moved apart. Nicole now looks at things philosophically: she acknowledges that wrestlers, like athletes and musicians, face many temptations on the road.

Nicole met Maurice's mistress when she joined him in Minneapolis that summer. The young woman was young enough to be his daughter. She was a wrestling fan going through a dark time and considering suicide; Maurice wanted to reach out to help, and eventually he couldn't resist the temptation. Even though Nicole was barely thirty years old.

"Maurice loved women and he knew how to be charming. He attracted many women. But we never got into fights as a couple," Nicole says today.

Nicole was a positive influence in Maurice's life. Once Maurice had divorced Dorothy, their eldest son, Mike, quickly learned to love Nicole. Mike learned to see things differently.

"Thanks to the years my mother and father had together, we lacked nothing. We had a big house, a swimming pool, and great Christmas parties. After the divorce, he came to see us regularly, but my father was always a divorced father with visiting rights. He was a modern-day gypsy. I realized pretty quickly that I would never have a full-time father and I decided then and there to enjoy every moment I spent with him."

Nicole says the years she spent living with Maurice in their home in Sainte-Thérèse-de-Lisieux were the best of her life. Their children were the ones who suffered most from their separation. But she has no regrets about what she long considered to be her one true love. "I was a shy person, but with Maurice I learned how to loosen up, and I gained a lot of self-confidence. We had so much fun together."

Maurice wasn't a bad father — quite the contrary. He just couldn't be tied down to a single place. He belonged to the whole world. And he didn't just belong to the world — he often felt the need to take care of everybody else. Maybe it was because he was the son of a police officer, but he never accepted people taking advantage of the little guy. He had something of a vigilante streak when it came to helping out friends — and sometimes even strangers.

One time he was wrestling in Matane, in the eastern part of Quebec. The wrestlers were eating at their favorite restaurant when the female owner came to their table to explain she had a problem. She said some bikers were coming in, harassing the regulars, and causing a lot of trouble. The wrestlers listened, then Maurice told her he would be back in the restaurant after that evening's matches. He stuck to his word and turned up later. He took a seat and waited. The two bikers in question turned up. One of them began making fun of Vachon, while the other poured a glass of soda on his head. With one hand, Maurice grabbed the second biker by the throat, and with the other he plunged a fork into his eye socket and yanked the eye out!

Clearly, Maurice and the other wrestlers traveling with him had to leave the premises immediately. Every policeman in town was looking to arrest him, but he was already on his way home. He finally received a summons to appear in court, but he got off with an acquittal. His lawyer told the judge the bikers in question were intimidating the restaurant owner and Maurice had come to her defense. The judge told Maurice not to take the law into his own hands but then let him off. Today, it's difficult to fathom the reasoning behind the judge's ruling: was it the bikers' criminal record, Maurice's reputation, or the fact that it was a completely different era? One thing is for certain: a man who pulled out another man's eye wouldn't get off as lightly today.

Maurice might have gotten up to a lot of mischief with his gang of buddies in his younger days in Ville-Émard. But that was a different era and Maurice was no longer a child. He believed it was simply a question of justice. "I could never stand seeing a big guy abusing his strength against a little guy, or seeing four or five guys attacking someone alone. I have to jump into the fray and defend the guy who's all alone."

Mike also remembers how his father got special consideration from the police in Quebec. In some ways he was like a comic book superhero. Whenever he got involved in something, the police looked away. On the way to an event in La Tuque, Maurice was stopped by the police with a case of beer next to him. The police officer at the roadblock wished him good luck in his match that evening and let him go.

Police in the United States also showed Maurice a lot of consideration. Maurice was driving one time to Houston, with Buddy Wolfe to his right, and Mike and the wrestlers Hans Schroeder and John Tolos in the back. Wolfe didn't just hand Maurice a beer — he also passed him a joint. Maurice missed his exit. He decided to back up on the highway. And just like in any good story, that's when the police turned up. Tolos panicked, telling the police he was a hitchhiker and he had no idea who the other passengers were. That's when Maurice stepped out of the car, exuding self-confidence — or maybe thoughtlessness. After all, he was holding a beer in one hand and a joint in the other. Tolos started yelling that they were all going to jail. The police talked to Maurice in the patrol car. Then, he returned to his wrestling buddies, and the group were free to drive on!

"They were wrestling fans. They just wanted autographs," Maurice told his buddies. But for Tolos, the damage was done: he swore never to travel with Maurice again.

Mike adds, "I think he didn't even take a puff of the joint. My father loved to drive, but more than that he loved talking.

Unfortunately, it would have been dangerous for him to drive and talk at the same time. It was safer for all of us to have someone else do the driving!"

In 1977, Maurice did a last tour in Japan. Most of the time he was teaming up with Gypsy Joe, his former arch-enemy, and he also lost in the tournament final against Rusher Kimura. In 1978, he cut back his schedule considerably, though he continued to wrestle for the AWA and returned to Montreal more regularly. By 1978, the Montreal territory was nothing like it had once been. After All-Star closed in 1976 and wrestling was cut from television broadcasts, the territory was in the doldrums. Jack Britton tried to launch his promotion, but without television, it proved impossible. Wrestling had been through its glory years in Montreal, with promotions fighting each other in head-to-head competition, but now in the late 1970s anyone who wanted to keep the wrestling territory alive or make a decent living was bound to face multiple setbacks and frustrations. Maurice wouldn't get back onto Quebec wrestling shows until the International Wrestling promotion got going in 1980 and finally lined up TV coverage.

At the end of the 1970s, Maurice experienced several changes. Since Montreal was no longer an option, he decided to try his luck in Atlanta, where the promoter Ole Anderson brought him for a few matches. He had such a solid reputation with the AWA that Anderson made him the surprise partner of Dusty Rhodes against Ivan Koloff and Anderson himself. The staging was visually very effective. During the TV show, Koloff was stunned to discover Maurice hidden under a sheet in a cage. The match didn't produce a long-term run, but the event remains memorable. The announcer Gordon Solie explained to the crowd that the expression on Koloff's face showed just how terrified he was of Maurice. Koloff swore that he had no idea who was hiding in the cage because Anderson wanted to get a spontaneous reaction from him. Later, Koloff would team up in Atlanta with the late Buzz Sawyer, giving him the ring name "Mad Dog" Buzz Sawyer, because his face and wrestling style reminded him of Maurice. That ring name suited Sawyer perfectly and he kept it for the rest of his career.

Another big rivalry in 1979 pitted Verne Gagne and Billy Robinson against Pat Patterson and Ray Stevens for the AWA tag team championship. When Robinson got "hurt," Gagne had his back up against a wall. He had to find a rough-and-tough partner who could help him face Stevens and Patterson. According to fans and historians, Stevens and Patterson are considered as one of the best teams, not just in the AWA, but in the history of wrestling. Verne had no other choice but to choose a wrestler nobody could possibly have expected — in fact, his arch-enemy: none other than Mad Dog Vachon.

Fans were surprised by this choice, but that was nothing compared to the panic the champions got into: they refused to grant a title match to the new Verne–Vachon team, claiming the team had to prove itself before it could be considered a worthy opponent. This scenario was often used to allow champions to lose a match without losing the title. A rematch was therefore in the offing. Fans hoped to see their heroes win out again over the villains. The rematch offered an additional attraction since it would be a title match. That's what happened with Verne and his new teammate. Maurice didn't change the way he wrestled. Now, all he needed to get the crowd rooting for him was to team up with Verne, the hero of the AWA. Why complicate things? As a team, both Maurice and Verne could maximize their strengths, making sure to conceal the weaknesses that time and age were beginning to wreak on them.

On June 6, 1979, the two legendary wrestlers won the tag titles, and they kept it for over a year. It was the last important championship belt Maurice would wear. Still, despite his age, the fact was, Maurice still had star appeal in the key cities in Verne Gagne's territory.

He was still able to play the champion, and despite his age he was still ready to be a husband.

Maurice had just reached his fiftieth birthday. Like the French stand-up comic Florence Foresti says, "Turning fifty is like being a teenager again, but with a credit card!" Physically, it was not the same old Mad Dog. He was in better shape than many men his age, but he was also beginning to suffer from little health problems. Over the years, he hadn't been kind to his body and now, at fifty, that carelessness was coming back to haunt him. For example, he had knee troubles, which is very common among professional wrestlers.

But Maurice was still young at heart. Like a teenager, he felt he had the right to fall in love again . . .

LIFE STARTS AT FIFTY

Maurice experienced a lot of professional and personal changes once he reached the age of fifty. In fact, the 1980s gave him a completely new lease on life.

For some time, he had been going out with Kathie Jo Ustohal, the girl from Omaha. All these years he had kept in touch with her. Strange as it may seem, they realized they had a lot in common. Kathie had married and had a son, Mathew, with her first husband. Then, like Maurice, she divorced, only to find herself in a new but uncomfortable marriage. She got into a new relationship with Maurice, which was timely, because that was just when she got divorced from her second husband. Kathie and Maurice moved in together in Minnesota.

In 1980, Maurice finally got divorced from Nicole. Although Maurice and Nicole had been living apart for several years, the divorce was now official. Maurice would later admit he cried when they separated. Despite everything, he loved Nicole and he blamed wrestling — the other "woman" in his life — for his failed marriages.

Maurice asked Nicole to say he had been unfaithful — which was true — so she would have legal grounds for the divorce. He left the couple's home to Nicole, just as he had done years before in Dorothy's case. Normally they would have shared the house in Sainte-Thérèse-de-Lisieux, but Nicole's new spouse had opened a gym and was not exactly rolling in money. Maurice did this for the sake of their children. He gave her the house and provided generous support. He even helped her new spouse's business along, by appearing in commercials touting the gym.

A few years earlier he had declared bankruptcy, after taking a bank loan. His investment in Celebrity Wrestling provided no returns. The divorce did nothing to improve his financial situation. He had been floating in cash at the beginning of the 1970s, but that age of abundance was not destined to last. Like the grasshopper in La Fontaine's fable, Maurice was unprovided for and brought low when the north wind began to blow. This was also a time in his life when he didn't really care about money. In fact, the only reason he had ever wanted money in the first place was to be able to help his family and the people around him. It was mainly for them that Maurice had changed territory so often. He hoped to win more money in order to meet their needs and especially to support his young children. His wives and his children never lacked anything. They just missed having him around in person.

Still in 1980, his relationship with Kathie became official. She became his last wife on October 5, 1980, in Minnesota. Of his three wives, Kathie would have the longest marriage with Maurice, sharing in his life particularly after he permanently left the spotlight. Maurice didn't have a red cent to his name when they got married, so he had to get back to work. Kathie had to work too. Wrestling would fill most of his life during the first half of the 1980s.

A few months after the wedding, Maurice and Kathie moved to

Saint Boniface, a district of Winnipeg, Manitoba. Having already worked there, Maurice knew the city well. It was also a place where he had gotten into trouble. Back in the 1960s, after hitting a fan, the wrestling commissioner gave him a dressing down.

"You're not allowed to hit a fan," said the commissioner.

"Even if he hit my brother first?" Maurice asked.

"By no means," replied the commissioner.

"I don't care what you say. If a fan hits my brother, I'm going to hit him back."

"And you know what I'll do if you do that? I'll suspend you."

"And you know what I'll do if you do that?"

"Sure. You're going to sue me."

"No, you dirtbag. I'm going to kill you, piece of shit!"

Maurice then jumped on the poor commissioner. Paul had to intervene to prevent Maurice from going further. At the time, he still didn't understand that actions came with consequences — whether those actions were his or his opponent's. About the same time, Maurice beat the crap out of a guest at a hotel without realizing the guy was the head of Winnipeg's number one crime family. No, he still hadn't learned that this can be dangerous.

Maurice quickly became very popular in Winnipeg and made friends with a promoter named Merv Unger. Manitoba had a large French-speaking community, and this fan base identified with him. He became a local celebrity, sometimes proudly wearing the jersey of the Winnipeg Jets hockey team, to the delight of photographers. He got involved in the community (for example, by running several miles for charity along with Serge Savard, who was now playing hockey there, despite the state of his knees). He also built up a chain of seven opticians' shops with another French Canadian, Honoré Mecteau. Maurice appeared in the commercials. But he didn't have much business flair and this venture cost him a lot of money. Maurice wasn't the kind of man to bear a grudge, but he made an exception in Mecteau's case and long remained bitter about the failed partnership.

That said, the commercials were popular and displayed his sense of humor. In one of them, disguised as a spy, he turns to the camera: "In my business, you need good contacts!" The commercials all ended with the same last words: Maurice would say, "This is not an optical illusion!"

Maurice was always looking for a way to help his friends. He got Angelo "King Kong" Mosca involved in filming these commercials. Mosca was well-known in Canada. A member of the Canadian Football Hall of Fame, he had been dividing his time between wrestling and football when Maurice turned him into a full-time wrestler in the glory years of Grand Prix Wrestling. Maurice had also brought Mosca on a tour of Japan in recent years, where the two men worked as a team. Now they were wrestling in the AWA.

"Maurice was a fantastic partner who always managed to create the unexpected," says Mosca. "In Minneapolis, we were working against Adrian Adonis and Jesse Ventura. Ventura was scared to death of us. No one knew what would happen with Mad Dog. We were really stiff as a team, and if you didn't like that, you had to go work somewhere else." In 2002, twenty years after his heyday in Winnipeg, Maurice would headline a hugely successful tribute evening there, memorializing his career.

At the beginning of the 1980s, the AWA territory was booming, thanks to a rising star named Hulk Hogan. With Hogan, the AWA became the first promotion to capitalize on the marketing of wrestling souvenirs, and Maurice was a top-notch salesman. The AWA launched a series of wrestling figures, which are still highly prized by young and old alike. Strange to say, Maurice remains to this day one of the greatest wrestling stars to never have a wrestling action figure, despite his career with the AWA and WWE. In the 1980s, though, fans could pick up his T-shirt for the modest sum of $10, a T-shirt adorned with the phrase "It's a dog eat dog world!" — one of his favorite expressions, which he regularly repeated during interviews.

Despite his age and physical condition, Maurice remained a popular figure with the AWA. Fans were more interested in his storied past than in what he was doing at present. They were delighted to see he was still in action.

"Maurice was all over the territory; it was fun working with a guy who was so hot in a territory. He knew the psychology of the public. He had a perfect sense of timing even if he was no longer the wrestler he had once been," says Rick Martel, who fought for the AWA during those years as well.

Maurice didn't have the same edge in the ring, but behind the scenes nothing had changed. Maurice was so influential he convinced Verne Gagne to team up the Quebecer Neil Guay with Sgt. Slaughter, who was then playing the masked wrestler Super Destroyer Mark II.

"From day one, Verne disliked me," says Guay. "Maurice dressed me up as Super Destroyer, but Verne didn't notice the difference, and everyone laughed at him in the locker room. But Maurice got his way in the end because Verne hired me and I became Super Destroyer Mark III."

Verne wanted to fire Guay, but Maurice got him to change his mind. Then Verne got all hot and bothered a second time, and Maurice suggested to Guay that he should move to another territory. "Maurice told me, 'It makes no fucking sense. I'm going to call Vince McMahon Sr. and get you a deal in New York.' And that's just what he did. Maurice and Paul were my wrestling mentors!"

Maurice also gave sound advice to a young Hulk Hogan, who was often late in reaching fan-oriented events because he couldn't say no to anyone who wanted to talk to him on his way there. Maurice told Hogan, "Don't worry about us being late. They can always wait a little longer, and they will just love us a little more whenever we get there!" Hogan still applies this principle when making public appearances.

The whole crew, not just the wrestlers, admired Maurice for his ability to be so attentive to people. He always loved to laugh and he never played the star, although he had definitely achieved stardom.

"One of the referees was constantly talking about his caravan, and he wanted to show it to Maurice," Martel recalls. "This was by far the tiniest caravan I've ever seen in my life. But Maurice took the time to check it out and he complimented the referee. When we got back to the TV studio, he turned to me and said, 'Rick, did you see that god damn piece of crap?' We had a good laugh. I was impressed he had been so nice to the referee."

One of the most legendary stories in the history of professional wrestling dates back to this period. The story has been told so often over the last thirty years that it is hard to separate reality from fiction.

Gagne's company had a Cessna, and seven wrestlers went along for a flight from Minneapolis to Omaha. The aircraft was nicknamed Suicide 1 because passengers were regularly knocked around by turbulence and the pilot took off no matter the weather conditions.

This was a routine flight, and on the way down to Omaha, everything went like a dream. Maurice was aboard, along with Nick Bockwinkel, Greg Gagne, Steve O, Jim Brunzell, Adrian Adonis, and Sheik Adnan. Maurice asked Gagne a favor: could the local promoter Joe Dusek have him work early on the card so Maurice could meet Kathie and her in-laws at a restaurant? Of course, it was granted to him. Maurice didn't usually drink before a match, but on this trip, his knees were giving him a lot of pain. He took a little shot of whiskey . . . and Jim Brunzell and Adrian Adonis each gave him a painkiller that was way stronger than Tylenol.

After the matches, everyone headed to the airport for the return flight to Minneapolis. Maurice arrived by taxi much the worse for wear, along with Steve O. He had taken wine at supper and Steve O had just given him another whiskey to calm him down. Maurice was in really bad shape so he was sent to the back of the plane. He was in no shape to play cribbage with the others, which meant he was in a bad mood even before takeoff. Maurice just loved to play that game.

The return flight was an epic story that almost ended in tragedy. Once the plane reached 6,000 feet, Maurice suddenly opened the door of the cabin, to the horror of the other wrestlers. With the door wide open, 100 knots of wind shrieked past them like death incarnate, and the passengers were sure their last hour had come.

"We felt like we had been hit by another plane," said Gagne. "Maurice began throwing everything out the door, starting with litter and ending with his own wrestling gear. The pilot had to make an emergency landing on one wheel at a fort-five-degree angle, so the door wouldn't get sheared off and the plane wouldn't flip upside down."

To make matters worse, on landing Maurice ran out past the firefighters, paramedics, and police gathered on the airfield, and the police had to track him down.

The authorities now wanted to know what had happened. Nick Bockwinkel was put in charge of doing a little survey of the wrestlers. First, he asked who had been sitting next to the door. They answered Maurice. Then he took Maurice aside.

"What happened to the door?" Bockwinkel said.

"I opened it," Maurice said.

"Why?"

"It was a beautiful evening, I thought we should get some fresh air."

Baron von Raschke wasn't part of that epic trip, but he thinks he must have heard the story told and retold more than fifty times, and never quite the same way. The versions of the story have diverged over the years. For example, Sheik Adnan Al-Kaissie (formerly Billy White Wolf) wrote in his autobiography that Adrian Adonis had to take a dump, so he relieved himself in a plastic bag. The smell was so nauseating that Maurice opened the door to get some fresh air. According to another version Neil Guay heard, the other wrestlers were smoking a joint and passed it to Maurice, who took a puff for the first time in his life. This triggered an unexpected reaction.

The pilot was furious and ordered Maurice off the plane for good, telling him to complete the journey by bus. The pilot was a war veteran with nerves of steel and had coldly faced thunderstorms and many other kinds of nasty weather. But having Maurice on board was worse than a tornado. Finally, the pilot allowed Maurice back onto the plane, but on one condition: he had to sit directly behind the pilot and wear two seat belts. Maurice threatened the others he would kill them in Minneapolis if they didn't bring him back, but that didn't scare them: they were relieved to have survived the first stage of the journey.

When Verne found out about the flight, he was livid. Maurice was so sure he was going to be fired that he left the very next day to work in Hawaii without notifying Verne or anyone else in the office. After a week, Verne finally tracked Maurice down. He gave Maurice guarantees there was no question of his getting fired and told him to please come back to Minneapolis where he was needed. In fact, Maurice was featured prominently in the promotion's ads all over the territory and he was often billed in the main event. Gagne gave up on the idea of getting Maurice to pay $5,000 for a new door on the plane. Apart from Maurice, very few wrestlers could have gotten out of a situation like this unscathed.

Maurice gave only one interview about the incident. It appears on a DVD produced by RF Video. He said he accepted the situation and hoped one day to close the book on what happened that night. Unfortunately for Maurice, the story would be told at his funeral, when Greg Gagne recounted it "for the last time" at Kathie's request.

"I am trying to forget all about the story on the airplane," said Maurice, "but everyone wants me to keep telling it over and over. We all make mistakes in life, but this one could have killed us all."

This episode fed a steady stream of jokes, and other wrestlers teased Maurice mercilessly on practically every flight. People laughed about the story even when he wasn't on board.

A few weeks after losing the AWA tag team title in July 1980, Maurice was booked in a program with a behemoth named Jerry Blackwell. He weighed about four hundred pounds and was very agile despite his size. On TV, Maurice nicknamed him "Fatwell." Blackwell was also very strong, sometimes jumping off the top rope and performing stunts such as bending iron bars with his neck or driving nails with his forehead into a wooden board. In the wrestling world, Blackwell was widely respected for his style. He worked hard and he was the perfect opponent to face Maurice at this stage of his career.

Blackwell teamed up with the gigantic "Big" John Studd, while Maurice teamed up again with the Crusher. Sadly, Maurice had lost ground as a pro wrestler. At the beginning of his career, he had made the piledriver into one of his signature moves, literally terrorizing fans. Now, in the 1980s, he was no longer able to perform the move safely. Maurice no longer had the strength to lift behemoths like Blackwell and Studd, and on one occasion, Maurice almost dropped Studd on his head. The four men wrestled in many matches in late 1980 and up to late January 1981, when Blackwell "injured" Maurice in Minneapolis.

Maurice needed a break, so he decided to leave the territory for a while. He wrestled in Ontario and Winnipeg until the summer of 1981, but he then felt drawn back to Quebec like in his younger years.

"I always returned to Quebec in the summer. We always miss our country, which is first Quebec and then Canada. There is an extraordinary mindset there that you can find nowhere else. You can find American, Canadian, French Canadian, and French influences in Quebec, all bound together in the same package. This is our homeland after all — there isn't any other."

The wrestling scene in Quebec had changed a lot since the years when All-Star Wrestling had competed head-on with Grand Prix Wrestling. Gino Brito took over the promotion from his father, Jack Britton, following Jack's death in February 1980. Brito wanted to regain a foothold in the Quebec market, so he joined up with two major partners: the wrestlers Frank Valois and André Roussimoff, better known as André the Giant. Brito built up the credibility of his territory by lining up stars from another era. Johnny and Jacques Rougeau were no longer wrestling, so Brito turned to the stars of Grand Prix Wrestling, Maurice and Carpentier. Maurice had slowed down considerably in the ring, although Carpentier could still be spectacular at times. Brito used the AWA strategy of presenting Maurice as a legend, then putting him in a team where his limitations would be less noticeable. The ring name Mad Dog still drew media attention and brought fans to see new wrestling stars like Dino Bravo, Rick Martel, and Raymond and Jacques Jr., the new generation of Rougeau brothers. Besides, Maurice trusted the promoter to treat him fairly and didn't demand big guarantees.

Varoussac Promotions would later become International Wrestling. For now, it was in its second year. In the summer of 1981, Varoussac used Mad Dog Vachon for the first time. He had feuds with his old friend the Destroyer, as well as Michel "Justice" Dubois, but especially with Pierre Lefebvre, in what Quebecers called "the

Battle of the Mad Dogs." Lefebvre was from L'Assomption, an off-island suburb of Montreal. Like Maurice, he was hairy and had a hoarse voice, so the Detroit promoter George Cannon nicknamed him "Mad Dog." Brito saw this as a natural rivalry and Maurice accepted without batting an eyelid.

This was a major rivalry for Pierre Lefebvre, who would unfortunately die in a car accident in 1985. Lefebvre's best friend Raymond Rougeau recalls: "At first, Maurice Vachon made life difficult for Pierre. He really bashed him around. He wanted to know whether Pierre deserved the ring name 'Mad Dog.' I told Pierre to do a better job defending himself. But he only defended himself as needed. He soon realized this was a test. This was the biggest opportunity of his career, and it would lead to him being acknowledged as another 'Mad Dog.' This could have led to some great things if he hadn't died so young. In the summer of 1981, Pierre really earned Maurice's respect."

Generosity was one of Maurice's signature qualities. By agreeing to share a nickname that had enabled him to build up such a fantastic career for himself, he helped a younger man get ahead in wrestling. If Maurice had not been so generous, he could have prevented Lefebvre from using his name. He could even have refused to wrestle with Lefebvre altogether.

In this program, Raymond teamed up the most with Maurice. The two men were still suffering from the aftereffects of the war between promotions back in the 1970s. The Rougeau clan wasn't exactly on intimate terms with Maurice outside of the ring. Raymond and Maurice would meet in the town where they were wrestling, they would wrestle, then they would meet up again in the next town. There was no partying together, no socializing.

On August 3, 1981, Maurice teamed up with Raymond and Jacques Jr. — these were the sons of Jacques Sr. and the nephews of Johnny, two of his all-time greatest enemies in Quebec. This was a unique moment considering the rivalry that had raged between Maurice and Jacques in the 1970s and the everlasting one he had with Johnny. Another important event occurred the following week when Maurice teamed up with his son Mike against Michel Dubois and Pierre Lefebvre. A crowd of 4,200 people came to see the match at the Paul Sauvé Arena in Montreal. This was one of the last times Mike wrestled with his father: Mike ended his active career the following year, although he did a few matches now and then up to 1992.

There was no obvious winner in "the Battle of the Mad Dogs" and it would pick up again the following summer. On the other hand, Maurice had clearly reached a point of no return: he couldn't be both a villain and a legend. Fans had too much respect and love for him to be a true heel.

After a few matches in Winnipeg and a good long rest, Maurice was back in Quebec in July 1982, where he wrestled a unique and exceptional match against the bloodthirsty Abdullah the Butcher. Moreover, Varoussac organized the first card in years at the Montreal Forum. Maurice was delighted to return to the legendary arena, where he teamed up with Carpentier.

Then, his rivalry with Lefebvre was revived. Maurice played his character to the hilt, cutting Lefebvre apart in public statements. For example, in an interview conducted by Édouard Carpentier he said, "I heard that Lefebvre, that dog, broke his leg. Édouard, you have no idea how sad that makes me." He also returned the favor to Raymond and teamed up with him against Lefebvre and Maurice's old protégé, Pat Patterson.

On September 27, he challenged the British Empire and international champion Billy Robinson, in what would be his last match for a singles title in Quebec. He sounded like the belligerent youth from Ville-Émard of yore: "There's no way the English are going to lord it over me. This guy's going to have a hard time eating fish and chips with a broken jaw!" Maurice would have no particular fondness for the English right up to his dying breath!

The summer of 1982 also marked Maurice's return to Saint Paul for the AWA, a triumphant return after an eighteen-month absence. Things naturally picked up where he had left them. On August 8, Maurice faced Blackwell and his manager, Sheik Adnan Al-Kaissie. Maurice needed a teammate, so he asked his old enemy Verne Gagne for help. After all, Maurice had helped Gagne years before, at which time Gagne had told Maurice he owed him one! The combination of Verne and Maurice on the same team drew 19,000 fans, who were now seeing two legends fighting side by side: it was like a dream come true. And for the fans, it created some uncertainty over the new pair: would Maurice actually betray his partner? Wrestling fans love questioning what could happen and what crazy ideas the different promoters can come up with. Whatever the story is, it's always a good idea to create doubt about the outcome of a storyline.

Maurice continued in his rivalry against Blackwell until the end of the year, sometimes teaming with Jim Brunzell. Fans remember this rivalry largely because of a famous interview Maurice gave at the time. When the interviewer Gene Okerlund came to meet him, Maurice was in his workshop building a pine box for Blackwell that would force him to "quit" wrestling after sustaining an "injury." The word "coffin" never came up during the interview, but viewers didn't need a dictionary to understand what Maurice was planning. The interview gave a striking visual impression: Maurice seemed to be possessed, with his flashing eyes that came out at you from the TV screen, and the hammer he kept driving obsessively into the pine planks. He explained to Okerlund what would happen to Jerry "Fatwell" once he laid hands on him. This wasn't the first time he had built a coffin to dramatize a rivalry: he had already built one back in Portland in the 1960s, for his rival Lonnie Mayne. In wrestling, nothing is lost. Everything can be recycled.

"Maurice was the perfect wrestler in an interview," says "Mean" Gene Okerlund, a former AWA and WWE announcer. "He was perfect in every sense of the word, whether he was in a cage or building a coffin in a workshop. He was one of my favorite wrestlers, and one of the favorites of other wrestlers as well."

"We were doing interviews every Wednesday in Saint Paul," says Rick Martel. "Even though he was nearing the end of his run, his interviews were still as in-your-face as ever. The boys never missed those interviews. Seeing him transform himself into 'Mad Dog' was always something."

Maurice had also developed a particular style of wrestling that made his rivalries that much more intense. At *WrestleMania VII* in 1991, Jake "The Snake" Roberts and Rick Martel wrestled blindfolded, wearing hoods that prevented them from seeing their opponent during the match. This kind of wrestling probably went back — at least in part — to the "Algerian Death Match" that Maurice had used since the 1960s.

"The first blindfold match I ever saw was Mad Dog Vachon against the Crusher in Saint Paul, Minnesota, in 1968," said Bill Watts. "I don't know if Maurice invented this style of matches, but he sure made it better known by incorporating it into his. He played on his supposed Algerian origins and used it against multiple opponents, particularly in his rivalry at the time against Blackwell."

Maurice used several partners in his war against the stable of Blackwell, Adnan, and Ken Patera. He also teamed up with the most popular babyfaces in the territory, Jim Brunzell, Greg Gagne, André the Giant, Baron von Raschke, and Verne Gagne, as well as Dick the Bruiser, the Crusher, Rick Martel, and even Hulk Hogan.

On April 24, 1983, in Saint Paul, Verne and Maurice had their rematch against Blackwell and Adnan in front 18,000 spectators, plus more than 5,500 others on closed circuit TV, beating all attendance and gate records of the AWA. This match was one of the two main events of the evening. In the other one, Hulk Hogan was trying to become AWA champion by facing the defending champion, Nick Bockwinkel. This match is still remembered today because Hogan won, only to see his victory overturned, much to the chagrin of the audience. Hogan was hugely popular, but Maurice and Verne were still the evening's finalists.

In May 1983, with Maurice wrestling full time in Minneapolis, sad news hit Quebec wrestling. Johnny Rougeau had died after a long battle against cancer. Johnny and Maurice had never been friends — quite the contrary — but Johnny's passing marked the end of a chapter in Maurice's own career.

Johnny had retired from the ring several years before his death, but Maurice's career was going full-tilt. He played his character so well that it seemed perfectly credible for him to challenge the champion, Bockwinkel, a few times during this period. On October 23, 1983, before 19,500 spectators, he won a battle royal, which meant he would face the champion the following month. The illusion was perfect. Fans still believed in him, as if time stood still at some point in the 1960s. His championship match against Bockwinkel took place on Thanksgiving, and the rematch was held on Christmas Day. Both events drew large crowds, and even if Hogan was the promotion's main attraction, Maurice's popularity was still a big drawing card. On December 25, 1983, in Saint Paul, Maurice won by disqualification. This would be his last important singles match for the AWA.

From that point onwards, things would really change in the realm of professional wrestling. By 1984, wrestling was already becoming more "entertainment" and less of an athletic discipline. The advent of cable TV meant fans could follow what was happening in different territories and compare different wrestlers. Maurice was now visibly older, he was losing ground physically, and he could no longer be considered a serious contender or real threat. He was fifty-four years old, and his wrestling career was winding down. But a second career awaited just around the corner. Maurice would become more than a mere wrestler. Now he would become a legend.

THERE'S NO BUSINESS LIKE SHOW BUSINESS!

"Pro wrestling is a thankless career. When I made my debut, people only had eyes for the winners. At first, I got beaten up a lot. In the ring, opponents busted my teeth and fractured my larynx. People told me I would never amount to anything as a wrestler. I fought constantly to represent French Canadians everywhere in the world. Some people tried to get the better of me, but they never succeeded. As long as there is a single drop of blood left in my body, nobody will ever get the better of me, whether from the U.S. or anywhere else."

Maurice was reaching the end of this thankless road his career had led him to. He would actually finish his active wrestling career in 1986, but just before that he would take part in the biggest change affecting wrestling up to that time. In 1984, Maurice quit the AWA, giving up the personal independence that had allowed him to wrestle whenever and wherever he wanted. Now he would wrestle for the WWF, which was expanding rapidly throughout the United States.

Until then, most wrestlers agreed verbally with the promoter about their working conditions. When a wrestler wanted to leave a territory, or when a promoter judged his character no longer had growth potential, either party could give a few weeks' notice to terminate the arrangement. The wrestler then moved on to pursue his career elsewhere, while a new wrestler entered the territory to take his place.

Maurice and the manager Bobby Heenan were among the few who actually gave notice to Verne Gagne before leaving the AWA. Verne generously thanked Maurice for his many years of dedicated service. Verne even saved his honor by allowing him not to wrestle in his last scheduled match on June 10 in Saint Paul against Bruiser Brody. But Maurice was in the arena that night. Brody was a really tough guy in the prime of his career and he was infamous for never wanting to look weak. If the two men had actually found themselves in the ring, Maurice would certainly have tried to take control of the match. Given Maurice's volatile personality, there would have been a real battle. And this time around, Mad Dog might have lost. It was the end of an era. The AWA was his favorite promotion — the one he was most dedicated to, and for which he had worked the most often, and also the longest. For Maurice, wrestling for the AWA had been a twenty-year-long epic adventure. He owed Verne Gagne big time.

So it came as a real surprise to see Maurice in Minneapolis a week later, on June 17, 1984, wrestling for the WWF (he had debuted with them two days earlier, on June 15). This decision surprised fans, who didn't have a clue he had left the AWA and didn't realize Verne had done him any favor. Maurice was not the only one in this situation. Other wrestlers had also abandoned their old allegiances to sign exclusive agreements with Vince McMahon Jr., who by now had replaced his father as head of the family business. The system of territories had existed a long time: a given territory never or almost never intruded on another. But McMahon was planning to spread his product throughout North America, which amounted to breaking the old rules. He recruited the best and most popular wrestlers in each territory, bringing them into his own organization to better invade rival territories. Sometime later, he would use this same tactic in Quebec, recruiting the Rougeau Brothers, Dino Bravo, and Rick Martel.

June 1984 also marked Maurice's last trip overseas as a professional wrestler. He had started wrestling abroad when barely eighteen. Now he would finish his international career in Austria. Before returning to America, Kathie and Maurice made a stopover in Paris, where they sat a few minutes in front of the Eiffel Tower. Maurice was thoughtful. He remembered how important travel had been to him.

Back in America, he wrestled almost exclusively for the WWF until February 1986. This proved to be the finest hour of the latter part of his career. He wrestled five or six times per month, which was less often than before, but was still enough to make some good money. He wrestled in cities like Minneapolis and Chicago — the traditional heart of AWA territory — and also on the U.S. West Coast, where the AWA had a foothold. But he rarely wrestled on the U.S. East Coast. This was more a business decision than a sentimental one. He realized his career was winding down. Actually, the character he played still worked well in territories where the AWA maintained a strong presence, but in the new markets where the WWF was now expanding, fans saw him as a little old man who didn't do much in the ring. In interviews, he was as brash and full of energy as ever, but in the ring his performances left something to be desired, and fans didn't believe in him the way they used to.

Maurice certainly is one of the most important wrestlers in AWA history. According to many experts, he ranks in the top five to this day. He had become famous for terrorizing fans. But by the mid-1980s he could no longer strike that trademark terror in their hearts.

In cities that were key for Maurice, the WWF put him in the main event, where he teamed up with Hulk Hogan or André the Giant. With these same wrestlers, the AWA had managed to draw bigger crowds the previous year, but the matches Maurice took part in still made sports news in Minnesota. "I have nothing but good memories of having rubbed shoulders with Maurice, who was a great wrestler, a great man, and a great friend," says Hogan.

The WWF sought out Maurice, not just because he could bring in good crowds in the American Midwest, but because he could have a big impact in Quebec. He didn't wrestle in Montreal before 1986, but Maurice was hired for French-language broadcasts of the WWF to interview other wrestlers in a segment called *Brunch with Mad Dog*. Unfortunately, Maurice came off better when promoting himself than when he interviewed other wrestlers, where he was supposed to help them promote their upcoming matches. Video clips on YouTube nowadays show some of the interviews Maurice did with young Luc Poirier or veterans like André the Giant. The evidence shows the interviews didn't work. When it turned out that broadcasting Maurice live from ringside didn't work, his segments were prerecorded in studio. But the results were the same. These interviews were all recorded at the beginning of 1985. The interview with Jesse Ventura was so bad that Maurice lost the gig. The truth was, the segments were really poor and nothing that bad could possibly make it onto TV today.

Pat Patterson took over the brunch segment. He liked playing the antagonist, like Roddy Piper on *Piper's Pit*. Patterson was much better suited to this type of segment than a good guy like Maurice who tried somehow to ask real questions. Maurice would certainly have been more effective as a manager, but in the long run, a manager can only be effective by playing the bad guy, which Maurice couldn't really do. In December 1985, Maurice was invited onto *Piper's Pit*.

Many fans were surprised that Piper was so nice to him during the interview segment, but Piper found that quite normal.

"When Maurice came to the WWF, I wanted to give something back to him," Piper explained. "Because I owed him so much, there was no way I could return the favor. I was proud of the things he had taught me. I've never said this before, but the interview I did on *Piper's Pit* with Mad Dog stands as the most important one for me, personally. Hitting Snuka with a coconut and André vs. Hogan were all about selling tickets. When I did the show with Maurice, I wanted to tell the world how great he had been and to show viewers all he meant to me."

Maurice also showcased his acting talents while doing the TV segment for the WWF. He helped stage a fake wedding for his brother Paul on the USA Network's *Tuesday Night Titans*. He showed during this segment the attitude that would bring him success on Quebec television later on. He wasn't afraid of being the butt of a joke, he had a great sense of humor, and he came off as an exceptional person who left nobody indifferent even if he was not wrestling. The wedding ended with a food fight: Maurice got a custard pie in the face, just like Vince McMahon Jr., who was ready to take it on the chin, doing just as much as he asked out of his own wrestlers. The staging was hilarious and seemed like something out of a Benny Hill skit.

On February 24, 1986, Maurice's adventure with the WWF ended with the first show the WWF ever put on by itself at the Montreal Forum. Maurice was one of the wrestlers in the main event, a battle royal. Maurice was eliminated and headed for the locker room, only to return to the ring shortly afterwards brandishing a chair. He whacked Pat Patterson's head with it, drawing blood, thereby getting Patterson eliminated. In the lead-up to the event, Maurice promoted tickets sales by intensifying his rivalry with Patterson on French television; the issue was who should host the brunch segment. Patterson was then nicknamed "the Dream of Quebec." Maurice gave interviews before the show, shouting a single inflammatory sentence with that husky voice of his, to whip up fan hatred for his rival.

"There's just one thing I dislike about Pat Patterson: it's the fact he's breathing! He isn't the Dream of Quebec — no, he's the Nightmare of Quebec . . ."

Maurice had played a key role in Patterson's American career and now Patterson was going to return the favor at the Forum — a true temple of pro sports Maurice had been dreaming about ever since boyhood. Some 17,300 fans packed the stands to witness the two men settle scores.

Réjean Tremblay wrote in the Montreal daily *La Presse*: "Mad Dog can still cheat in the ring. Monday night, he set the crowd on fire by entering the arena in a fit of rage, waving a Quebec flag as he toured around. He battled with the other wrestler until he drew blood, administering a chair shot to the poor guy's head. Nobody got the better of him; nobody dealt him dangerous shots. Mad Dog was in an ebullient mood upon leaving the Forum. He had stolen the show!"

This was an important show for the WWF, and late-night television newscasts on Channels 10 and 12 were all abuzz about Maurice's presence. This would be his last match working for McMahon's promotion.

Surprisingly, a few months earlier, in October and November 1985, the AWA had used him, but only in Winnipeg. He was paired up there with the AWA champion Rick Martel, playing a Canadian this time. TV color commentators had always said Maurice was Algerian-born, then he had moved to Paris, then on to Canada, but great stress was laid on his Algerian origins. For McMahon, the AWA was no longer a threat by then. He knew Maurice was nearing retirement so he had no problem with Maurice working in Winnipeg, especially since Verne wasn't the promoter there any longer: the city was now Blackjack Lanza and Nick Bockwinkel's territory, under the banner of the AWA. Meanwhile, for the first time, the AWA taped shows in Winnipeg for the Canadian market and was broadcast from coast to coast on the sports channel TSN. Maurice was the character Canadian fans knew best, thanks to his years with Grand Prix Wrestling, whose matches were broadcast across the country.

In April 1986, after completing his contract with the WWF, Maurice wrestled one last time for the AWA, in South Dakota. This was actually his last match in the United States.

Now fifty-six, he had reached the end.

For journalist Réjean Tremblay, the biggest question of all was why Maurice wanted to keep punishing his fifty-six-year-old body. The wrestler's answer was straightforward: "Because the crowd, the fans, is like a drug. The payoff for a wrestler lies in smelling a good crowd who get drawn right into the action. I still can't live without that."

But what Maurice didn't tell the journalist is that he wasn't in a strong enough financial position to retire. He was making good money but it was nothing compared to what other wrestlers made in the 1980s, let alone today's wrestlers. At the peak of his career, Maurice earned U.S. $150,000 per year. But this was far from the norm. In the 1960s, wrestling for the AWA earned him between $45,000 and $75,000 per year.

"When I was young, I wrestled in a town for $10, and now they pay me $1,000 dollars to do the same. I'm too banged up to continue, but I don't know how to do anything else," he said.

In the last few years, he had been able to make up to $2,000 per week with the AWA. The WWF wasn't known for being stingy. But Maurice hadn't put money aside for his retirement. He was lucky to have come across a level-headed girl like Kathie.

According to Mike, "She managed their finances as a couple, something my father, Maurice, had never been able to figure out on his own. She was smart and she made good investments. Once he was done with TV in Quebec and was forced to retire, she made sure he could live the rest of his life without working."

Maurice had always demonstrated flair for making the right decisions in the ring. But he lacked flair in the business world. He bought five acres of land he didn't need, a farm in Minnesota, condemned apartment buildings in Nebraska, a convenience store and a country house in Glen Sutton, Quebec — a house that would cause him many problems, mainly with his own family. And all that despite the fact he couldn't spend large sums without Kathie's prior approval. He even bought properties in Kathie's name, something she hated: this was also the only time she seriously thought of leaving him. Maurice definitely had no talent for business!

He had no understanding of the principles of investing, but he evidently could earn a living doing something other than professional wrestling.

He felt most comfortable in the world of mass communications. If truth be told, Maurice's experience as an interviewer in French for the WWF had been disastrous, but he had an incredible sense of comedic timing for the camera. He had charisma and he was an instantly recognizable public figure. In fact, he would make an ideal spokesperson.

He developed a very successful relationship with Labatt Breweries. He made good enough money to pay off the mortgage he and Kathie had taken out in 1983 to buy their home in Omaha, Nebraska. There is an old adage: "A lady who takes a husband adopts his country." But the opposite was true in Maurice's case, because he was the one settling with Kathie in her hometown.

In the early 1980s in Quebec, Maurice did a Labatt Lite commercial with two other wrestlers, André the Giant and Little Beaver, before becoming the company's sole spokesman. At the end of these ads, done for the French market only, Maurice would say: "You don't need a dictionary to get the point." The French version of this ad slogan is still a popular expression across Quebec to this day, to point out that something is so evident that a dictionary would be pointless.

The ads were so popular that on October 5, 1985, Maurice was invited to the première of a Saturday evening comedy show similar to Saturday Night Live, *Samedi de rire*. The show, hosted by Quebec's most popular stand-up comic of all time, Yvon Deschamps, reached cult status and was broadcast by Radio-Canada, the French network of the CBC, early on Saturday evenings, just before hockey games featuring the Montreal Canadiens.

Maurice played in several skits. Reciting verse by the French Renaissance poet Ronsard might have sounded like a good idea to scriptwriters, but it was easier said than done. But a scene with Deschamps, two other actors, and future singing superstar Céline Dion — then just seventeen — was a huge success. Céline had viewers in stitches when she imitated Maurice's gravelly voice, and Maurice sang a modified version of Céline's hit song, "Une colombe."

The critics were fairly harsh, especially *La Presse*, who described Maurice's performance in these terms: "Mr. Vachon is funny but only in small doses, such as TV commercials, where the script calls for him to say just one sentence. But when he has more dialog than that, he gets all flustered and simply can't deliver." This appraisal might seem to have been unkind, but it was accurate. As subsequent events would show, Maurice had a hard time learning his lines.

But Maurice had fond memories of the comedy show. "Actually, appearing on that Saturday evening show opened the doors of show business to me." Despite the thumbs-down from the critics, a star was born.

Maurice wasn't getting any younger. He was just beginning to discover new talents for himself, so he started thinking about retirement. He still loved getting reactions from the crowd, he loved the sport, but his body was no longer up to the challenge. Kathie wasn't exactly complaining about his decision to retire, although she had no role in his decision.

After talking things over with his son Mike, Maurice decided to organize a grand farewell tour of the province of Quebec in the summer of 1986, working with Michel Longtin, his longtime manager. He couldn't have known at the time that his appearance on the Saturday evening comedy show would open the floodgates to the second career he had been longing for.

"My agent and I are preparing a big tour throughout Quebec that will take us to about sixty cities. It will be a non-profit tour wherever possible. My little sister Vivian will be there: she's coming back from Germany and hasn't been in Canada for the last ten years. Gustave the Giant will be there too: he has bigger hands than André the Giant and is simply the biggest French Canadian on the face of the Earth. We want to hold a big show in Quebec City and one more in Montreal so I can finally retire. If you want your city to be added to the tour, contact Promotions Grand Prix 86," he added with a wry smile on many talk shows in Quebec.

Between June and October, the tour ultimately held shows in forty cities, with three or four shows a week. They were sold to the local arena or an organization in the region for around $5,000. Maurice cleared about $300 per show, the remainder being used to cover various expenses and pay other members of the troupe. The tour didn't make a fortune, but the Vachons created a nice family atmosphere. Vivian made a wrestling comeback, Mike served as referee, Paul was the ring announcer, and Maurice's children Stéphan, Jean-Pierre, and Denis all played a role. Unfortunately, these last two didn't stay with the troupe very long. Even Kathie played along, selling popcorn. The wrestlers had a good time together, but sharing life on a daily basis with so many people was hard on Kathie and Maurice's children. In addition, some nights the troupe stayed in Maurice's mother's house in the Eastern Townships, a house that saw up to eighteen people sleep over one night!

The tour was a resounding success, drawing on wrestlers like Armand Rougeau (as Maurice's teammate), Richard Charland, Gino Brito Jr., Georges Guimond, Little Beaver, Sailor White, and Sky Low Low. International Wrestling served as the agent for several wrestlers and promoted the shows in Quebec City and Montreal under their banner.

Maurice helped other Quebecers right up to the end of his career. He now gave a helping hand to Armand Rougeau's career. Armand was Jacques Sr.'s son and the latest Rougeau family member to enter the wrestling world. During the tour, Maurice often teamed up with Armand, who learned a lot from Mad Dog.

"I loved him so much; we had lots of fun together," Armand later recalled. "We even roomed together. I am definitely the member of the Rougeau family who knew him the best. He was a remarkable human being. He taught me a lot about how to behave outside the arena, how to react when people challenge you in a bar, how to conduct interviews, and how to enjoy life on the road. My brother Raymond taught me half of everything I know about wrestling, and Maurice taught me the other half. I applied this knowledge later on dealing with promoters."

The best way to ensure the tour's success was to get people talking about it on TV. Maurice had above all to be front and center on TV if people were going to come out in any numbers to see him one last time. Michel Longtin, the promoter and intermediary, had the talent and drive to make things happen, transforming the image of Mad Dog in the eyes of Quebecers.

"Longtin did the rounds and sold Mad Dog to the media," Mike says. "My father always took the time to talk to people even when he was late. In a way people paid him back a hundred times over for showing them so much respect over the years. His retirement could have been rushed. Longtin was the magic ingredient that had been missing. He believed in my father more than my father believed in himself."

The marketing campaign for Maurice's farewell tour was multi-faceted. Nothing was considered impossible. Everything imaginable was tried out. Maurice even sang some rap music in French. His brothers Paul and Guy, his sister Diane, and their parents were all known for their singing talents, but not Maurice. He didn't need to be an opera singer when the music was a tongue-in-cheek rap song for marketing purposes. The song was simply called "The Mad Dog Rap." It was played on the radio to some extent. It served mainly to get Maurice onto variety shows. Composed and produced by the producer Denis Pantis, a big fan of Maurice's, and Pierre Gervais, the song completely changed what ordinary people thought about Mad Dog the "brutal" wrestler.

Unknowingly, Maurice was following in the footsteps of one of his own fans, the late singer Prince. Growing up in Minnesota Prince had often watched AWA television in the years when Maurice was regularly wrestling there. In an interview, Prince admitted he developed his unique voice by imitating Mad Dog. One day, a radio host asked about this. Maurice — a man never to be shy about his opinions — shot back: "I don't like Prince's music. I actually prefer Bing Crosby and Quebec's own Fernand Gignac!"

The lyrics of "The Mad Dog Rap" were relatively easy to learn and they were catchy. At least in French, they were!

My name is Mad Dog, you know me.

Don't need nobody to introduce me.

I'm looking forward to meeting you

One last time in your neighborhood.

Now you know the truth, I always loved wrestling.

I'm moving on: to big-time singing.

Watch out, Springsteen, Fernand Gignac,

Mad Dog's coming to give you a whack.

Becoming a rock star ain't bad . . .

And it doesn't hurt that bad!

Issued as a 45 rpm single, the song sold 17,000 copies.

Mike recalls: "I heard that song so many times during the farewell tour that if I never hear it again I'll be happy." Kathie says the same, even though she never understood the original French lyrics. The song played wall-to-wall during every second of the farewell tour when nobody was in the ring. This was high adventure and Maurice couldn't help seeing the funny side of it all: "I never thought I would make a record, and now that I've made one, I don't think I will ever make another!"

Maurice the rapper left an indelible mark in the minds of Quebecers, thanks to popular TV appearances on many well-known programs such as *Ad Lib*, *Showbizz*, *Star d'un soir*, and *Via Québec*. Maurice had dreamed forever of doing comedy one day, and now he was in his element. On the morning program *Café Show*, Maurice even cooked his favorite dessert, a peanut butter pie.

He had a natural talent for this type of show. He knew how to adapt his style to get into back-and-forth verbal sparring that was all improvised just like a wrestling match. And he always came out the winner.

The most amazing aspect of Maurice's new career was when

he became Michel Jasmin's gourmet inspector on TV. Jasmin, who had been one of Quebec's most popular late-night television hosts, had a new show airing in the afternoon in Quebec City. The two men developed a strong bond, displaying an innate mutual understanding. They played the role of food critics, crisscrossing Quebec to shoot funny TV spots for *Via Québec*, Jasmin's show on Channel 4. Maurice performed well and his kidding style really got across to viewers, whether he was critiquing fast food or haute cuisine.

"Maurice wasn't too sure about things at first, but I reassured him: I told him I would help him along with his comeback lines," Jasmin recalls. "When he was uncomfortable with something, we would work around it. After the very first spot, people would come up to him in the street and talk to him about the inspector. It was an instant success, and he just loved it."

The two men worked together in a very unusual way: the spots were shot in the evenings and Maurice got to take a little nap while technicians were setting up the lighting and sound gear! Jasmin and the production crew had an infallible technique for waking Maurice up. They would ask him if wrestling was all fake! Maurice almost always bolted awake, in a very shocked state. Once he calmed down, he would remain awake during the entire shoot.

The chemistry between the two was really perfect. When Jasmin made a comeback in Montreal with *Jasmin Centre-Ville* (*Jasmin Downtown*) on a new TV station, Channel 35, Maurice was part of the cast, acting as a butler escorting the guests onto the show. He was Jasmin's version of what Ed McMahon was on *The Tonight Show* with Johnny Carson. Jasmin quickly dreamed up this idea because it gave Maurice the chance to barge into interviews, injecting regular doses of humor. For the station, Maurice was an important acquisition: on September 7, 1986, he took part in the launch of the station's first season.

The connection with Jasmin played a decisive part in Maurice's

TV career: it moved him from star status to superstar status, something he had secretly hoped to do for a long time. "If I hadn't been a wrestler, I would have been an actor," he once confided to his second wife, Nicole. With Jasmin's help, he developed his character for the show and perfected the timing of his improvisations. The province of Quebec discovered the man behind Mad Dog.

"Like everybody else," remembers Jasmin, "I thought of him as a Mad Dog, a guy full of rage and totally out of control. So when I met him, I realized he was human, deeply human, and also very open-minded. We were shooting and people would come up to talk to him, so we would stop the shoot and he would speak with people."

Jean-Pierre Coallier, the host of *Ad Lib*, has a similar story to tell. "The wrestler and the man were two completely different people. He was a gentleman, extremely nice and delicate. He was always good to me and my audience. In the 1960s, when I announced wrestling shows on Channel 10, I realized it was different to have wrestlers right there with you in the same room. I was a little surprised, but I realized Maurice wasn't going to pull my shirt off. If you scratched him up, you would find a heart of gold! He was a no-brainer to be featured on our show, and he left no one indifferent."

On air, Jasmin never referred to Maurice as Mad Dog: he always called him by his first name. This was an important step towards making the public more aware of the person. In fact, Jasmin did exactly for Maurice on TV what the latter had already done for so many others in wrestling: he took the wrestler under his wing and gave him the boost he needed to start his second career.

"I think the greatest talent Maurice had in terms of TV was the confidence he placed in the people around him. He trusted them completely," Jasmin added.

Throughout his wrestling career, Maurice had been accustomed to entrusting his body to his opponent in the ring. This was the one place where you really had to trust the person facing you. So trust was a quality he had known about for a long time.

During this period, Maurice was even more present in the media in Quebec City than in Montreal. In addition to his television appearances, he landed a job on the radio. He was the star guest on CHOI-FM's morning show, also taking part in skits. The station was then trying to compete with Quebec City's single most popular radio show on CJMF. This was just like wrestling: there were no rehearsals and everything was live. This explains the charm of the show. Unfortunately, the experience only lasted a few months because the ratings weren't any good. Not everyone in Quebec City wanted to wake up on weekday mornings to Mad Dog's gruff voice!

During this period, the Keystone electronics store in Quebec City used Maurice excessively as spokesman, with two new ads every month (there would be about thirty in total). Maurice's ads made him so popular that he lectured in Quebec City as an advocate of nonviolence in Quebec schools.

"I love children. If I am able to do my part and make a contribution, by talking to young children and getting them to think twice, then I will."

Several other companies took advantage of Maurice's instant recognition factor. Ultramar, General Motors, and the chain of sports restaurants La Cage aux Sports all hired him as a spokesman. Maurice was so well-known to the public that he made the cover of the Quebec humor magazine *Croc* (something like *Mad Magazine* in the United States).

The sustained public campaign accompanying Maurice's farewell tour was simply unprecedented in Quebec wrestling. He was down to his last two matches, the first on October 8 at the Quebec City Coliseum, and the second on October 13 at the Paul Sauvé Arena in Montreal.

"At the end of the tour, he said he couldn't take it any longer, he was too tired," remembers Mike. "Promotion for the show started at 8:00 a.m. in the morning. By the time he finished his match that evening, he had been on the run for ten or twelve hours. He was tired but he still loved it. It was a perfect end to his career."

One is tempted to assume that with Maurice's maturity and wealth of experience, he could get through the tour without incident. But he still had a problem controlling his impulses, especially when he had been drinking. One evening after a show in Carleton County, New Brunswick, Maurice was having a drink with the other members of the troupe when he sucker punched a man who questioned the legitimacy of wrestling. So Maurice still had a way to go on the personal level.

With Maurice's last matches, International Wrestling managed to draw some of its last good crowds: when Maurice wrestled at the Quebec City Coliseum, the stands were one-third full; he drew a crowd of 3,200 spectators in Montreal. The problem wasn't him — it was wrestling. In October 1986, only the WWF managed to draw fans in droves. Maurice's fans would say they could continue seeing him on television in any case.

The idea for the Montreal match was to revive the kind of crowd passions stirred up by the famous match of 1973. Killer Kowalski came up from Boston to serve as referee for a match pitting the team of Jos Leduc and Maurice against Gilles Poisson and Man Mountain Moore, the same match held in Quebec City for that matter. Gilles Poisson knew he had only one thing to do in these last two battles against Maurice: he had to make his mentor look good. Poisson had volunteered to be part of the matches and Maurice in turn had asked for Jos Leduc as a partner. Moreover, right after the match in Montreal, the TV cameras captured an interesting conversation between two living legends:

"It was a pleasure being on the same team as you," Jos told Maurice. "This was the first time, and unfortunately it's going to be the last time."

"We should have teamed up a long time ago," Maurice replied.

"My favorite opponent was Jos Leduc," Maurice later said in an interview. "He was definitely one of the biggest drawing cards in all of wrestling."

Before turning the page on his career, Maurice spoke in a spirit of serenity: "I have represented my country at the Olympics, because I love wrestling, and today is my last day and I still love my job. When I look back, I wonder how I managed to get over all the bad luck I had throughout my career."

A new career was dawning for Maurice, and a lot of people believed he would enjoy success for many more years. Maurice wanted above all to please the fans. Whether he was in the world of wrestling or of entertainment, the same root impulse was at work.

"My real boss is the public. People use us to vent all the frustrations they encounter in their everyday lives. When they go to the matches, they scream like hell. They're releasing their safety valves. I've always given the fans more than their money's worth. People often ask whether I am good or bad. I've always been on one side — the winning side."

There was no way he could know it, but the biggest battle of his life lay just ahead. It would be an unfair fight, and it would literally change the course of his life. His last victory would cost him dearly.

MAURICE CHEATS DEATH, PART THREE

Maurice met with resounding success on Quebec's show-business scene during 1986 and the first half of 1987. But on October 9, 1987, fate suddenly intervened and changed everything.

Towards the end of the year, Maurice had several new projects lined up, including a play and a children's program that would see Maurice playing the role of a pirate. With October 5 coming up, Kathie wanted the couple to reunite in Omaha to celebrate their sixth wedding anniversary. Maurice had been spending a lot of time in Quebec getting his second career going, particularly in his home in Glen Sutton, while Kathie stayed in Nebraska working. They were both pursuing careers, which meant they didn't have a lot of personal time together. Their wedding anniversary was an ideal time to meet up. During Maurice's stay in the Midwest, the couple decided to spend a few days with Kathie's sister Susan, in Des Moines, Iowa, just east of Nebraska.

The fateful morning of October 9 started like any other.

"I heard him down in the kitchen," Kathie said in the days

following the accident. "He made some noise and I thought he was making coffee before reading the paper and watching early morning news on TV. When I came downstairs, he had already left. I knew he had gone for his daily walk and I expected to see him again in two or three hours as usual."

But Maurice made a decision that morning that changed the course of his life. Around 6:30 a.m., when Maurice decided to go for his walk, it was still dark. He knew the area well and usually walked along the service road of Interstate 80. He had been running since the London Olympics of 1948, but by the mid-1980s his knees had gotten so bad he had switched to long walks. City workers had put a layer of new crushed gravel down and the ground was too soft, so he decided to walk right in the middle of the road.

At more than forty miles per hour, a 1977 Ford LTD hit him hard. Maurice was thrown to the ground, unconscious.

The driver was Fred J. Fackler, a fifty-nine-year-old resident of Des Moines with a history of mental health problems. He didn't stop to assist Maurice and left the scene of the accident. He drove on to a house and told the occupants he thought he had hit a deer on the roadside. He didn't wait for the police to arrive, and he didn't return to the scene. Instead he went to a little diner nearby — a truckers' hangout.

The inhabitants of the house immediately called 911. When paramedics arrived on the scene, Maurice was conscious, but he obviously had a concussion. Since he had just gone out for a walk, he didn't have his wallet or any ID. He couldn't remember his sister-in-law's phone number. But he managed to tell the paramedics his brother-in-law was Larry Dawson and worked at the post office. At 7:18 a.m., the ambulance took him to Broadlawns Medical Center in Des Moines.

He arrived there in serious condition, with an open fracture on the left leg, a head laceration, a concussion, a badly bruised right leg, a few other bruises, and unbearable pain.

Meanwhile, Maurice's brother-in-law reached Kathie at her sister's place. She headed straight for the hospital.

The medical center had no trauma unit, so the doctor on duty, Dr. Julie Wood, consulted the orthopedist on call, Dr. Thomas McClain, and both concluded Maurice needed to be transferred to the University of Iowa Hospital in Iowa City where McClain worked most of the time. This was the only place in the entire state able to treat the kind of trauma Maurice had just experienced. However, the orthopedist didn't even bother to examine Maurice in person and based his decision solely on the written report describing his injuries.

No medical helicopter was available. Maurice was transported by ambulance with the siren switched off. After two hours on the road, the ambulance reached Iowa City at 11:05 a.m. On arrival, he was examined and evaluated, then sped on to the operating room for surgery on the compound fracture of his left leg. It was during this first operation that Dr. James Nepola, one of the surgeons operating, noticed something abnormal about his right leg.

A group of muscles, vessels, and nerves are contained in the fascial envelopes in the upper and lower limbs. In the event of trauma — for example, when a person gets hit by a car — the pressure inside this compartment gradually increases within a few hours. This is called compartment syndrome, which is a conflict between the content (the muscles and neurovascular system) and its container. This increase in pressure on the affected limb requires a medical intervention, called a fasciotomy, which involves making an incision in the fascia, the fibrous membrane surrounding the muscle. The fasciotomy reduces pressure. This is an emergency procedure and should be practiced six to eight hours after the accident. Late detection, as in Maurice's case, can lead to nerve and muscle necrosis. Maurice showed no clinical symptoms that would allow for diagnosis. But he felt unusually severe pain — one of the symptoms of compartment syndrome.

"I didn't believe a human being could endure so much suffering and yet survive. I felt like I was dead — dead a million times over."

This type of injury must be diagnosed quickly to improve the patient's chances of recovery, but even then, it is hard to treat the patient even once a fasciotomy is performed. The patient is susceptible to several kinds of infection after surgery.

The test to detect compartment syndrome only takes a few minutes. But the problem in Maurice's case was that the Broadlawns Medical Center hadn't performed the test, and even once he reached Iowa City the test wasn't performed right away.

For once in his life, Maurice was sure he was about to die. He was so desperate he asked his wife to bury him in the family plot in Quebec, next to his father's grave.

Thanks to Dr. Nepola's observation, the doctors finally performed the fasciotomy — the last operation of the day — at around 5:00 p.m. Maurice would have to undergo a total of seven operations, including five during his first week in the hospital.

Kathie was told everything was going well and Maurice's right leg would be saved, so she returned home to Omaha to take care of things. On October 15 at 11:00 p.m., she got an unexpected call from her sister Susan saying Maurice would have his right leg amputated the following morning. The fasciotomy had been performed too late and the tissues were already dead. And if Maurice's leg wasn't amputated, he could contract gangrene, a kind of necrosis caused by critically insufficient blood supply that spreads in the body and can kill the patient. The only option was to amputate the affected limb before the onset of gangrene.

So, on October 16, the surgeons amputated his right leg just below the knee. Maurice didn't want to die: he preferred to keep fighting, even if it meant he was missing a good part of his right leg. His left leg was healing, meanwhile, thanks to a skin graft.

It had been a week of hell for Maurice, and he told reporters about his desperate ordeal. "I have never experienced such a terrifying experience in my life," he said. "This is terrible. Worse than death. What I felt into my soul and in my mind was incredible."

Journalist François Ferland went on to say Maurice was a superman for showing such courage during the ordeal. But Maurice told him he had been affected by this accident and would never be the same man again.

His family was stunned to see how resilient he was. They had no doubt Mad Dog would pull through. "I can't believe it. What fortitude!" Michel Longtin said, over and over. Maurice's son Mike added: "If I were him, I wouldn't be able to get over it, but he's different: he won't let anything destroy him."

But things weren't quite as they seemed. Maurice had a long way to go.

Kathie took the accident just as hard as Maurice did, and she admired the moral courage he showed in adversity.

"He accepts much better than I do what has happened to him," she told reporter Mario Brisebois. "When the doctors told him the facts, it just broke his heart. He was silent about the way he felt but you could read his emotions on his face. But since then, he has impressed me. He accepts his fate. And he insists he has always fought to succeed in life and he will continue fighting on his remaining leg. Even though he is going through hell, I can assure you he is in excellent spirits."

In large part, Maurice found the courage to survive because Kathie loved him. "Before his leg was amputated, he asked me if I accepted the situation, if our marriage would be affected forever by this disaster. It was normal for him to speak to me like that. The question was bound to come up during an ordeal like this. If I were him, I would react the same way. I would also wonder whether my spouse would continue loving me and wanting me. When he spoke to me about that, I told him nothing would change."

The accident led to a media saga that is hard to explain to people living outside Quebec. Kathie often said Maurice was as well-known in Quebec as Johnny Carson in the United States. The province transformed Mad Dog, the terror of the wrestling ring, into a national hero who was fondly remembered. In 1987, Réjean Tremblay summed up the situation in the Montreal daily *La Presse*:

> Quebecers aren't sharing the misfortunes of a former gold medalist at the Commonwealth Games. We aren't giving our total support to the former professional wrestler — one of the best in the business. No, we are supporting a sincere and honest man in his fight against gangrene — a man whose commitment to the vocation of acrobat in the ring has earned our respect. People know the difference between what's genuine and what's phony. Sometimes it takes more time but people end up recognizing the difference.

During Maurice's close to two-month stay in the hospital in Iowa City, he received more than 40,000 letters of support from across Canada and the United States. Maurice was alone in a double room, but he ran out of room with all the bouquets of flowers fans sent him!

The hospital staff showed him exemplary kindness and devotion, and they often wondered who this patient could be, who received phone calls or telegrams from the likes of Canadian prime minister Brian Mulroney; Montreal mayor Jean Doré; the leader of the

New Democratic Party (NDP), Ed Broadbent; the president of the Montreal Canadiens hockey club, Ronald Corey; Hulk Hogan; and WWF officials. This was before the era of emails and text messages! Jos Leduc told the weekly magazine *Échos-Vedettes* he would have gladly given his own leg if it meant saving Maurice's leg: Mad Dog had helped him launch his wrestling career around the world. Mad Dog was his idol.

Verne Gagne made a long tribute to Maurice during his TV show. "I have known Mad Dog since 1948, when he represented Canada in the Olympics. There is no tougher man alive than Mad Dog Vachon. The most unpredictable man I have ever met in my life. Like a few other wrestlers, I bear scars on my body that were dealt to me by Mad Dog. He is an intense man and a competitor who goes all the way. In everything he does or promises, he can deliver the goods. He is a man of his word and I respect him a lot. I wish him the best of luck during this ordeal."

In Quebec and elsewhere, many people gave him their support during events like the Défi Mark Ten International strongman contest, hockey games, and other sports events. But individuals weren't the only ones to show their support. The Quebec Nordiques hockey team sent him a jersey signed by the entire team. Thanks to Jim Fanning, coach of the Montreal Expos baseball team, Bob Oldis, the Expos scout in Iowa, accommodated Paul Vachon and Kathie in his home. Fanning had become friends with Maurice during various activities organized by the Labatt Brewery, an Expos sponsor.

"It was as if the very moment Maurice fell, the entire country came to help him stand up again," Paul Vachon said a few years later.

In the months following the accident, Maurice said: "This tidal wave of affection from Canada was beyond my expectations. I also want to take the opportunity here to thank the people of Quebec for the thousands of cards and letters of encouragement I received. Without your support, I am convinced I might not have been able to get through this ordeal. *Thank you.*"

This was quite an admission from a man who projected the public image of a superman throughout his career.

Several journalists went to Iowa to meet Maurice and get his comments during the ordeal. He even shot a commercial for Keystone from his hospital bed. The University of Iowa Hospital had all the equipment and facilities Quebec journalists needed to conduct their interviews. The Keystone ad campaign called on Maurice's services more than any other company. He needed to continue earning a living, so doing the ads seemed natural.

Maurice was recovering in hospital, without much income, receiving private care costing several tens of thousands of dollars, since his Canadian public health insurance didn't cover his stay in the United States. At first the Quebec government took the position he was not a Quebec resident and therefore not eligible for government assistance. Michel Jasmin, who had also recovered from a serious road accident, had begun working with Labatt to launch a fundraising campaign in the event the Quebec government did nothing to help Maurice. Jasmin got help from Kathie to line up a trail of documents proving Maurice had lived only five days in the United States in the year preceding the accident. His Canadian taxes were all paid, and since 1986 Maurice had lived most of the time in Glen Sutton, Quebec. With all this information in hand, the SAAQ (the publicly funded Quebec Automobile Insurance Corporation) reimbursed the costs of his stay and hospital care in Iowa, which amounted to $62,000 in 1986. Without this government intervention, it goes without saying that Maurice would definitely have had to file for bankruptcy again. All the Quebec government asked in return was that he did his rehab in Quebec.

However, this posed a new problem. Given his condition, what was the fastest and safest way to bring Maurice back to Canada? Once again, his friend Michel Jasmin found the solution. With the help of Prime Minister Mulroney, federal energy minister Marcel Masse, and the president of Blue Cross, Jasmin got the oil company Petro-Canada to fly him home by private jet. Petro-Canada was going to sponsor the 1988 Calgary Olympics, and as a former Olympian Maurice qualified for their help. Maurice would carry the Olympic flame a few months later, on its way out to Western Canada.

"My father told me that by competing in the Olympics, people would remember me for the rest of my life," Maurice said.

On November 21, Maurice took the plane from Iowa City to Montreal, accompanied by Michel Jasmin, Michel Longtin, Éric Fournier of the Channel 35 station, and a nurse.

"When I got on the plane, Maurice began to cry like a baby," said Jasmin. "He was so happy to see me and happy about what we had done for him. That day marked me for the rest of my life."

Long before, Maurice had returned home from London and Auckland in relative anonymity. This time, in November 1987, Mad Dog Vachon returned to a hero's welcome at Dorval Airport, where a crowd cheered him.

"I'm really happy to be back in Canada and Quebec. I think this must be the best day of my life," he said during an impromptu press conference once he got off the plane. Although Maurice had a heavy heart, he was the very image of strength and courage. He was met at the airport by his family, friends, former wrestlers, Marcel Masse, Petro-Canada vice-president Gaston Beauregard, and the federal minister of state for fitness and amateur sport, Vincent Della Noce.

Maurice underwent rehab at the Lucie-Bruneau Rehabilitation Center. Michel Jasmin was spokesman for this renowned institution and got a big hand from managing director Jacques-Gilles Laberge internally to make things easier for Maurice. Mad Dog described his recovery as a long journey through the desert, a journey with both ups and downs. At the time, Michel Jasmin was one of his closest confidants.

"I experienced the same thing in 2005. You know, a person never accepts an amputation. It is something you just have to deal with. Maurice told me: 'I have made my living using my body, and I'll end my life without one limb.' It's clear that with this accident, the Big Man upstairs picked the wrong guy!"

Maurice was no spring chicken, and the many injuries he had sustained slowed the progress of his physical therapy. Rehab isn't easy and involves a lot of suffering. But Maurice realized there was hope and anything was possible when he met a double amputee worse off than he was.

By February 1988, his left leg had recovered completely and the screws were removed. There was talk of his doing a daily show called *The Adventures of Mad Dog the Pirate*, plus other projects such as writing an autobiography, opening a restaurant chain, and returning to Jasmin's TV show the following spring. But his amputated right leg still had an open wound and he continued to suffer a lot. He would suffer from phantom pain the rest of his life. Maurice didn't manage to get back onto his friend Jasmin's show. But Jasmin has many wonderful memories from this period and will always be proud of his association with Maurice.

The harsh and even sad reality was that for Maurice, life had to continue. In fact, he would return to his first love: professional wrestling . . .

DEAL OR NO DEAL?

The WWF organized a tour that brought Maurice to cities where he was still a big attraction; Denver, Minneapolis, Omaha, Milwaukee, Winnipeg, Chicago, Toronto, and Montreal would get to see Mad Dog Vachon take his first steps in public after the operation. You can amputate a wrestler's leg and put him out of commission, but you can't take away wrestling from a wrestler.

On March 14, 1988, Maurice drew a crowd of 18,000 spectators for a great evening at the Montreal Forum. In the final match, Hulk Hogan and Bam Bam Bigelow faced André the Giant and Ted DiBiase. Maurice got a thunderous standing ovation. This was the first time he got up from his wheelchair and walked a few steps in front of his fans, and he was deeply moved. The fans loved and admired him, and, hero-like, he paid them back with his determination and courage. The WWF did things with style. The Canadian national anthem was performed to underline his status as an Olympian. His mother, then aged eighty-two years, was at ringside beside her son. Paul Vachon and several other family members were also present, as well as TV personalities and several wrestlers like Bob Langevin, Ovila Asselin, Jos Leduc, and Omer Marchessault. Gino Brito, promoter at the time in Montreal, presented Maurice with a TV set and a WWF plaque. This would be Maurice's last time as the star attraction at the Montreal Forum, and he really delivered. His eyes brimming with tears, a stifled sob in his throat, he called out to the crowd that he would "always be a wrestling fan."

Just as the promotion for this new tour got under way, newspapers reported that Maurice and his wife were suing the State of Iowa, Broadlawns Medical Center, and Drs. Julie Wood and Thomas McClain for one million dollars. The suit held them all responsible — but above all Dr. McClain — for failing to test Maurice for compartment syndrome. In addition, the couple questioned the fact that Maurice was sent to the hospital in Iowa City, whereas two other hospitals in Des Moines — Mercy and Methodist — were just ten minutes away from the Broadlawns Center. Following the advice of their lawyers, Maurice and Kathie refused an out-of-court settlement of $125,000.

To everyone's surprise, the couple's lawsuit was dismissed in court on November 21, 1990, three years after Maurice's triumphant return to Montreal. The couple lost again on appeal in 1992, and a last time in 1994, when Maurice sought to sue the State of Iowa on the grounds that the test should have been performed when Maurice reached the university hospital, not after his operation. Michel Longtin was even called to testify about the financial losses that Maurice had sustained in Quebec following the accident, providing additional evidence of his status as a television star. In its final judgment, the court concluded the couple had possessed the medical record of the incident for more than two years and it was now too late to start new proceedings.

This setback stemmed from the fact that medical negligence

can't be invoked if it is based solely on a wrong decision being taken. Negligence can only be demonstrated where the doctor, in choosing a diagnosis and treatment, doesn't follow the proper procedure. In fact, the law was so confusing to jurors that it has since been amended.

Fred J. Fackler, the hit-and-run driver, was arrested minutes after the ambulance was called. He had no money or insurance, since at the time residents of Iowa didn't need insurance to drive a car. When Kathie tried reaching him by phone, she heard Fackler say he had heard Maurice wasn't doing too well, after which he hung up. He didn't even bother to turn up for his court appearance. He was eventually fined $114. The Vachons decided not to sue him. Maurice accepted the blame for the accident: he shouldn't have walked in the middle of the road. At the same time, he bore a grudge against the hospital: "They made a medical error and they committed a crime against me."

Maurice wasn't used to defeat, but he continued moving forward with the publication of his autobiography, co-written with Louis Chantigny. Like other wrestling books of the time, this rather short work protected the secrets of the profession. The book was launched to considerable fanfare on May 26, 1988, at the Metropolis in Montreal.

New projects began piling up, and they were increasingly varied. Once Maurice retired, there were newspaper reports of a fast food chain; this was the brainchild of lawyer Jean-Marc Béliveau, former head of the provincial party Union Nationale.

Mike recalls: "The idea was good, my father's name was instantly recognizable, and Béliveau convinced me. I told my father he had nothing to lose since he wouldn't have to put any money into the project."

The company was set up as "Mad Dog Burger Ltd." The original concept was to take existing restaurants and convert them into

Mad Dog Burger outlets. Each franchise cost $50,000, but when additional expenses were factored in, the cost was closer to $250,000. The decor was reminiscent of a wrestling arena and employees had to wear referees' uniforms. All franchises had to serve square hamburgers (in the shape of a wrestling ring) and a simple maple sugar pie. Otherwise, each franchise could offer what it liked. Maurice tried out a few different burger recipes before agreeing to associate his name with the chain.

Montreal had three franchises in all. The first was located at 223 Sainte-Catherine Street East. It opened on May 21, 1988, days before the launch of Maurice's autobiography. On November 1, 1988, a second franchise opened on Masson Street, and a third opened at Place d'Armes in October 1989.

In an interview, Maurice set the record straight about his involvement in the project: "I am not just lending my name. All important decisions concerning franchises will be made by me and nobody else. I want to prove that French Canadians are capable of great achievements. That's why I got started in the restaurant business."

Maurice failed to mention that Béliveau gave jobs to Mike and Paul. Both had space in the lawyer's office, but in practice they didn't work for him a single minute. Mike was paid $500 a week to do nothing and Paul got a rented car in the bargain, which he would keep for three years! As usual, Maurice bent over backwards to help his people. The little-known backstory of Mad Dog Burgers helps us to understand his decision.

Unfortunately, the chain completely disappeared about a year later. According to Pierre Garceau, CEO of the Quebec Franchise Council, the formula of restaurant franchises was all the rage in Quebec at the time. "Many athletes and artists lost a lot of money in ventures like this," he says.

In the only interview Maurice ever gave on the topic, he confirmed out loud what people closest to him felt deep down. "Béliveau was dishonest and he fooled me too. He convinced many people to invest their money. It was a very bad experience and many people lost a lot of money. The idea and name were good, but Béliveau wanted to make all the money."

In this respect, Maurice was not entirely wrong. A few years later, Béliveau would be disbarred as a lawyer for having "borrowed" $150,000 from the franchisees to finance an outside transaction that should have brought him $1 million.

On the positive side, in 1988 TQS finally launched the children's TV show *The Adventures of Mad Dog the Pirate*.

It is hard to imagine today that a children's show could be entrusted to a wrestler who once promised to kill himself if he didn't beat his opponent, but the character Maurice was now portraying was nothing like the rough-and-tumble wrestler back in the 1970s. He was now playing a pirate, captain of a submarine, who discovered the ship's hold was full of child prisoners. This discovery stirred him to leave his evil ways and devote himself entirely to providing children with love. He starred alongside a few child sailors and the chief engineer, the marionette Piston, played by Michel Ledoux.

Unfortunately, Maurice was still having a hard time recovering from his accident. He struggled to deliver on the set. Michel Ledoux recalls a typical day of shooting and explains why it was difficult for Maurice to learn his parts.

"It was weird. Maurice had just had surgery, and his memory wasn't so good with all the anesthesia. On set, he had to learn a page at a time. When he read through five pages of a scene, you had to explain to him what he had just learned. When the cameras started shooting, he would face one camera then another without noticing which camera was focused on him. He spoke facing whatever camera his instinct told him to face. The director adjusted to the situation by passing from one camera to the next. Except that Maurice forgot his lines. So when he was trying to remember what to say, the director Raymond Decary told me to improvise, to fill in the blanks, to say what he was supposed to say. I would improvise with Piston's voice: 'So if I understand correctly, my dear pirate, you want to tell me about a treasure buried on the beach.' He could have picked up where I left off. Instead, he started all over again. So we went past the allotted time and everything had to be done all over again. It took a lot of time. Seventy-five episodes with Maurice . . . But he was a really nice guy."

Clearly, Maurice was no longer able to manage in a competitive environment where time and money were everything. The production team tried everything, even providing him with an assistant to help him learn his lines, but they had to face the facts. It was too soon for Maurice to be back at work. He wasn't in good enough health for regular appearances on a children's show.

This would prove the end of his media career.

Maurice sometimes felt the world of wrestling was harsh, but TV wasn't much better. Quietly and discreetly, he retired from public life in Quebec, returning to Omaha with Kathie. He would continue to spend a few months a year in Canada, whether in Quebec or with his children in Windsor, Ontario.

He reappeared briefly in 1993 when he unsuccessfully tried to become the Liberal candidate in the federal election. His neighbor Donald Johnston, the former minister of justice, had suggested he make the run. But the Liberal Party did not feel that Maurice, with his gravelly voice and disability, was right for their plans. Politics, too, was a harsh world.

Maurice had already sought medical advice about his voice, which had been an asset in the wrestling ring but was now a liability in politics . . .

"I once went to see two specialists in the United States. I thought I had throat cancer. But no. They explained to me that my vocal cords weren't working normally, and it was probably because of the many blows I took on the larynx. Besides, they told me I had papilloma on my vocal cords."

Maurice's media career was short but intense. He took the bull by the horns and soon became an attraction the media were all fighting over. Tragically, the car accident in Iowa brought this exciting time of his life to an abrupt end.

After the accident, Réjean Tremblay explained to English-Canadian media the special status Maurice enjoyed in Quebec: "We Quebecers love people when we can feel their sincerity . . . We call this kind of person 'genuine.' Mad Dog has reached the point in life where he is a fighter, like [former Quebec premier] René Lévesque during the last two years of his life. After the battles are done, we just want to keep hearing the stories, and we love the stories."

Maurice's media career was definitely over, but this wasn't the end of the road. Actually, it was the beginning of a new life.

23

THE ROAD TO HAPPINESS

Maurice found himself in a unique situation: he couldn't come out of retirement to take part in one last great match. For the first time since the end of his amateur career, he had completely broken away from wrestling. In quick succession, he mourned the end of his wrestling career, and then the loss of his leg cut short a promising public career. Maurice, however, was the kind of man who never said "die": he always fought for what he earned, and while fate might have imposed some limitations, there was no way he was going to give in. He preferred enjoying life and his family. Having his wife Kathie with him was definitely the best thing that could possibly happen to him at that time. For Maurice, retirement meant playing cribbage with his friends over a beer or a glass of Crown Royal, his favorite whiskey.

But his drinking complicated things. Maurice had always loved having a drink, but he was now in his sixties and he couldn't tolerate hard liquor the way he once could. Besides, he used alcohol to vent his frustrations. He might seem to be at peace, but deep down he was boiling. Kathie had to put up with his mood swings.

"Alcohol could spoil things for Maurice. I think he was an alcoholic," says Kathie.

He sometimes blamed his wife for the misfortunes that befell him. First off, the car accident wouldn't ever have taken place if she hadn't insisted on their spending their anniversary together in the United States. So Kathie was now his scapegoat, and she put up with it until the night Maurice punched her.

They had gone to a restaurant with a couple of friends, and there had been a lot of drinking followed by a pointless argument. Right in the middle of the street in full view of their friends, Maurice reacted to a comment Kathie made and struck her. She didn't flinch, she didn't fall, but back home, she told him to leave the house and return to Quebec to think over what he had just done. Kathie had experienced a violent relationship before marrying Maurice, and she flatly refused to live through another one. Maurice realized she was serious and he had to control his hot temper now that he could no longer count on wrestling to drain away his raw energy. When he came back, he promised her he would never drink alcohol again.

It was day and night for Maurice from that point on, and Kathie remembers the years that followed as the best of their relationship.

"I would gladly have taken another punch if it meant he would no longer touch alcohol," says Kathie now.

Maurice became more patient, nicer than ever. This was the exact opposite of everything alcohol had caused him to be. When he drank, he was rude and aggressive and he forgot a lot of things. One time he had come back from a tour in Alaska and he simply didn't have the slightest idea what he had done with his dentures. His decision in the early 1990s to abstain from alcohol brought on a new openness on his part to religion and the existence of a supreme being. For a long time, Maurice had rejected the notion of God, and in this he was like many other Quebecers who had been saturated with religion in their youth. Kathie was very religious, and she was glad to see her husband face life with greater serenity. He was born again; he experienced a spiritual renewal of his relationship with Jesus Christ.

Maurice was also a modern husband who did the cleaning, dried the dishes, cooked up a storm, and, according to Kathie, was the world champion when it came to folding towels. He liked simple food, such as shepherd's pie and baked beans with bacon. He also loved taking care of the yard — he really was in love with nature. Kathie was his lady love: he called her "angel" and his "better half." And Kathie wouldn't want to do anything to destroy his rough-and-tough image, but she remembers Maurice was extremely sensitive and expressed his love by writing letters and poetry. He was always ready to help, especially where children were concerned: their innocence and vital joy brought him great comfort.

One day, one of Kathie's friends working in an Omaha school asked whether the WWF would be willing to have a wrestler visiting the city come talk to the students about the dangers of drugs. Maurice had been out of touch with the WWF for a long time, but he got the WWF to send Fred "Tugboat" Ottman. He had always been generous and that would never change.

But there were also setbacks that changed life forever. In 1981, Ferdinand Vachon died of complications from Alzheimer's disease. Maurice was living at the time with Kathie in Winnipeg. He hated funerals and didn't like having to deal with his feelings and grief. His own father had never attended the funerals of even his closest friends. "My father always said, 'Why should I go? He won't be coming to my funeral,'" says Paul.

This was definitely a major loss for Maurice. His father had been his idol. It was for Ferdinand that Maurice had won a gold medal. For his part, Ferdinand had always shown great admiration for his son. Ferdinand was a born athlete and vicariously enjoyed Maurice's major exploits in sports, exploits he never could have pulled off himself.

"I once told my father: 'I was in the Olympics, I won championships, I did all of this for you, Daddy. In the bottom of your heart, I know you brought me to the YMCA because you loved me. You were setting me on the right path.'"

Ferdinand and Maurice had always had a very solid relationship, but in the end, Ferdinand could no longer recognize his own children. Maurice just bottled up his emotions and stayed away from the funeral.

In 1991, when his sister Diane (Vivian) died in a tragic car accident with her daughter Julie, Maurice found this all the more devastating because she had been the youngest in the family. He was still very proud of her achievements and reputation in wrestling. Funerals are often a way for the living to mourn and express their pain. They are a moment of catharsis that helps the living to recover. Maurice didn't cry and he couldn't bring himself to attend the funeral of his close relatives. He wanted to remember them the way they had been when alive, in the most positive light. Diane was no exception. In 1992, when his mother Marguerite died of natural causes, Maurice couldn't bring himself to attend her funeral either.

Mike recalls: "My father didn't like the way everybody cried and everybody is miserable. I am even surprised he attended his own funeral . . ."

These events took place just before Maurice started changing his relationship with alcohol and violence. He was coming to the end of a long personal process that finally taught him to better manage his emotional life and to enjoy retirement in peace.

Maurice was never rich. The end of his career had gone well and he was married to a woman who managed their finances wisely, so he wasn't in need. He had always liked the good things in life. He was a generous man who gave freely to others. For example, one day, he bought his sister Vivian a fur coat after seeing it in a shop window: he wanted to please her. He behaved the same way with strangers: he picked up the tab in restaurants or paid a round in bars. In his heyday as a wrestler, he bought animals for his parents' family farm, even though he didn't live there. Maurice sometimes wondered where all his money had gone, but he didn't fret about it because money didn't really matter to him.

Once Maurice had recovered sufficiently from the car accident, he jumped at the opportunity of reconnecting with his great love, wrestling. He loved seeing other wrestlers and fans, not to mention that he couldn't exactly turn down a good payday.

On May 23, 1993, WCW invited him to Atlanta for Slamboree, a pay per view event honoring wrestling legends. During the evening, he reconnected with Verne Gagne, Stu Hart, Greg Gagne, the Crusher, and Red Bastien. Maurice was interviewed by the voluptuous Missy Hyatt, who was startled by the intensity of his performance.

When you reach a certain age, you learn to be more patient. Slamboree rekindled his love of appearing in the spotlight, but it would take three long years before the wrestling world was talking about him again.

On April 28, 1996, he was the surprise guest on *In Your House 7: Good Friends, Better Enemies*, a PPV event presented by the WWF. This appearance was literally about to unleash a storm. World champion Shawn Michaels was defending his title against the villainous Diesel at a card held in the brand-new Omaha Civic Auditorium. After being introduced to the crowd, Maurice and other wrestling . legends sat in the front row to enjoy the show. Suddenly, Diesel — Kevin Nash — went up to Maurice and started launching into him.

Diesel outraged the fans by tearing off Maurice's artificial leg, using it to clobber Shawn Michaels. But Michaels managed to grab the limb and won the match by knocking Diesel out. Some fans and well-meaning souls have consistently vilified WWE for coming up with this idea, which they claim exploited Maurice and his disability. But in fact, Maurice was the one to come up with the idea of using the prosthesis as a weapon during a discussion with the office some time before. Maurice couldn't be pressured into doing something he didn't want to do. Besides, Nash and Michaels had meticulously rehearsed the scripted moves with Maurice earlier in the day, to make sure Nash removed the limb the right way. Maurice proved once again he was ready to give everything for the sake of a good wrestling show.

There is a tendency in wrestling to want to recreate key segments that have worked well in the past. So it should come as no surprise that Maurice would lose his "wooden leg" yet again. On May 31, 1998, Maurice and the Crusher were honored by the WWF in Milwaukee, on the pay per view show *Over the Edge*. They were awarded a plaque by the announcer Michael Cole. Suddenly, Jerry "The King" Lawler jumped into the ring and grabbed Maurice's artificial limb. But there was a very good reason he couldn't yank it off!

According to Lawler's biography, Vince ordered him over his headset to enter the ring and interrupt the ceremony. He was supposed to attack Mad Dog and remove his artificial leg, then clobber the two wrestling legends with it. The segment didn't seem well prepared and everyone was uncomfortable, especially the spectators. Initially, Lawler grabbed Maurice by the right leg, then by the left, and he obviously didn't know how to remove the artificial leg. The Crusher was now seventy-one and wasn't fast enough to react properly, and Maurice fell awkwardly once Lawler attacked, which made the segment far less entertaining than in 1996. Besides, there were consequences: Maurice got hurt and had a hard time sleeping for a few months. Sadly, this was the last time Maurice would appear in a ring.

Maurice didn't feel sorry for himself. He continued enjoying life and appearing at wrestling conventions. Thanks to these independent events, he picked up honors and played cribbage. Maurice had played the game with his father since childhood, like other members of his family. By pure coincidence, cribbage had also been the most popular game in the locker room during his wrestling career. At the time, promoters didn't like their wrestlers playing poker and rummy since they could lose considerable sums of money and would then need cash advances. Cribbage cost almost nothing and was easy to play at a time when wrestlers traveled by train and car. Maurice was considered a good player. He took the game too seriously sometimes, but he used cribbage to socialize with peers. At the very end of his life, despite his failing memory, he would continue to surprise his entourage by playing cribbage, keeping better track of the score than his opponents.

In 2003, the Cauliflower Alley Club (CAC) bestowed on him one of the most moving honors he ever got — the Iron Mike Mazurki Award. Founded in 1965 by former wrestler and actor Mike Mazurki, the CAC was an association of wrestlers, boxers, and stuntmen in Hollywood. It now comprises mostly wrestlers and through its annual convention in Las Vegas, it helps members with financial and other assistance. Maurice attended the convention regularly as long as his health permitted, and he held the organization in high regard right up to his death. Over the years, the CAC also honored his brother Paul, his sister Vivian, and his niece Luna. Attending the convention together as a family was a great experience: it was like traveling together in the old days. Maurice's acceptance speech in 2003 was one of the best interviews of his life, and it was very moving for people in the audience.

In 1999, a comic documentary about Maurice's career aired on the Comedy Network. Some of the filming took place in a church in Pointe-Saint-Charles, near the Montreal neighborhood where he grew up, and he attended a wrestling show there. It was a rare public appearance for Maurice in Quebec, particularly in this kind of setting, and Michel Piché the promoter brought in three times the usual number of fans.

In 2007, on a visit to Quebec to promote a documentary about the history of Quebec wrestling, Maurice talked about his life in retirement on the popular Radio-Canada show *Tout le monde en parle*, the most popular talk show in the province. The in-studio audience and TV viewers across Canada were happy to see Maurice finally enjoying the pleasures of life.

"I take care of my children, my grandchildren, and my great-grandchildren, plus I watch poker on TV," he said. The show host has a resident sidekick, Dany Turcotte, who put a question to Maurice that would have driven him into a fit a few years earlier: "Is wrestling all fake?" With his usual ready wit, Maurice invited him to the ring to find out whether it was fake or not . . . Turcotte then paid Maurice a tribute by offering one of his famous trademark cards, which read: "Joe Louis the boxer had his cake. Mae West the actress had hers. To immortalize you, I propose that Vachon Cakes create the 'Little Mad Dog': two solid parts filled with a tender and creamy heart in between." He couldn't have found a better way to describe Maurice.

Family life was now calmer and happier for Maurice, but there were downturns as well. In addition to his divorces, Maurice's children gave him cause for concern throughout his life. Some, like Denis and Jean-Pierre, resented their father's absence when they were little and eventually went to prison. Others remained aloof from him for several years for seemingly trivial reasons. Maurice also had seven grandchildren and nine great-grandchildren. As if a curse had stricken the family, the lives of his grandchildren weren't always easy: one of his grandsons went to prison, while one of his granddaughters was murdered at the age of seventeen. This was a true ordeal for Maurice. In 2010, his brother Paul's adopted daughter, Luna Vachon, also died. She had a husky voice and aggressive attitude in the ring just like Maurice, and many wrestlers and fans thought she was Mad Dog's daughter. She was very close to the brothers: "My father and my uncle mean a lot to me. When I was honored by the CAC, I was crying because they were both right there with me." For ten years Maurice hadn't been on speaking terms with Kathie's son but they finally reconciled in his last few years. Maurice told him straight out, "I love you, son." And it was as if the years of suffering both men had endured were suddenly wiped clean. Kathie would never forget those words.

In 2008, disaster struck again when Maurice lost the use of his left leg. After a fall, he had to undergo surgery to replace his left knee. He had to wait several months for the operation to be performed, and during these eight months of inactivity he stayed in Windsor, Ontario, with his daughter. In the meantime, his muscles atrophied: keeping the use of his leg muscles would have required him to do three physiotherapy sessions per week. At Maurice's age and in the absence of medical supervision, this was a lot to expect. He now had to use a wheelchair at all times and couldn't do anything without someone else's help. Every day, people came to care for him and his medical needs.

He made his last visit to Quebec in 2009, to promote the documentary *Mad Dog: The Man Behind the Beast*. This Quebec hero bore the ravages of time. Directed by Yves Thériault, the documentary humanized Maurice, showing him for the first time with a natural, uncut, white beard, not the stage beard that was dyed charcoal black. Deep inside, he seemed like the same person as ever. He did the rounds of the media, winning over a new generation of viewers with each appearance. In TV studios, he radiated an unusual kind of aura, and people found his presence riveting.

It was becoming increasingly difficult to interview Maurice on a subject because he often told the same old stories. It was around this time that doctors diagnosed him with dementia. The principal and most striking symptom is memory loss, especially in the short term, although some older memories remain vivid. Dementia made Maurice even quieter. Alzheimer's can be temporarily stabilized with medication, but nothing can be done for dementia. Concussions have become a big public issue in full contact sports. But in Maurice's day they weren't diagnosed, which definitely did nothing to help his condition. Maurice said he once didn't remember having wrestled the day before.

Also in 2009, Maurice was invited to an NCW show, a Montreal wrestling promotion, which welcomed him and his brother Paul to honor their achievements over the years. For the first time in over thirty years, they met up with Fernand Ste-Marie, the voice of Grand Prix Wrestling, during a moving evening rich in emotions that brought back nostalgic memories of a bygone era. For many viewers, it seemed like their youth was passing once again before their eyes. Maurice even gave a brief impromptu interview — definitely a crowd-pleaser.

"The name is 'Mad Dog.' I am Mad Dog Vachon. If you don't like my face, come and tell me to my face. Don't talk about me behind my back. I am Mad Dog Vachon and I approve this message."

Part of the proceeds from the event went to the Lucie-Bruneau Rehabilitation Center, where he had stayed during his convalescence and rehab in 1987 and then again during his last visit in his beloved homeland.

He was also invited for a guest appearance by the Montreal Canadiens, and the crowd cheered him one last time at the Canadiens' arena. His charisma and personality were still definitely intact, because fans lined up to take a photo with him or shake his hand.

During this last tour of Quebec, Maurice repeated several times that he had worked hard all his life to be hated: seeing the reaction of the fans, he realized he had failed to reach his goal.

But the most important reason for visiting his home province this time was to accept the highest honor for a Quebec athlete: induction into the Quebec Sports Hall of Fame. Founded in 1990, this institution aims to highlight the sporting achievements of Quebec athletes who have distinguished themselves on the international or national stage. Other inductees include Gary Carter, Louis Cyr, Jacques Villeneuve, Mario Lemieux, Patrick Roy, Maurice Richard, and Jean Béliveau.

"To be honored by this induction is both a tremendously moving experience and a real pleasure. The Mad Dog I played throughout my career has finally found his niche in this prestigious Hall of Fame," Maurice said with humility.

Yves Thériault had come up with the idea of the induction, timing it to coincide with the launch of his documentary. "It was relatively easy to convince the selection committee, given Maurice's amateur career," he said. "When I saw the reaction he got that night, I was happy for him, because I was seeing his health deteriorate and I had the feeling this would be his last visit to Montreal."

On November 9, 2009, Maurice became the second professional wrestler, and probably the last, to enter the pantheon of Quebec sports. Yvon Robert Sr., Maurice's model and idol, had been the first in 1992. Claude Raymond, former pitcher for the Expos, introduced Maurice during the evening and insisted Maurice was the genuine article. As in his best years, Maurice main-evented the evening and received a standing ovation. The undoubted highlight of the evening was when many stars came on stage to immortalize a moment with him. From diving Olympic bronze medalist Annie Pelletier to former Montreal Canadien Réjean Houle, everyone wanted to be photographed with him or simply shake his hand.

"I grew up in the east end of the city [of Montreal] and I regularly watched wrestling on TV with my father," said Pelletier, who thanked Maurice for all the memories going back to her youth. "He is a colorful and friendly man," said former hockey player and fellow Hall of Fame member Marc Tardif. The induction provided the Vachon family with one more opportunity to come celebrate with him: they were now scattered all over North America, and it was rare to get them all together. Maurice's induction into the Hall of Fame was his last chance to visit Quebec and to meet up with the entire Vachon clan and close friends. A large dinner was put on for family and friends.

Honors like this allow athletes like Maurice to gain the recognition they deserve for dominating their discipline. This was as true of Maurice in wrestling as it was of Maurice Richard or Jean Béliveau in hockey. Maurice had often said his gold medal at the Auckland Games was an honor that went straight to his heart, and Quebec continued to honor him the same way, straight to the heart, until the very end.

"I was impressed by his personality and his pride in being a Quebecer," said Yves Thériault. "A charismatic man, certainly one of the best people I have encountered during my career making documentaries."

Many might have considered this last trip to Quebec the last chance for wrestling fans to say goodbye, but the WWE paid him the ultimate tribute in 2010. At the request of Pat Patterson, Vince

McMahon agreed without hesitation to induct Maurice into the WWE Hall of Fame. Maurice was still healthy enough to travel and join in the festivities, which take place the day before *WrestleMania* each year. "It's a great honor. I am very proud. I always had a good relationship with Vince Jr. I can't wait to see my old friends, but also my old enemies," he said in an interview with *SLAM! Wrestling*.

On March 27, the Dodge Theater in Phoenix, Arizona, was packed full when Maurice was inducted into the Hall of Fame, joining the greatest wrestlers in history, like Hulk Hogan, Bret Hart, Steve Austin, Pat Patterson, Killer Kowalski, André the Giant, Verne Gagne, and Roddy Piper. Maurice had a short career with the WWE, but the promotion sought to honor all deserving members of the wrestling industry, not just stars whose years of glory had been primarily with the WWE.

For Patterson, it was important to honor Maurice publicly — while there was still time — and to say "thank you" in front of 70,000 spectators at *WrestleMania XXVI*. This was the biggest evening of the year for the WWE, and the veteran wrestlers honored the day before were now presented to the crowd. Without Maurice, Pat Patterson would never have existed, and he was not alone in this respect. This was also the last time Patterson would see his mentor. He remembers above all the pleasure he read in Maurice's eyes during the different activities in Phoenix.

"Maurice loved it to the hilt; he stayed in the hotel lobby, and people lined up to chat with him and get him to sign autographs."

Patterson was saddened to see Maurice showing such obvious signs of degeneration. He was now confined to his wheelchair, and Patterson had served as a guide during his speech, prompting him through his memories.

This was Maurice's last significant public appearance, because his health continued to deteriorate. In 2012, Kathie began turning down interview requests, since her husband was no longer able to engage in conversation. On the other hand, she would go with him once a year to participate in activities organized by the George Tragos/Lou Thesz Hall of Fame at the National Wrestling Hall of Fame in Waterloo, Iowa. That's where, in July 2013, Maurice Vachon made his last public appearance in the world of professional wrestling. During the traditional banquet, he received another standing ovation from the fans, but also, and especially, from his peers gathered for the occasion. Immediately afterwards, he told those closest to him: "Wow — what a feeling — it's still as impressive as ever." As if each testimony of love for him came as a complete surprise.

Throughout the weekend, he was all smiles. He proudly wore his *WrestleMania XXVI* cap. And despite his diminished faculties, he gave autographs or accepted to have his picture taken with fans.

"For me, my duty, my role, my job, my profession was to raise the crowd and give them their money's worth. So at this point, I guess I succeeded pretty well!"

The signs of disease were increasingly apparent: it was hard for him to sign his name.

A few months later, Quebec lost a larger-than-life hero, a man who had become a legend.

"I always thought he would live forever," Patterson says candidly.

Unfortunately, Maurice Vachon died peacefully in his sleep on November 21, 2013 — twenty-six years to the day after his triumphant return to Quebec.

Up to his very last breath, Maurice had an exquisite sense of timing . . .

THE PASSING OF A LEGEND

The man passed away, taking his qualities and faults with him. But the legend will be with us forever. His exploits will be glorified and he will be remembered at his best. A new generation who never knew Maurice, who never knew Mad Dog, will get to learn about him.

Maurice had the fiber of those exceptional beings who never accept their dreams are impossible, who refuse to let trials and weaknesses thwart their deep thirst for adventure in life. Maurice simply tried to be happy while doing what he wanted to do.

Maurice would often say, and quite rightly, "Professional wrestlers are the toughest men in the world. Men out of the ordinary. In life, we are constantly fighting against poverty, misery, and disease. Life is a constant struggle."

He left a stirring legacy in the world of wrestling and his peers spoke about him with eloquence.

"Maurice Vachon represented us Quebecers everywhere in the world. He proudly stood up for Montreal and Quebec wherever he went without ever playing the star. He was simply 'Mad Dog,'" says his most famous protégé, Pat Patterson.

"One of the pillars of this business. He can be compared to the greatest wrestlers like Lou Thesz, Buddy Rogers, and Bruno Sammartino. He is part of a highly select group in our midst. Despite his size, the world believed he could beat anyone. He was larger than life," says Raymond Rougeau.

"Maurice symbolizes the French Canadian who fears nothing. Despite all the problems I had with him, he represented me. Quebecers believed in him, because he was genuine," said Yvon Robert Jr.

"He was extremely hard-working. He had a good head for wrestling. His interviews were masterpieces. Can you imagine that in the WWE today? No, because he didn't need anyone scripting what he was going to say. He was the kind of fighter I idolized because of the way he used his time on television," says Terry Funk.

"You can't say you know anything about wrestling until you've seen an interview with Mad Dog Vachon," says former champion Ric Flair.

"He was a wrestling genius. He understood things before other people did — he knew how to make them work. I found him remarkable," adds Jim von Raschke.

"Maurice was the strongest one among us. In real life, he would have beaten us all one by one. In the arena, he was professional. He was a businessman doing his job. But if we did something he didn't like, he reminded us who he was. I loved him," said Abdullah the Butcher.

"Maurice Vachon built up the prosperity of several territories, giving them credibility through his style and presence. He earned the respect of fans both on the personal level and for pro wrestling in general. I'm not sure that wrestling would have continued on for generations without men like him. Without him, 'Rowdy' Roddy Piper would never have existed. I want you to put that in your book, and also that I really loved him," said Piper, speaking of the man he considered his father. Piper would meet death himself a short time after.

"The last time I saw him, he said he was proud to have contributed to my career. In twenty-five or thirty years, I am convinced we will still be talking about Maurice. Quebec will never forget him," says Armand Rougeau.

"Maurice's legacy is: you have to respect your profession, no matter what it is. He took wrestling seriously. You give 100%. You show respect for others and yourself," says Rick Martel.

"When I learned he had died, I couldn't really believe it. I didn't want to believe it. It was hard for me to accept. He was such a good friend. I loved Maurice," says Don Leo Jonathan.

"His death saddened me. He was really unique. I loved him a lot," said Nick Bockwinkel.

"Maurice was the greatest wrestler Quebec has ever known. I have to rank him ahead of Yvon Robert for the entire body of his work. In wrestling, Maurice carried the Quebec torch high. I've never been in a territory where the wrestlers didn't respect and admire Maurice," concludes Paul Leduc.

Paul Vachon's last meeting with his brother is etched in his memory: it took place in the last few years, when Paul stopped at Maurice's place during one of his many road trips. The brothers played cribbage, and throughout the day, Paul wasn't sure whether Maurice recognized him or not. Finally, when Paul was on the point of leaving, Maurice said, "I love you, brother!" This is the last memory Paul wants to keep of his "big" brother.

It's true Maurice was a wrestler and a brother, but he was also a TV star.

"Maurice got bored when there was nobody around him," says Michel Jasmin. "He needed the energy of other people to feel good inside. The world of television played that role for him at a critical moment of his life. He had a mysterious kind of charisma; he was a fascinating paradox combining tenderness and violence in a single harmonious whole. He was very important to me. We made an improbable team, but we were also terrific together. It's strange to see how many things we had in common — things that bound us together in our lives and our personalities. Today, I sometimes catch myself thinking I could call him anytime: he will always be present for me, in one way or another."

Michel Jasmin is undoubtedly the Quebec public figure most marked by Maurice. There is, however, a long list of other public figures, from all over the province, who have also been marked by his presence, such as former hockey players Patrice Brisebois and Luc Robitaille, politician Mario Dumont, and boxing promoter Yvon Michel, just to name a few. The TV and radio host Paul Houde sums up what all these people think:

"When we were students, we would go to the matches for our weekly emotional release. Maurice Vachon was the ultimate lunatic of the ring. We saw him as a mega star!"

Maurice has inspired many other people like him, but he was also able to find inspiration in others during his later years, and it helped him keep the faith.

"Life sends you all kinds of trials. When I think of a guy like Christopher Reeve, Superman, this guy was paralyzed from the neck down. He had so much courage. A case like that inspires me, a man like that. The message is clear: we have to continue fighting. Life is one long wrestling match!"

This sums up the attitude that enabled Maurice to have such a great career, a career filled with all kinds of honors.

A panel of specialists deemed him to be the second best wrestler of all time in Quebec. He and Paul formed the second best tag team.

He is also ranked the fourth best heel in the history of wrestling and the fourth best Canadian wrestler. He was inducted into all the different wrestling Halls of Fame. In addition to the Halls of Fame already mentioned, he was inducted into the Wichita Falls, Texas, Pro Wrestling Hall of Fame, the one for Quebec wrestling, and the one maintained by the *Wrestling Observer Newsletter* — the *Wall Street Journal* of professional wrestling.

In 2011, the CROP polling firm undertook an opinion poll for the Quebec game show version of *Family Feud*, asking respondents to name a famous wrestler. Only Hulk Hogan and Jacques Rougeau Jr. were mentioned more often than Maurice. He also garnered awards abroad: he was considered the fifth most hated athlete in the history of Minnesota, ahead of football player Randy Moss.

Finally, he is on the short list of Quebecers among the one hundred best wrestlers of all time and on the list of Quebecers who won a recognized world championship.

Despite all the honors and all the praise, Maurice remained humble throughout his life. He didn't take fame seriously, although he wanted to take the discipline of wrestling seriously.

And even if he brought honor to his country, he also regretted living the life of the wandering Canadian. "It will always be very difficult for me to live somewhere else, because my heart, my mind, my soul, and my memories all remain in Quebec!"

His legacy in popular culture is also significant. Before his time, criminals were the only ones to be taunted with the nickname "Mad Dog." Nowadays, this nickname is seen positively: of course, a "Mad Dog" is a dangerous person, but a "Mad Dog" is also someone who goes all the way, who never gives up. Several athletes have taken on this nickname in sports ranging from baseball to soccer, hockey, basketball, rugby, and football. Over the years, a dozen wrestlers have taken on the nickname. In a 1992 episode of the American animated TV series *The Ren & Stimpy Show*, Ren plays a professional wrestler nicknamed "Mad Dog" Hoek. Not Hulk or Macho Man, but "Mad Dog."

A British black humor TV series running since 2011 is called *Mad Dogs*. After Maurice died, a bar in Montreal launched a craft beer named "Mad Dog" in his honor.

The last few years were difficult for his family and friends. René Goulet, for example, maintained steadfast contact with him but couldn't stand it when Maurice was no longer able to recognize him. It came as a big shock to others to learn of his death.

"I was in the hospital when my son called me," says Michel Longtin. "I was simply stunned. I hung up the phone, and I asked the doctor to leave me alone. My eyes filled with water, and I could see the experiences I had with Maurice pass before me like a movie. What I remember most is the way we would have to stop on the roadside when traveling together because we were laughing too hard to continue driving. What a wonderful man!"

His son Mike expected the sad news any day, but when the fateful call came from Kathie, he was filled with different emotions. "I would have expected to be the most affected," he says, "but he had reached the end of the road. He must have packed two hundred years of adventures into one short life. He lived a beautiful life. All the attention his death got made me happy but also surprised me. He had been out of the limelight for almost thirty years. How many famous people get barely a paragraph in the newspaper when they pass away? He must have been important to many people and he fully deserved that importance. He was paid a touching and representative tribute. It wasn't always easy being Mad Dog's son. Nowadays I can appreciate it. I can say I'm glad he was my father. He was like Louis Cyr, a legendary person who is going to be remembered for generations. I still catch myself thinking he's going to ring the doorbell some morning. I always waited for him to come see me between trips. This trip is just lasting a little longer. I can't really miss him. He's all over YouTube when I need to see him. It's as if he were still alive — at least the character he portrayed will always be with us."

Mad Dog's death generated impressive media coverage. He made headlines overseas and pretty much everywhere in the United States, primarily in Minnesota and Nebraska, but also in Oregon, Florida, and California. Even the prestigious *New York Times* mentioned his passing. In his native Canada, his life was celebrated from coast to coast. It was rare for a Quebec wrestler to be honored like this in the United States and English Canada. But in Quebec, his death was covered by the media wall-to-wall.

For two full days, newspapers, radio, and television stations devoted nonstop coverage to him, in countless articles and news segments. This coverage was full of nostalgia: many people had fond memories of wrestling, and many more had memories of Mad Dog Vachon.

"I remember that on Sunday mornings, I would watch wrestling on TV with my father. Quebec has lost an icon," said Michel Therrien, former head coach of the Montreal Canadiens. "This is sad news. We don't want people like that to disappear. He was definitely part of Quebec's heritage."

Montreal mayor Denis Coderre got the city council to observe a minute of silence. The mayor tweeted, "When I think of Mad Dog Vachon, I relive fantastic times at the Paul Sauvé Arena and shows with the Rougeau and Leduc brothers, legendary fights with Édouard Carpentier, Gilles 'The Fish' Poisson and Michel 'Justice' Dubois, etc. #RIPMadDog."

Then Leader of the Opposition in Ottawa, Thomas Mulcair, remembered Maurice as a legend and offered his condolences to the family. Former Quebec premier Lucien Bouchard recalled seeing him in action in person in the Chicoutimi territory.

A tribute evening was held on December 11, 2013, in Montreal. A commemorative plaque was unveiled on that occasion. As soon as the tribute ended, another round of media coverage started. Maurice was a TV star: he had built a reputation and a name, reaching out to the public through the camera lens. Even after his death, this practically symbiotic relationship continued.

Maurice began his career in an era when television was in its infancy. The Olympics weren't massively covered the way they are nowadays. Professional wrestling was extremely popular. But if Maurice had emerged as a pro wrestler at any other time over the last sixty years, he would have been just as successful. In his younger years, he had the personality and raw look of a Hollywood actor. If he had taken part in the London Olympic Games in 2012, and not in 1948, he would instantly have become a TV star like fellow Quebecers and Canadian Olympians Alexandre Despatie, Annie Pelletier, and Jean-Luc Brassard. If he had left amateur wrestling in the 2000s, his status as a former Olympian and talented streetfighter would have ensured him a successful career in mixed martial arts, like three-time former UFC welterweight champion, Quebec's own Georges St-Pierre.

"If Mad Dog were young now, he would be world champion in mixed martial arts," said the late Billy Robinson, former coach in this discipline.

But Maurice was a man of his time and he lived exactly the life he wanted: a life filled with travel, friends, and fun. In fact, life brought him everything he could have imagined with his child's mind, and then some more. Through his trials and tribulations, he continued growing, while maintaining an unusually determined attitude. In the end, he lost his last battle, but he never surrendered. His final performance was truly magnificent. He did everything to meet the challenge of this final adventure.

Over the last few years, Kathie had to find ways to keep Maurice safe despite himself. He loved nature and enjoyed spending time outdoors, but she wouldn't let him get out on the street. He wanted to wander, but he couldn't go out alone — it was too risky. She thought up a scheme to keep him in the driveway by forbidding him to cross a line, but that scheme didn't work for long. Kathie then installed garden hoses to set out a perimeter he wasn't allowed to cross. It ought, in principle, to have been impossible for him to cross the garden hose with his wheelchair, but he found a way to roll right over it. She then thought up a new scheme: tying a rope to his wheelchair to limit how far he would go with it, but only when he was outside. Despite all these measures, Maurice was clearly still looking for a way to escape. He had the same taste for adventure as ever.

One Saturday morning, a few weeks before his death, Kathie came home from grocery shopping with friends. Maurice was in his room in the basement where he had been living for years, long before his health problems of late. Just as he was finishing his breakfast, Kathie took a moment to bring the grocery bags inside. Maurice realized the garage door was open, but Kathie did not. He headed outdoors. His movements weren't restricted; there was no rope holding him back.

A few minutes later, much to Kathie's surprise, a child in the neighborhood rang the doorbell, asking if her husband was the one in a wheelchair. She said yes, Maurice was safe in the basement. The child insisted the gentleman had zoomed down the hill and his wheelchair had flipped over. He was at an intersection about three hundred feet down the hill.

Kathie ran down and, rescuing Maurice, asked if everything was all right. Maurice smiled mischievously, the way he always did. He was proud of his escape. Miraculously, he hadn't broken anything and got off with a scratch on his knee. He had flipped over onto the median in the middle of the street. The needles and tubes from medication didn't come off, which could have injured him. Above all, no car had driven by. Paramedics called to the scene drove him home. On arriving, they asked if they could do something for him, to which Maurice replied: "I would like to get back into the garage."

In fact, he wanted to escape all over again. When a person is sick or weakened, his strongest instincts, the ones deepest inside him, sometimes take over. During those few moments, Maurice became once again the little boy setting out by train to travel the wide world.

The day before his death, he wasn't doing well and even had a hard time swallowing. In the last while he sometimes let his head drop backwards with his mouth open as if he had just died. The doctors were convinced he suffered a series of small strokes, but he always came back to normal. That night, he had another of these episodes. He was left feeling tired, but no more than usual. Kathie took his head in her hands and said softly in his ear: "Maurice, you were a wonderful husband for me. I love you so much. See you tomorrow morning." Maurice smiled, and Kathie tucked him in the way she did every night and then went to bed upstairs.

The next morning, she poured herself a cup of coffee as usual, then headed down to the basement. Going down the stairs, she called out "*Hola!*" — her customary greeting in Spanish. There was no answer from Maurice. Kathie felt perhaps he was still asleep, but when she reached his bedside, she could see Maurice lying there peacefully. He was no longer breathing. His body was still warm. This time, Maurice was gone for good.

The funeral was held in Iowa, and many came to pay their respects, including old friends like Baron von Raschke, Greg Gagne, and Jim Brunzell. But there were a lot of friends without any connection to wrestling, his caregivers, or his family. It was a sober funeral — one he probably would have found a bit too sad. But it was far happier than the kind of funerals he had always dreaded. Once the funeral was over, the Canadian national anthem was played in the funeral home.

A man had died. Maurice had died. An incredible artist had died. Mad Dog had died. His family was in mourning. His country was in mourning. The little guy from Ville-Émard had died in Omaha, confirming that up to the very end and even up to his very last breath, Maurice "Mad Dog" Vachon was still . . . a wandering Canadian.

EPILOGUE

Dear readers,

My name is Kathie Vachon and I was married to Maurice for over thirty-three years. As you have learned in this book, my husband didn't always have an easy life.

But he never quit. He was a fighter. He was a wrestler.

My husband left me with a thousand and one souvenirs comprised of people, places, and adventures that I keep locked up in my mind and heart. I can visit them at any time.

We loved each other and we each made the other a better person. There were times when some giant, dark clouds lingered overhead, but the sun eventually broke through.

Living with Maurice was not dull. He had more lives than a cat! I do believe he kept his guardian angels on their toes throughout his whole life. I also believe when he took his last breath here on Earth, his next breath was in the arms of his Savior.

I found this little paragraph in the newspaper recently and I immediately thought Maurice would have identified with this:

> Life is not a journey to the grave with the intention of arriving safely in a pretty well preserved body, but rather, to skid in broadside, thoroughly used up, totally worn out and loudly proclaiming, "Wow! What a ride!"

Maurice didn't waste any of his life. Wrestling kept him busy more often than not. He often said he would have done anything for wrestling, and that he had loved every minute, despite all the obstacles along the way.

But he never quit. He was a fighter. He was a wrestler.

Thank you for taking the time to read his story, his life. And as Maurice used to say: "God bless you!"

Kathie Vachon
October 2014

MAURICE "MAD DOG" VACHON: STATISTICS

This is an overview of the 3,001 amateur and professional known matches Maurice Vachon took part in, as well as important dates in his career and life. The initial list of matches was compiled by Vance Nevada with the help of files from Matt Farmer, Tim Hornbaker, Jim Melby, Mike Rodgers, Jim Zordani, Jeff Sharkey, J Michael Kenyon, Pat Laprade, and Bertrand Hébert.

PROFESSIONAL RECORD

1,298 wins; 1,086 losses; 251 draws; 357 no-contest matches.

MAJOR CHAMPIONSHIPS

Stampede International Tag Team (Calgary), Pacific Northwest (Portland), AWA Heavyweight (Minneapolis), AWA Tag Team (Minneapolis), International Heavyweight (Quebec), IWE Tag Team (Japan), IWE (Japan), Grand Prix Heavyweight (Quebec), Grand Prix Tag Team (Quebec)

TIMELINE

September 1, 1929: Birth of Maurice Régis Vachon (Ville-Émard, QC)

July 29, 1948: Defeats K. P. Roy at the Olympics (London, England)

July 30, 1948: Loses to Adil Candemir at the Olympics (London, England)

July 31, 1948: Loses to Paavo Sepponen at the Olympics (London, England)

February 6, 1950: Defeats Peter Fletcher at the British Empire Games (Auckland, NZ)

February 7, 1950: Defeats Callie Reitz at the British Empire Games (Auckland, NZ)

February 7, 1950: Defeats Bruce Arthur, winning the gold medal at the British Empire Games (Auckland, NZ)

May 14, 1951: Draw against Al Tucker, his pro debut (Montreal, QC)

June 20, 1951: Defeats George Mann in his debut at the Montreal Forum (Montreal, QC)

October 30, 1954: Birth of his son Maurice Jr. (Mike) (Montreal, QC)

December 4, 1958: Birth of his son Denis (Montreal, QC)

December 16, 1961: Birth of his daughter Cheryl (Honolulu, HI)

May 4, 1962: Loses to Dick Garza by disqualification; for the first time he is said to be from Algeria (Portland, OR)

June 22, 1962: Wins a battle royal; for the first time, newspapers call him "Mad Dog" (Portland, OR)

October 20, 1964: Defeats Verne Gagne, winning the AWA World Championship (Minneapolis, MN)

January 24, 1967: Defeats Hans Schmidt, winning the International Championship of the Montreal Athletic Commission (Chicoutimi, QC)

August 14, 1967: Defeats Johnny Rougeau, winning the International Championship of the Montreal Athletic Commission (Montreal, QC)

August 23, 1967: Seriously injured in a road accident (Saint-Nicolas, QC)

July 28, 1968: Birth of his son Stéphan (Montreal, QC)

August 30, 1969: Together with Paul Vachon, defeats the Crusher and Dick the Bruiser, winning the AWA world tag team championship (Chicago, IL)

June 13, 1970: Loses to the Crusher in a cage match before a crowd of 12,076 (Milwaukee, WI)

August 14, 1970: Together with Paul Vachon, defeats Dick the Bruiser and the Crusher before a crowd of 21,000 people (Chicago, IL)

October 4, 1971: Birth of his son Jean-Pierre (Quebec, QC)

May 7, 1972: Defeats Édouard Carpentier, winning the Grand Prix Championship (Quebec, QC)

August 14, 1972: Together with Paul Vachon, loses to Jos and Paul Leduc before 17,008 people (Quebec City, QC)

September 18, 1972: Loses to Jos Leduc before a crowd of 15,000 people (Quebec, QC)

July 14, 1973: Defeats Killer Kowalski, winning the Grand Championship before a crowd of 29,127 people (Montreal, QC)

August 12, 1974: Loses to Jacques Rougeau before 10,000 people (Montreal, QC)

April 10, 1975: Defeats Mighty Inoue, winning the IWE Championship (Tokyo, Japan)

July 13, 1981: Draw against Pierre Lefebvre in "the Battle of the Mad Dogs" (Montreal, QC)

June 16, 1984: Defeats Steve Lombardi in his first match for the WWF (New York, NY)

February 24, 1986: Loses a battle royal to Pat Patterson in his last match at the Montreal Forum (Montreal, QC)

October 13, 1986: Together with Jos Leduc, defeats Gilles Poisson and Man Mountain Moore in the last match of his career (Montreal, QC)

October 9, 1987: Hit by a car in a road accident; his right leg has to be amputated (Des Moines, IA)

March 14, 1988: Tribute to Mad Dog Vachon at a WWF show (Montreal, QC) ·

May 23, 1993: Presented with other legends at the beginning of a
WCW show (Atlanta, GA)

April 28, 1996: Shawn Michaels uses Mad Dog's artificial leg to
attack Diesel at a WWF show (Omaha, NE)

May 31, 1998: Honored with the Crusher; Jerry "The King"
Lawler and the Crusher use his artificial limb (Milwaukee, WI)

April 6, 2003: The Cauliflower Alley Club bestow him with the Iron
Mike Award (Las Vegas, NV)

August 2, 2003: Inducted into the George Tragos/Lou Thesz Hall
of Fame (Newton, IA)

May 15, 2004: Inducted into the Professional Wrestling Hall of
Fame, along with Paul Vachon (Amsterdam, NY)

November 7, 2009: NCW tribute along with Paul Vachon, his last
appearance at a wrestling show in Quebec (Montreal, QC)

November 9, 2009: Inducted into the Quebec Sports Hall of Fame
(Montreal, QC)

March 27, 2010: Inducted into the WWE Hall of Fame by Pat Patterson (Phoenix, AZ)

March 28, 2010: Is introduced along with other new members of
the WWE Hall of Fame at *WrestleMania XXVI*, the only time he
attended WrestleMania (Glendale, AZ)

November 21, 2013: Dies at the age of 84 (Omaha, NB)

November 24, 2013: His death is announced during the match pitting
John Cena against Alberto del Río (Boston, MA)

November 25, 2013: The opening sequence of *Raw* highlights his
death (Long Island, NY)

A LAST WORD

"My world is a world of chaos. A world turned upside down, a sinister world, even a cloudy one. But sometimes the sun comes out. When you lose, when you have an accident, when you divorce, when you lose people you love, it's chaos, you're on the downward slope. But it's not always like that. Sometimes the sun comes out. If you ask me what kind of world we live in, my answer is: this is a dog-eat-dog world. If you want to get enough to eat, be prepared to fight every moment of your life. Call me Mad Dog but don't ever call me a loser. I am the Mad Dog who wins in life. I love life!"

Mad-Dog Vachon

REFERENCES

Apart from the references cited below, we have also benefited from access to the archives of CBC, Radio-Canada, TQS, and the Archives Nationales du Québec.

BOOKS

Al-Kaissy, Adnan, and Ross Bernstein. *The Sheikh of Baghdad*. Chicago: Triumph Books, 2005.

Allyn, Robert, Pamela Allyn, and Scott Teal. *The Solie Chronicles*. Gallatin, TN: Crowbar Press, 2009.

Anderson, Ole, and Scott Teal. *Inside Out*. Gallatin, TN: Crowbar Press, 2003.

Atlas, Tony, and Scott Teal. *Too Much . . . Too Soon*. Gallatin, TN: Crowbar Press, 2010.

Berthelet, Pierre. *Yvon Robert: Le Lion du Canada Français*. Montreal: Trustar, 1999.

Brisco, Jack, and William Murdoch. *Brisco*, Newton, IA: Culture House Books, 2003.

Dillon, James J., Scott Teal, and Phillip Varriale. *"Wrestlers Are Like Seagulls": From McMahon to McMahon*. Hendersonville, TN: Crowbar Press, 2005.

Duncan, Royal, and Gary Will. *Wrestling Title Histories, Fourth Edition*. Waterloo, ON: Archeus Communications, 2000.

Flair, Ric, Keith Elliot Greenberg, and Mark Madden. *To Be the Man*. New York: Pocket Books, 2004.

Funk, Terry, and Scott E. Williams. *More Than Just Hardcore*. Champaign, IL: Sports Publishing LLC, 2005.

Giroux, Lionel, and Jean Côté. *Un nain dans l'arène de la vie: Little Beaver*. Montreal: Éditions Québecor, 1979.

Graham, Billy, and Keith Elliot Greenberg. *Tangled Ropes*. New York: Pocket Books, 2006.

Hansen, Stan, and Scott Teal. *The Last Outlaw*. Gallatin, TN: Crowbar Press, 2011.

Hart, Bret. *My Real Life in the Cartoon World of Wrestling*. Toronto: Random House Canada, 2007.

Koloff, Yvan, and Scott Teal. *Is That Wrestling Fake? The Bear Facts*. Hendersonville, TN: Crowbar Press, 2007.

Laprade, Pat, and Bertrand Hébert. *À la semaine prochaine, si Dieu le veut!* Montreal: Libre Expression, 2013.

Laprade, Pat, and Bertrand Hébert. *Mad Dogs, Midgets and Screw Jobs*. Toronto: ECW Press, 2013.

Lawler, Jerry, and Doug Asheville. *It's Good to Be the KING . . . Sometimes*. New York: Pocket Books, 2002.

McCoy, Heath. *Pain and Passion: The History of Stampede Wrestling*. Toronto: CanWest Books, 2005.

Molinaro, John F., Jeff Mareck, and Dave Meltzer. *Top 100 Pro Wrestlers of All Time*. Toronto: Winding Stair Press, 2002.

Mulligan, Blackjack. *True Lies and Alibis: The Blackjack Mulligan Story*. Groveland, FL: Headlock Ranch, 2008.

Oliver, Greg. *Pro Wrestling Hall of Fame: The Canadians*. Toronto: ECW Press. 2003.

Oliver, Greg, and Steven Johnson. *Pro Wrestling Hall of Fame: The Heels*. Toronto: ECW Press, 2007.

Oliver, Greg, and Steven Johnson. *Pro Wrestling Hall of Fame: The Tag Teams*. Toronto: ECW Press, 2005.

Rougeau, Jean. *Johnny Rougeau*. Montreal: Éditions Québecor, 1982.

Sarrault, Jean-Paul. *Fais-le saigner*. Montreal: Logiques, 1993.

Snowden, Jonathan. *Shooters: The Toughest Men in Professional Wrestling*. Toronto: ECW Press, 2012.

Sullivan, Kevin. *The WWE Championship: A Look Back at the Rich History of the WWE Championship*. New York: Gallery Books, 2010.

Vachon, Maurice, and Louis Chantigny. *Une vie de chien dans un monde de fous*. Montreal: Guérin Littérature, 1988.

Vachon, Paul. *The Rise and Fall of Grand Prix Wrestling*. Laval, QC: Impressions Prioritaires, 2009.

Vachon, Paul. *The Territories and Japan*. Laval, QC: Impressions Prioritaires, 2009.

Vachon, Paul. *When Wrestling Was Real: Memories and True Stories, "The Early Years."* Laval, QC: Impressions Prioritaires, 2009.

Watts, "Cowboy" Bill, and Scott Williams. *The Cowboy and the Cross: The Bill Watts Story; Rebellion, Wrestling and Redemption*. Toronto: ECW Press, 2006.

WEBSITES

Ancestry: www.ancestry.com

ClubWWI: www.clubwwi.com

The Dan Gable International Wrestling Institute and Museum: www.wrestlingmuseum.org

Fédération de lutte amateur: www.quebecolympicwrestling.ca

Gary Will: www.garywill.com/wrestling

History of WWE: www.thehistoryofwwe.com

Kayfabe Memories: www.kayfabememories.com

Legacy of Wrestling: legacyofwrestling.com

Maple Leaf Wrestling: http://mapleleafwrestling.4t.com/canadianpage.html

Mid-Atlantic Gateway: www.midatlanticgateway.com

Newspapers: www.newspapers.com

Online World of Wrestling: www.onlineworldofwrestling.com

SLAM Wrestling: slam.canoe.ca/Slam/Wrestling/home
Sports Reference Olympics: www.sports-reference.com/olympics
World Wrestling Federation: www.wwe.com
Wrestling Classics: www.wrestlingclassics.com
Wrestling Observer: www.wrestlingobserver.com
Wrestling Title Histories: www.wrestling-titles.com

NEWSPAPERS AND MAGAZINES

Allo Police

Le Droit

Échos-Vedettes

Le Journal de Montréal

Le Journal de Québec

Le Lundi

The Montreal Gazette

Le Nouvelliste de Trois-Rivières

La Patrie

La Presse

San Francisco Chronicle

Le Soleil (Saguenay)

La Tribune (Sherbrooke)

SPECIALIZED MAGAZINES

Boxe

Le Journal de la lutte

Le Livre de la Lutte

Lutte et Boxe

Main Event: The World of Professional Wrestling

Pro Wrestling Illustrated

La Revue de lutte professionnelle du Québec

The Ring Wrestling

The Wrestler

Wrestling Observer Newsletter

TV SHOWS AND DVDS

La Lutte. Directed by Michel Brault, Marcel Carrière, Claude Fournier, and Claude Jutra. Canada: NFB, 1961.

Mad Dog: L'homme derrière la bête [Mad Dog: The Man Behind the Beast]. ORBI-XXI Productions, 2008.

Mad Dog Vachon Shoot Interview. RF Video interview collection

Les Saltimbanques du ring [Acrobats of the Ring]. Directed by Bernard Lafrenière. ORBI-XXI Productions, 2006.

Wrestling Queen. Directed by Patrick Vallely. USA: Snowman Productions, Inc. 1973.

GET THE EBOOK FREE!